A VIOLENT PEACE

GLOBAL SECURITY AFTER THE COLD WAR

Also available from Brassey's

BORAWSKI
Security in a New Europe

BROWN
The Strategic Revolution

HARTCUP
The Silent Revolution:
Development of Conventional Weapons 1945–85

IISS
Strategic Survey

LEECH
Halt! Who Goes Where?:
The Future of NATO in the New Europe

ORMAN
Faith in G.O.D.S.

A VIOLENT PEACE

GLOBAL SECURITY AFTER THE COLD WAR

By

Paul Rogers and Malcolm Dando

BRASSEY'S (UK)
LONDON ★ WASHINGTON ★ NEW YORK

UK editorial offices: Brassey's, 165 Great Dover Street, London SE1 4YA
orders: Purnell Distribution Centre, Paulton, Bristol BS18 5LQ

USA editorial offices: Brassey's, 8000 Westpark Drive, First Floor,
McLean, VA 22102
orders: Macmillan Publishing Company, Front and Brown Streets,
Riverside, NJ 08075

Distributed in North America to booksellers and wholesalers by the
Macmillan Publishing Company, NY 10022

Library of Congress Cataloging in Publication Data
available

British Library Cataloguing in Publication Data
A catalogue record for this book is
available from the British Library

ISBN 0-08-036694-5   Hardcover

Printed and Bound in Great Britain by
Hartnolls Limited, Bodmin, Cornwall.

Contents

Contents

Preface

It is a calm winter's day in northern England, a few months after the failure of the coup attempt in Moscow. Whatever the problems to be faced in the Soviet republics, the Cold War is over and the talk is of a New World Order. But what kind of new world is being constructed out of the old East–West confrontation? Are the structures which resulted from a half century of worldwide militarisation going to be easily rearranged to more constructive tasks? Indeed, are the mind-sets of the élites who directed the East–West confrontation going to be able to cope with the design of a stable and just new world order?

The reader of this book will have asked some of these questions already. What follows is an attempt to assist in the process of thinking through this crucial issue. We should begin by making our own position quite clear. We believe that a stable world order can only come about through an intensive effort to address the problems of world poverty, the destruction of the environment and the continuing militarisation of international relations. We believe that a new axis of conflict is now in the process of becoming established, a North–South axis, and that the deep polarisation of the world community into the wealthy and the impoverished, coupled with the limits on human activity being set by global environmental constraints, could combine progressively to create a gravely unstable and conflict-ridden world.

Given the nature of the global problems we now face – in part because of the waste of the last 50 years – partial and half-hearted measures have little chance of successfully preventing further devastating conflicts and mass human suffering.

Our starting point is the process of militarisation which overlies

i

these global problems, and the manner of its development during the Cold War years. We examine the attempts to control this process, try to identify its interaction with political and economic trends in North–South confrontation, suggest the likely outcome of this combination and indicate some alternative approaches to security which recognise the fundamental dangers of allowing a 'crowded, glowering planet' to develop.

We suggest that the North does have a chance – similar to that available to the United States at the end of the Second World War – largely to structure a new world order. We argue that the nature of the relations with the Third World will dominate that new order. We suggest that too ready a recourse to the use of economic and military strength to coerce and control the Third World, rather than finding imaginative and radical new means of co-operation, will lead to a repetition of what happened over the past decades in the West's relations with the Soviet Union.

However strong the states of the North might be, and this means essentially the states of the old Western alliance, it seems unlikely to us that it can ultimately coerce countries of the size and potential power of China, India, Pakistan, Nigeria and Brazil for the next several decades. If we attempt to operate from a 'position of strength', we believe that they will progressively militarise in return. Given the impossibility of restricting scientific knowledge and the lethality of modern weapons, we will witness a series of interlocking arms races, often regional in nature but broadly orientated on a North–South axis of conflict.

The book is divided into 12 Chapters. The introductory Chapter contrasts the choices available to the US and its allies in the immediate post-war years with the opportunities now available to create a genuinely peaceful new world order which is not just a group of Northern states exerting control by any means necessary.

Chapters 2 and 3 review the process of global militarisation, with emphasis on the East–West confrontation which has provided the driving-force for this process since the late 1940s. These Chapters concentrate on the most dangerous developments, principally weapons of mass destruction, and chronicle the initial halting attempts to come to terms with the new nuclear weaponry in the first détente of the 1960s and 1970s. These, and the more thorough efforts of the Gorbachev regime after 1985, are investigated in order to point out the role of the growing understanding of the nature of our global problems in international relations.

Chapters 4 and 5 give an account of the continuing process of militarisation – both East–West and in the South, with emphasis on one of the most dangerous legacies of the Cold War, the proliferation of nuclear, chemical and especially conventional weapons of mass destruction across the world.

In Chapters 6 to 9, we examine the capacity of the North, and especially the United States, to project military force to any part of the world in pursuit of its perceived security interests, and focus particularly on those economic interests, especially control of resources, which have underpinned the systematic development of military power projection in the 1980s.

In doing so, we offer a detailed analysis of the 1991 Gulf War, demonstrating two key features of that conflict – a resource war over control of the world's largest concentration of oil reserves, and a war fought with the devastating new conventional weapons of mass destruction.

In Chapter 10, the combined global pressures of population, resource depletion, huge disparities in wealth and environmental constraints are reviewed, and the likely patterns of North–South conflict indicated.

Chapters 11 and 12 then offer some alternatives. First, in Chapter 11, an appropriate arms control agenda for the 1990s is offered, which would reverse the recent process of militarisation, using the institutions developed in recent years to form a basis for control of proliferation in its many forms.

Finally, in Chapter 12, we attempt to draw our argument together by indicating some of the approaches to the creation of a peaceful new world order which seem essential in the coming decades. This involves not just demilitarisation, but a radical change in trade and development policies of the North towards the South, the evolution of ecologically sustainable development strategies, and the development of a system of global inter-state relations adequate to address global environmental threats.

Given that the book was written largely during August and September 1991, we have had to recognise the rapid pace of change in the former Soviet Union, and the likelihood that it may be more accurate to use the term Soviet Federation or Commonwealth in due course. Whatever the long-term outcome of the reform process in the Soviet republics, we would expect a powerful entity to emerge, based not least on the core of the Russian heartland, although this may follow a period of instability. Concern with developments within the Soviet republics may well dominate Western thinking on international relations, but we would argue that this is an inadequate and even parochial response to global trends.

Finally, it will be obvious that we end up calling for a great deal of 'new thinking' and action. We do not apologise for this given the probable outcome of the alternative 'steady as she sinks' strategy.

Acknowledgements

We would like to thank our colleagues at the Department of Peace Studies at Bradford University, especially Oliver Ramsbotham and James O'Connell, for their comments and suggestions. We are also grateful to Jenny Shaw and Angela Clark of Brassey's and Josephine O'Connor Howe for their patience in seeing this book through to publication.

Paul Rogers
Malcolm Dando

1 January 1992

1

A New World Order?

In late 1986, *The Washington Post* carried an article entitled 'Arms Talks: 20 Years of Duds?'[1] The article was based on a major study carried out by Harvard University's John F. Kennedy School of Government for the US Arms Control and Disarmament Agency. The study concluded that superpower arms control agreements had not significantly altered the military plans of either side. Indeed, it argued that even modest arms control negotiations would become deadlocked if the relevant arsenals were not roughly equivalent.

Thus the fears of conservatives in the West that arms control negotiations might lead to complacency, and the hopes of liberals that military plans would be affected, were shown to have been groundless. Despite the ups-and-downs of the superpower relationship – the coming of détente followed by the second phase of the Cold War during the 1980s – what mattered was military strength not arms control.

Attempts to cap or reverse this process of militarisation did not, of course, just fail from the mid-1960s to the mid-1980s. The Cold War set in during the late 1940s. For the whole of this period, the international system was dominated by the confrontation between the United States and the Soviet Union and little progress was possible.

The United States had emerged from the Second World War as by far the world's strongest power. It proceeded, as had other such powers in the past, to arrange an international order to its own best advantage. As one study noted:

> . . . The overriding US national security imperative, as revealed in scores of military planning documents, intelligence reports and inter-agency

papers, was to prevent Soviet control of the raw materials and manpower of Europe and Asia lest the Soviet Union use these resources to enhance its long-term capabilities to wage war against the United States.[2]

Thus the Soviet Union came quickly to be regarded as the hostile ideological foe and a policy of containment became dominant.

While a 40-year period of military confrontation may have been inevitable between East and West, it is important to appreciate that people at that time did not see such inevitability in the degeneration of the wartime alliance. Even within the US State Department, opinion varied from advocation of active collaboration with the Soviet Union and sharing of atomic secrets through to hard-line atomic sabre-rattling.

Even at the highest levels of the State Department, Bohlen and Robinson were arguing that the possession of the atomic bomb gave the United States a period of decisive superiority, during which time it should act to influence Soviet behaviour for the better before that country, too, developed nuclear weapons.[3] The policy they favoured was a long period of non-confrontation and attempts at compromise, in the belief that this might moderate the USSR's intentions before its military capabilities increased.

Nearly 40 years later it was the Soviet Union that began an out-and-out policy of concession and compromise. In the field of arms control after 1985 we saw a series of major treaties agreed, all asymmetrically favourable to the West. The Soviet Union was not expected to accept the 'zero-zero' INF deal, it gave up hugely greater forces in the CFE Treaty, and the START Treaty – for example in the bomber-counting rule – is moulded to US interests. Moreover, it radically changed its stance on verification in order to increase Western trust in what had been agreed.

One way in which these events are viewed is that the West 'won' the Cold War and the Soviet Union had to accept defeat when its economy and political system were no longer able to support the military confrontation. While the Soviet Union's parlous economic state was certainly a major factor in the Gorbachev revolution, it would be hard to argue that he and his liberal advisers were not also motivated by a view that continued military confrontation was an inappropriately dangerous way to proceed in the nuclear age.

The UN has pronounced that the 1990s will be the Third Disarmament Decade.[4] It is therefore appropriate to ask whether we in the West have also understood well enough that the advance of military technology makes a policy of co-operation and regulated intercourse a much less dangerous option than relying on military strength. For it is clear that the Western group of states in North America and Western Europe, together with Japan, face an analogous problem to that faced by the United States in 1945. Then, it was how to relate peacefully and constructively with the Soviet Union. Now it is how to relate to the majority of the population of the entire world.

US Secretary of State, James Baker, may talk of a Euro-Atlantic Community that 'extends from Vancouver to Vladivostok' and which is based on the ideals of the Enlightenment.[5] But will we end up with co-operation amongst the rich Western states, envelopment of the former socialist states and a heightened exploitation of the Third World?

Surely, Jerry Saunders was right to argue that in such a type of new world order:

> . . . nationalism will beget nationalism and we will be that much further removed from the real world order challenges . . . the transition from conflict to co-operation between East and West, the redress of inequality that divides North and South, and the harmonising of economic needs with environmental requirements, to name but a few . . .[6]

Baker's dream of a Euro-Atlantic Community may seem a vision for the future to people whose thinking and hopes have been dominated by the tensions and dangers of the Cold War. Peace will replace confrontation and a new world order will be ensured. But the reality is that such a Euro-Atlantic Community, narrowly conceived, will be a minority, and a small minority, of the people of the world, barely one-fifth of the total yet controlling three-quarters of the world's wealth. Such a Community will all too easily become a basis for a new form of confrontation unless our thinking can encompass the radical changes necessary to develop a truly just and peaceful world order.

What is required for properly addressing these real questions of our age is a recognition of the need for pluralism, multipolarity and interdependence. An attempt to strong-arm the poor will, we believe, lead to a new period of unstable military confrontation, made much worse as a result of the military legacy of the Cold War – 40 years of sustained development and proliferation of those 'higher forms of killing' embodied in the many new military technologies.

This book is written on the assumption that such a new period of militarisation is not inevitable – just very likely. It is written accepting that the North will have to take the lead in constructing a new world order, not least because it must bear responsibility for most of the developments which threaten that very order, but hoping that a sophisticated policy can begin to produce the structures of a just and stable world.

Sophisticated new policy, however, can only result from a proper understanding of how we have arrived at our present position. It is therefore to the history of the past five decades – particularly the process of global militarisation and the distortion of human policies – that we turn first.

2

The Nuclear Arms Race and Global Militarisation

After the end of the Second World War, there were hopes and expectations of general demilitarisation. While the massive armies of the victors, especially those of the Western states, were demobilised within a few years, a new military momentum had become established as part of the developing Cold War. Militarisation in the following decades was fuelled primarily by the East–West competition and, while it covered most forms of military technology, it could be seen most clearly in the development of nuclear weapons, especially strategic systems. This nuclear arms race will be explored first, before drawing some conclusions on the global implications of military momentum.[1]

Origins

Nuclear weapons were first developed in the Manhattan Project over the period 1942–45, a massive military-industrial project funded and staffed primarily by the United States but also involving scientists and engineers from several other countries, especially the United Kingdom and Canada.

By early 1945, the possible use of the atom bomb against Germany was no longer likely, as the war against Germany was nearing its end, but the Pacific War was continuing, with Japan increasingly on the defensive. After the first test of an atomic device, the Trinity Test at Alamagordo in the New Mexico desert on 16 July 1945, the decision was taken to use the new weapon operationally, and two devices were used against Hiroshima and Nagasaki in early August 1945.

The Strategic Continuum

While the atomic bomb was a weapon which was several orders of magnitude more destructive than any other weapon at that time, it was seen by military strategists as an extension of existing tactics rather than an entirely new entity.

The development of strategic conventional bombing in the later stages of the Second World War had led to the capability to deploy up to 2,000 medium-range bombers against a single target area in one massive air-raid. Such raids could deliver over 7,000 tons (7 kilotons) of conventional high-explosive munitions against cities and other targets, producing levels of destruction similar to those of the Hiroshima and Nagasaki bombs. Certainly, the conventional air-raids on Hamburg, Dresden and Tokyo all produced casualties of a similar order to the nuclear raids.

Within this context, the atom bomb was seen, at least in part, as an extension of conventional strategic bombing, and the whole ethos of early nuclear targeting was of weapons available for strategic aerial bombardment of major centres of industry and population rather than, in any sense, an 'ultimate weapon'. To the strategic planner in the mid-1940s, the atom bomb extended warfare, it did not supersede it.

The Early Years

After the end of the Second World War, the US government determined to continue the development and production of nuclear weapons in isolation from its war-time allies, a policy codified in the McMahon Energy Act of 1946. By 1948 the United States already had an arsenal of some 50 nuclear bombs and was developing the B-36 strategic bomber as a means of delivering such weapons over intercontinental distances.

The Soviet Union had commenced an atom bomb programme towards the end of the Second World War but did not commit major resources to the project until 1945. An existing strength in nuclear physics helped the Soviet Union develop and test an atomic bomb by 1949, considerably earlier than had been predicted by most Western analysts.

This Soviet development came at a time when post-war tensions had risen rapidly and a Cold War was already in progress. This had reached a peak with the Berlin crisis in 1948 which resulted in the Berlin airlift and the subsequent failure of the Soviet Union to achieve a neutral and weakened Germany. By 1949, partition of Europe into two quite rigid spheres of superpower influence was largely complete and this, coupled with the Soviet nuclear test that year, resulted in a marked hardening of US attitudes to the USSR.

A subsidiary but direct effect of the US policy of retaining complete control of its nuclear weapons research was the determination by the Labour government of Clement Attlee that Britain should become a nuclear power. A programme was initiated during the late 1940s which led to Britain testing a device in 1952.

New Weapons and Frequent Tests

In East Asia, China had, by 1949, come under Communist control, with the US-supported nationalists relegated to exile on Formosa (Taiwan). This heightened US fears of the spread of Communism, a perception exacerbated by the 1950–53 Korean War. Initial Soviet political and material support for the North Koreans in their invasion of the South was overshadowed within months by direct and massive Chinese military participation in the war.

As the US and other allied forces succumbed to initial Chinese advances and then became bogged down in bitter fighting around the 38th parallel, there were calls for the US to use its nuclear arsenal, especially as the Soviet Union had few, if any, operational nuclear weapons and China had none. In the event, Truman and then Eisenhower decided against such use and there is little evidence that it was seriously considered at the senior levels of political leadership.

This did not make for any reconsideration of the utility of nuclear weapons; indeed the deepening East–West tensions were more than adequate to ensure a massive investment in nuclear programmes. By the early 1950s, the United States and the Soviet Union were already embarked on two further developments, the production of the thermonuclear or fusion bomb, often termed the H-bomb, and the development of rocket-propelled missiles as delivery systems for nuclear weapons. Although the Soviet Union followed closely on the United States in developing the H-bomb and was narrowly ahead of the US in testing an intercontinental-range ballistic missile (ICBM), it was the United States which had the overwhelming preponderance of nuclear weapons and delivery systems throughout the 1950s.

The reality of this US superiority was not received wisdom in the public arena, where there were constant reports of massive new Soviet programmes. The 'Red Threat' was given an added dimension by the launch of the first Soviet space satellite, Sputnik, in 1957, which appeared to be proof of a Soviet technological superiority.

Even so, by the late 1950s, the US Strategic Air Command had many hundreds of medium- and long-range bombers, the former based largely in Europe, and the tactical air force, army and navy were all beginning to deploy tactical nuclear weapons. Throughout this period, the essence of US targeting policy was the planned large-scale use of nuclear weapons in response to any significant Soviet aggression, the so-called 'trip-wire' approach, a policy which was only feasible given the overwhelming US nuclear forces.

United States policy towards the Soviet Union and China had become primarily one of containment and involved the strengthening of NATO with the stationing of substantial US armed forces units in Europe. Containment was considered to be particularly important in South-East Asia where the establishment of SEATO followed US provision of financial support for the French in the closing stages of the Indo-China war up to 1954. During the mid- and late-1950s, the US provided considerable military and financial support to a number of states, and containment ultimately led to prolonged and bloody involvement in Vietnam in the 1960s.

China, meanwhile, developed its own brand of Marx-Leninism and embarked on the long and halting path towards industrialisation. This included programmes to develop advanced military technology, at least in part with the aid of the Soviet Union, a policy which included the development of nuclear weapons. Ironically, this programme was not to be completed until 1964, well after the political break with the Soviet Union.

Britain was able to deploy a small aircraft-based nuclear force by the late 1950s, although this was aimed primarily at responding to strategic nuclear attack. By the early 1960s, Britain was also deploying its own tactical nuclear bombs, including carrier-based aircraft among the delivery vehicles. Britain's commitment to nuclear weapons was only in part related to the East–West conflict; much of the motivation was concerned with a vain attempt to maintain great power status. This eventually extended to the basing of nuclear weapons in Cyprus, occasional deployments to Singapore and the provision of a tactical nuclear capability for aircraft-carriers.

France, too, was intent on developing its own nuclear capability, with a similar mix of motives to which was added a concern that Britain should not be the only Western European nuclear power. Intensive research and development throughout the 1950s resulted in the testing of the first French atomic bomb in the Sahara in 1960.

During the course of the mid- and late-1950s, both superpowers engaged in large-scale and frequent testing of nuclear weapons in the atmosphere. Even though scientific understanding of the direct and indirect radiation effects from nuclear detonation was relatively poor, the sheer extent of the testing programme led to growing public concern over the environmental and medical consequences.

Public concern, especially in Europe, developed into major campaigns, initially against nuclear testing but, by the end of the decade, against all nuclear weapons. The Campaign for Nuclear Disarmament in Britain was the best-known of a large number of activist movements which developed in several countries.

Thus, by the end of the 1950s, the Soviet Union and the United States were involved in an immensely costly nuclear arms race as part of their wider political confrontation and, for differing reasons, three other major powers had embarked on their own nuclear weapons programmes.

Confrontation and Nuclear Détente

By the early 1960s, there was intense nuclear competition between the United States and the Soviet Union, especially in the area of long-range missile technology. The Soviet success in launching the first artificial satellite in 1957 had had a considerable impact on US self-perceptions, not least during the 1960 Presidential campaign, and a result of this was a massive technological effort by the United States to 'regain' supremacy in all significant areas of nuclear and related technology.

In reality, early Soviet ICBMs were crude and unreliable, and the US retained a broad superiority well into the 1960s. Even so, the Soviet nuclear forces were now sufficiently large to be able to threaten effective retaliation against any US nuclear attack. Consequently, the previous US nuclear strategy of massive nuclear retaliation against a Soviet conventional attack was no longer viable. Thus, during the early 1960s, the US nuclear planners evolved a much wider range of targeting options which included Soviet command and control facilities, nuclear forces and conventional military targets as well as urban-industrial targets. US nuclear strategy was codified in the Single Integrated Operational Plan (SIOP); the first of these Plans, SIOP-62, included only 210 non-military targets out of a total target list of around 1,900.

In the late 1950s, Soviet nuclear planners had adopted an outlook rather similar to that of their US counterparts – early and massive use of nuclear weapons after the outbreak of a war – in the belief that a nuclear conflict could be won by whichever party used nuclear weapons most forcefully in the early stages. This quickly changed to a wider yet more selective use of nuclear weapons, a change which accelerated after the end of the Khrushchev era in 1964.

Meanwhile, the Cuba missile crisis of 1962 was recognised by the US and Soviet leaderships as coming uncomfortably close to nuclear confrontation. This, coupled with continued public concern about nuclear issues, helped to produce a climate in which negotations on nuclear arms control and disarmament were politically appropriate (*see* Chapter 3).

These negotiations in the 1960s, coupled with the obvious results of the multilateral Limited Test Ban Treaty in controlling most atmospheric tests of nuclear weapons, resulted in a marked easing of public concern with nuclear issues. This continued through the 1960s, even though China tested a nuclear device in 1964, and a wide range of new nuclear weapons was being developed by the United States and the Soviet Union.

The Decade of Lost Opportunity

During the 1970s, a new series of strategic arms control negotiations took place, the so-called SALT 2 talks, and these led to the SALT 2 Agreement of 1979. This sought to control the total numbers of deliverable strategic nuclear warheads deployed by the United States and the Soviet Union, but the pace of technological development was so fast that the negotiations themselves were constantly overtaken by events. During the seven years of talks, the numbers of warheads in the strategic inventories of the super-powers actually doubled, due largely to the new practice of fitting a single strategic missile with several warheads.[2]

This kind of technical development had been continuing in the late 1960s and early 1970s, even against a background of cuts in the US defence budget. The budget had peaked in 1969, at the height of the Vietnam War, and declined substantially in the early 1970s, but this was largely due to the withdrawal from Vietnam. Research and development of new nuclear weapons continued with few budgetary limitations.

During the 1960s, the United States and later the Soviet Union deployed submarine-launched ballistic missiles (SLBMs), and this was followed by the practice of fitting several warheads or re-entry vehicles to each ICBM or SLBM. These multiple re-entry vehicles (MRVs) could spread out over an extended target such as a city, giving a shot-gun effect, and were claimed to have two advantages: they made ballistic missile defences more difficult to develop and a major target would still suffer massive damage even if some warheads failed to detonate.

The MRV idea was subsequently developed into the multiple independently-targetable re-entry vehicle (MIRV) in which each of the several warheads in a missile could be targeted on a separate target within a 'foot-print' or area of land which could be as large as 250,000 square kilometres.

By the early 1970s, the United States was able to deploy the Poseidon SLBM which could carry up to 14 small MIRV warheads on each missile. This led to a huge increase in strategic warhead numbers, even though the number of delivery vehicles remained more or less constant. The Soviet Union lagged behind the United States in both MRV and MIRV technology but tended to produce missiles which carried smaller numbers of much more destructive warheads.

Over the same period of the 1970s, strategic bombers continued to be deployed, even though air defences improved substantially. By the end of the decade, bombers were being equipped with short-range stand-off nuclear missiles which could be fired at air defence facilities ahead of the flightpath of the bomber, to clear a way through to the target. A further development was the long-range air-launched cruise missile (ALCM) which could actually be launched from a strategic bomber outside the air space of the target country. Such ALCMs were developed in the 1970s but were not deployed until the early 1980s.

During the 1970s, the superpowers continued to develop and deploy a wide range of tactical and intermediate-range nuclear weapons. Apart from free-fall nuclear bombs for strike aircraft, these weapons included surface-to-surface missiles of 50–5,000 km range, surface-to-air-missiles, anti-ship missiles, sea-launched land-attack missiles, anti-submarine depth bombs, torpedoes, land mines, sea mines and a variety of artillery-fired atomic projectiles (AFAPs).

In addition to strategic nuclear targeting, complex targeting scenarios for tactical and intermediate-range nuclear weapons were developed by the United States and the Soviet Union as well as the middle-ranking powers.[3] NATO nuclear strategy is a good example of the type of approach adopted in the 1960s and 1970s. NATO's policy of flexible response, first codified on 16 January 1968 in Military Committee Document MC 14/3: 'Overall Strategic Concept for the Defence of the NATO Area', and nominally still in force in 1991, involved maximum flexibility in responding to Warsaw Pact attack, including a wide range of nuclear options.

It was a development of MC 14/2, the 'trip-wire' strategy of the 1950s and early 1960s, which involved a massive nuclear response to any Warsaw Pact aggression. Such a policy was unsustainable in the face of a growing Soviet nuclear capability, and flexible response sought to erect a strategy in which limited use of nuclear weapons could be envisaged as a deterrent to Warsaw Pact attack.

NATO's nuclear operations plans were co-ordinated with the US strategic nuclear targeting programme, the SIOP, through a joint NATO/US team based in the United States, and NATO's plans called broadly for two levels of nuclear response to Warsaw Pact attack. The lower level was so-called 'selective use' and involved a small number of nuclear weapons used against advancing Warsaw Pact forces before the latter employed nuclear weapons. The nuclear forces used could be between 5–100 nuclear weapons, mostly small-yield artillery shells and bombs and aimed at large concentrations of Warsaw Pact forces and their logistic support. The aim would be to force the Warsaw Pact forces to cease their aggression and withdraw, a policy based on the presumption that the Warsaw Pact would not escalate to nuclear use on its own, or even try to pre-empt NATO nuclear first-use.

Should the selective use of nuclear weapons fail, NATO's main nuclear targeting plan would then come into operation, the so-called 'general response'. This would involve a general nuclear attack on Warsaw Pact forces in Eastern Europe and the Western part of the Soviet Union, including attacks on nuclear forces, conventional forces, command, control and communications facilities, transport networks and ports. This level of nuclear attack would probably involve some thousands of nuclear weapons and would be undertaken in conjunction with elements of US strategic forces.

On a smaller scale, the middle-ranking nuclear powers – Britain, France and China – followed suit in their development of tactical as well as strategic nuclear weapons. In Britain, for example, the strategic force of Polaris missiles was paralleled by the deployment of free-fall bombs and depth bombs, the Lance artillery missile and two calibres of nuclear artillery shell.

Although the feared proliferation of nuclear weapons to many different countries did not materialise in the 1970s, there were some relevant developments. India test-fired a nuclear device in 1974. It has since maintained that this technological capability has not been diverted into producing an arsenal of nuclear weapons, but India clearly has the ability to do so at short notice. Israel appears to have developed nuclear weapons during the 1960s and to have acquired a weapons capability by 1970 at the latest, with free-fall bombs and artillery missile warheads available early in the decade. South Africa placed a high priority on developing nuclear weapons during the course of the decade, although the programme was probably not completed until the early 1980s.

Both superpowers were responsible for a form of nuclear pro-liferation – the basing of their nuclear weapons on the territories of allies. For the Soviet Union, this included Czechoslovakia, Poland, Hungary and East Germany, and for the United States it included the UK, West Germany, Belgium, Holland, Greece, Italy, Turkey and South Korea. Furthermore, the deployment of naval tactical nuclear weapons meant that nuclear weapons were present on warships in many oceans and seas.

In summary, by the end of the 1970s, the United States and the Soviet Union had built up strategic nuclear forces numbering nearly 20,000 nuclear warheads and comprising ICBMs, SLBMs and strategic bombers. They had, in addition, over 20,000 tactical and intermediate-range nuclear weapons and a complex set of targeting strategies which normally involved selective use of these weapons within a conventional conflict. A significant part of the US tactical and intermediate nuclear forces was integrated into NATO nuclear planning. Britain, France and China were substantial middle-ranking nuclear powers, with strategic and tactical nuclear weapons, Israel had a nuclear capability and India and South Africa had, at the least, a developing nuclear potential. The public perception of a static nuclear weapons environment was hardly accurate.

To the detached observer, the 1970s represented a decade when two quite different processes appeared to be in progress. Superficially there was considerable activity in nuclear arms control, but the reality was of a continuing enhancement of both the quantity and quality of nuclear armaments. SALT 2 sounded good but amounted to very little; meanwhile, nuclear developments continued unabated. It was in this context that from 1979 onwards increased tensions led to the so-called new Cold War.

The New Cold War

At the end of the 1970s, a number of factors combined to heighten East–West tensions, give a new impetus to the nuclear arms race and revive public awareness of nuclear issues. Significant among these factors were the Soviet intervention in Afghanistan, the political swing to the Right in the United States with the election of Ronald Reagan as President, itself partly a result of US reaction to the Tehran hostage crisis, and the coincidental development of a number of new weapons systems.

Led particularly by the United States and Britain, but by no means restricted to these countries, there was a greatly increased commitment to nuclear rearmament around the turn of the decade. In the United States itself, defence budgets from 1979–84 resulted in massive increases in funds for nuclear weapons research and development, and substantial increases in nuclear weapons deployments, including the resurrection of the B-1 strategic bomber and the deployment of the Trident C4 SLBM and the air-launched cruise missile. In Britain, the Thatcher government introduced plans to replace the ageing Polaris SLBMs with the Trident D5 system, involving at least an eight-fold increase in targeting capability.

Over the same period, the Soviet Union was improving and expanding its strategic nuclear forces, especially with the MIRVing of its SLBM force, and was also introducing large numbers of the SS-20 intermediate-range ballistic missile and the Backfire medium-range bomber. While Soviet nuclear forces were still technically inferior to those of the United States, the production rates of strategic and tactical systems in the late 1970s and early 1980s were remarkable. Soviet 'quantity' served to balance US 'quality', making it easy for hawks on both sides to continue their demands for more investment. France and China, meanwhile, were expanding their nuclear forces and there were persistent reports concerning the developing nuclear ambitions of Pakistan, Argentina and Brazil.

Many of the tensions concerned with the new Cold War were encapsulated in the controversy over new theatre nuclear weapons in Europe, especially the Soviet SS-20 missile and NATO's Pershing 2 and cruise missiles. Central features of the NATO missiles were their mobility and consequent distribution over several countries, together with their obvious connection with NATO's flexible response doctrine involving nuclear first use.

The Pershing 2 missile was seen as a particularly advanced weapon. Although its range was little more than 1,000 miles, it featured a form of terminal guidance which allowed it to combine speed with remarkable accuracy, with a circular error probable (CEP) of no more than 50 metres. The Pershing 2 was seen as a highly-effective weapon for employment in selective nuclear response, but it appeared to the Soviet Union to represent a firm shift towards a 'first strike' posture by NATO.

The Soviet Union itself was deploying several hundred triple warhead SS-20 missiles during the 1980s. While these were far less accurate than cruise or Pershing 2 missiles, they entered service in substantially larger numbers. Consequently, each side could argue that its nuclear expansion was a legitimate response to an escalating external threat.

Inevitably, an effect of this nuclear arms race in Europe was the development of powerful public opposition, especially in Britain, West Germany and the Netherlands. Much of the campaigning was directed against the so-called 'Euromissiles', but there was also a growing concern over new strategic developments.

At the strategic level, the major emerging trend was one of increased missile accuracy, with some multi-warhead ICBMs being developed with accuracies of below 200 metres CEP. This level of accuracy gave a significant capability against hardened missile silos and deep underground command bunkers and once again raised the problem of first strike weapons. The belief among critics of such developments was that the existence of fast accurate long-range missiles would cause considerable instability under crisis circumstances, as each side was tempted into adopting a 'use them or lose them' posture. Even if a complete disarming first strike was implausible, the act of striking first as part of a damage limitation policy, in conditions of crisis, was believed to be at least possible.

This kind of development aroused more concern in the United States than in Europe, and was one factor which led to the growth there of the Freeze Movement, concerned not so much with nuclear disarmament as with curbing any further developments.

The promotion of the Strategic Defense Initiative by President Reagan from 1983 onwards was partly a response to the growth of freeze campaigning, but was seen by its critics as another cause of instability, encouraging a further escalation in strategic arsenals in response to the development of defensive measures.

Thus, by the early 1980s, there was intense military competition between the superpowers, especially in the area of nuclear armaments, with considerable increases in the quantity and quality of strategic and intermediate nuclear weapons in hand. This led to a heightened public concern about escalation, especially in Europe.

Arms Control in the Early 1980s

In deciding to deploy cruise and Pershing 2 missiles, NATO chose at the end of the 1970s to adopt a 'twin-track' approach, linking negotiations on arms control and on the deployment of the new weapons, the discussions being designed to lead to an Intermediate-range Nuclear Force (INF) treaty. Similarly, efforts were made to embark on a new round of US-Soviet strategic arms control talks, the so-called Strategic Arms Reduction Treaty (START) discussions. Both sets of negotiations commenced in 1982 in Geneva, but were interrupted for some months by a Soviet withdrawal following the initial deployment of the new NATO intermediate-range missiles in 1983.

By 1985, the Western position was dominated by President Reagan's 'double zero' option – a willingness to withhold deployment of NATO intermediate-range nuclear forces if the Soviet Union withdrew all its equivalent forces. This involved the Soviet

Union in a much greater level of disarmament, and few analysts expected it to be acceptable.

The stage was thus set for protracted negotiations at a time of persistent escalation in nuclear arsenals. Prospects for curbing this arms race did not look good, and few analysts saw much prospect of any major arms control treaties being achieved in the late 1980s.

The Experience of Militarisation

While the process of global militarisation received by far its greatest catalyst in the East–West arms race, there were many examples of regional conflict and tension which developed their own dynamic. Most colonial wars of liberation were fought using small arms guerrilla tactics, although the colonial powers frequently retaliated with advanced systems and conventional tactics.

The long and costly war in Korea provided an impetus for rapid developments in land-based and naval aviation and early guided-missile systems, and the Vietnam War spawned a new generation of highly destructive anti-personnel weapons. In the Middle East, the combination of deep political tensions, oil wealth and East–West competition resulted in the deployment and use of many new weapons systems as well as the regional development of nuclear and chemical weapons and ballistic missiles.

Overall though, the core of the process of militarisation was the East–West axis of confrontation, even though it did entangle much of the global community. By the late 1980s, world spending on the military was approaching $1,000 billion each year, 83 per cent of which was spent by less than a quarter of the world's population that comprised the NATO and Warsaw Pact alliances.

3

Arms Control and Disarmament

From the record of global militarisation set out in the last Chapter, it might not seem unreasonable to conclude that over the 40-year period following the end of the Second World War attempts at arms control and disarmament had been a dismal failure. As we shall see, however, that is too simplistic a conclusion which denigrates the efforts of many people who were striving to come to terms with a new and very difficult situation.

With hindsight it is easy for us to see that the production of nuclear weapons introduced a major revolution in international relations. While, as in the past, many states could still fight wars in the hope of gain, given the developments in science and technology, war between the major powers in the nuclear age began to threaten destruction of the planet. This presented problems to those concerned with national security for which their previous experience had not equipped them.

For purposes of analysis the first four decades of the nuclear age, from the end of the Second World War until Gorbachev's arrival in power in the USSR, can be divided into three distinct phases:

- the first Cold War from 1945–62;
- the first détente between 1962–81; and
- the second Cold War from 1981–85.[1]

During the first phase of Cold War both sides – the US first and then gradually the Soviet Union – built up complete nuclear arsenals. Understandably, old ideas of seeking national security through military superiority reigned supreme, and attempts to achieve disarmament – particularly general and complete disarmament – were largely propaganda exercises.

In the first détente, following the Cuban Missile Crisis, no fundamental change took place in the nuclear balance between East and West, although a huge increase in the quantities of weapons, and qualitative improvements, occurred on both sides. Nevertheless, building on tentative foundations laid in the first Cold War period, certain people in the US developed a new set of ideas for attempting to stabilise the nuclear arms race. Rejecting both the impossible quest for meaningful superiority and immediate steps towards significant disarmament, they proposed internationally-agreed restraint through arms control measures as an effective way of dealing with the problem of avoiding nuclear war. Moreover, despite the momentum of the arms race, these ideas did have a direct effect and greatly influenced some of the major agreements reached. They also had an important indirect effect in influencing the thinking of some of the people who were to become prominent in the Soviet Union when Gorbachev came to power.

Unfortunately, by the time the second Cold War broke out in the early 1980s arms control seemed to have run out of steam. Even Thomas Schelling, one of the founding fathers of arms control, wrote an article in 1986 entitled 'What Went Wrong With Arms Control.'[2]

Arms Control Agreements in the First Period of Détente

Before we look in more detail at Western 'new thinking' of the late 1950s and early 1960s, we need to outline briefly what was later achieved in arms control measures. This will provide the necessary factual background for an analysis of the arms controllers' ideas and their successes and failures in implementation.

Arms control agreements concerned directly with nuclear weapons can be divided into five groups:
— the prevention of proliferation;
— reduction of nuclear arsenals;
— bans on testing;
— restrictions on distribution; and
— moderation of the dangers of deployments.[3]
Other agreements are concerned with:
— chemical weapons;
— biological weapons;
— other weapons of mass destruction; and
— conventional weapons.
Two major treaties were agreed in an attempt to prevent prolifer-

ation. The multilateral Non-Proliferation Treaty (NPT) of 1970 aimed to prevent the spread of nuclear weapons to other countries (horizontal proliferation). The Anti-Ballistic Missile (ABM) Treaty of 1972 prohibited the superpowers from attempting to construct nationwide defences against ballistic missiles, it being thought that this would have unleashed a compensatory growth in ballistic missiles (vertical proliferation).

While the growth in nuclear-weapon states has not been as fast as some predicted, critics have noted that the NPT did not, for example, include China, France, India, Israel or South Africa. Critics also noted that even with the ABM Treaty in place, the two superpowers massively increased the sizes of their strategic nuclear arsenals in the 1970s and early 1980s.

The SALT 1 and SALT 2 Treaties were initial attempts to restrict the sizes of the superpowers' nuclear arsenals. Again critics pointed out that the limits set had little real impact. SALT 1, for example, constrained the numbers of launchers, when the major problem was the MIRVing of warheads. SALT 2 was not ratified, and was eventually broken, by the United States. Moreover, the limits did not effectively restrict modernisation even during the period when the Treaty was observed.

The multilateral Limited Test Ban Treaty of 1963 banned the testing of nuclear weapons in the atmosphere, outer space and under water. This was criticised as being only a 'clean air act' because testing continued apace (and less noticeably to the public) underground. Two further superpower bilateral treaties on testing negotiated in the mid-1970s – the Threshold Test Ban Treaty and the Peaceful Nuclear Explosions Treaty – remained unratified by the United States until 1990. A series of multilateral treaties restricted the areas in which nuclear weapons could be deployed. The Antarctic Treaty of 1961 was followed by the Outer Space Treaty of 1967, the Treaty of Tlatelolco (Latin America) of 1968 and the Seabed Treaty of 1972. Clearly, critics argued, these were not areas where the military were strongly pressing to deploy nuclear weapons.

A further series of agreements between the superpowers (and some other nuclear-weapon states) attempted to reduce the danger of nuclear weapons being used in a crisis. Thus the original 'Hot Line' agreement of 1963 between the superpowers was supplemented by the Hot Line Modernisation Agreement and the Nuclear Accidents Agreement of 1971 and the Prevention of

Nuclear War Agreement of 1973. While the practical use of improved communications in crises cannot be denied, the Prevention of Nuclear War Agreement has been widely seen as being of little more than propaganda value.

Some restriction on chemical weapons results from the 1925 Geneva Protocol, but the reservations held by many state parties renders the Protocol effectively a 'No-First-Use' agreement in the view of many analysts. The Biological Weapons Convention of 1975 was hailed as a disarmament treaty in some quarters, but others have argued that its lack of verification provisions shows that the military did not at the time see such weapons as of much interest.

The multilateral Environmental Modification Convention of 1978 and the Convention on Inhumane Weapons of 1983 provide some, but very limited, protection against new forms of conventional weaponry. Finally, the Prevention of Naval Incidents Agreement between the superpowers in 1972 provided a model for a variety of operational confidence-building measures which were to follow later.

It should also be noted that these treaties do not encapsulate all the efforts to achieve arms control measures in the period. For example, the MBFR (Mutual and Balanced Force Reductions) negotiations in Europe continued unsuccessfully for many years; President Carter attempted to achieve an agreement to restrict the export of Conventional Weapons; and negotiations on a Comprehensive Nuclear Test Ban were considered to be very close to completion, but without final success, in the early 1980s.

Assessing Arms Control

In order to make a reasonable assessment of arms control we must ask what were the objectives of the Americans who developed the original ideas in the late 1950s; and to do that, it is necessary to understand something of the place of arms control in the maintenance of peace.

Most analysts believe that the fundamental causes of war are political: incompatible views on territory; ideology; nationalism and so on. In addition to such political causes, there are military factors. Thus, as there are few political reasons to fear war between the United States and Canada, no-one worried about the military balance between the two states after the Second World War. On the other hand, as there were political differences between the United States and the USSR there was great concern, on both sides, over the East–West military balance. In simple terms, there are two ways in which one might imagine war coming about between two such politically antagonistic and militarised states:

- a failure of deterrence (*ie* insufficient military strength) on one side might lead the other to think that a successful attack was possible; or
- a reciprocal build-up of weapons might lead inadvertently to war in a crisis because one side felt that it had to attack first or risk being attacked.

At one level, therefore, it can be argued that arms control measures cannot deal with the fundamental causes – the political roots – of war. Arms control does just what it says and no more. Yet, to the extent that the political causes of the original antagonism are based on, or exacerbated by, the military build-up on both sides, arms control measures could contribute to dealing with the underlying tensions that produce the danger of war.

On both sides, of course, there is likely to be a mixture of views on the nature of the competition with the other state and the best means of assuring national security. Again, to simplify, we might note that there could be three basic positions:

- hard-liners, who hold that the only safe course – even in the nuclear age – is military superiority, because of the inbuilt aggressive nature of the opposing state;
- liberals who hold that the only safe course – given the lethality of the weapons – is mutual disarmament; and
- those who believe that a prudent mixture of military measures and arms control restrictions is the only way to deal with both the preservation of political aims and the avoidance of nuclear war.

Clearly, hardliners worry about a failure of deterrence, but can be criticised for having no answer to the question of when the build-up will cease between antagonistic states. Liberals worry about the failure of control in crises, but can be criticised for having no answer to the question of how mutual disarmament is to be initiated and, just as important, how it is safely to be concluded. In the view of the arms controllers, therefore, both propositions involve dangerously destabilising possibilities.

In long-term interactions between antagonistic states there are likely to be ups-and-downs – periods of détente and Cold War – as the various groups gain more or less power. During periods of Cold War and non-negotiation, arms control will be of little direct relevance in guiding progress towards dealing with nuclear and other weapons. However, when détente and negotiations are possible, the ideas on arms control and disarmament that are available to political actors can be quite crucial in guiding progress. If there are no good ideas available, progress is likely to be limited. Thus, reasonable assessment of arms control would not look just at what treaties had been signed. If political conditions were inauspicious that would be somewhat unfair. A reasonable assessment would, of course, have to look at what had been achieved – there is little value in developing unacceptable ideas – but it would also have to ask how the ideas developed related to the realities of the nuclear age. Arms control might fail because it had no chance in the political climate of the time, or because it was not put forward in a usable way to political actors. But arms control might also fail, at a more fundamental level, if the ideas developed were not appropriate to the problems of the nuclear age.

Arms Control Objectives and Results

Thomas Schelling and Morton Halperin, in their classic book *Strategy and Arms Control*, suggested in the early 1960s that control should contribute to 'the avoidance of war that neither side wants, in minimising the costs and risks of arms competition, and in curtailing the scope and violence of war in the event it occurs'. The analysts who developed arms control accepted the political *status quo* and they carefully distanced themselves from the advocation of disarmament. Their approach was technical. They were primarily worried about how to ensure stability in crises, then about the costs of the arms race and finally about limiting the damage if war should occur. Yet, remarkably given the preceding intense period of Cold War, they argued that there were sound reasons for co-operation between nuclear adversaries.[4] The chief concern clearly was that the huge destructive power of nuclear weapons would lead to fear of pre-emptive destruction of either side's nuclear weapons by the other during a crisis. They argued that both sides would, therefore, be safer if both had secure retaliatory nuclear forces.

Arms controllers were particularly strong supporters of the ABM Treaty. They thought that the development of nationwide defences would lead to fears that such defences could be used to 'mop up' a weakened retaliatory force after a pre-emptive attack. This would therefore lead to even greater instability in crises and more rapid compensatory build-up of offensive forces, and was best avoided. Agreements on 'Hot Lines' were also welcome because they would reduce the dangers of misunderstanding in stressful circumstances.

As many critics have argued, however, there was obvious confusion over the idea of limiting damage if war came. If massive-scale disarmament was impossible, then the only possibility was to design for limited, accurate and controlled use of nuclear weapons. This, unfortunately, was likely to produce weapons systems and command and control arrangements which were indistinguishable, particularly to an opponent, from those needed to carry out pre-emptive first strikes.

Writing in 1986, Thomas Schelling argued that the 15-year period from 1957–72 was '. . . a remarkable story of intellectual achievement transformed into policy . . .' The high point in his view, was the achievement of the ABM Treaty, but he also felt that this was '. . . the end point of successful arms control'. Whilst he noted the value of the Partial Test Ban Treaty of 1963 and the Non-Proliferation Treaty of 1970, he argued that after 1972 '. . . the control of strategic weapons has made little or no progress, and the effort on our side has not seemed to be informed by any coherent theory of what arms control is supposed to accomplish . . .' He considered that there had been a 'mostly mindless' shift from a concern with the character of weapons to the numbers of systems involved. Schelling noted President Reagan's idea of SDI providing an impregnable defence and making nuclear weapons obsolete, but he did not see this as a realistic possibility. It has to be said that the very idea is a direct contradiction of the original arms control idea of achieving peace through maintenance of effective mutual deterrence.

Other critics have argued that while Schelling and his colleagues were obviously well-connected in Washington, the theory of arms control paid insufficient attention to how implementation was to take place. In particular, they have suggested that more attention paid to the way divergent lobby interests in the huge Washington bureaucracy operated would have led to greater success in seeing policies derived from arms control theory put into practice.

More seriously, other critics argued at the time, and have argued since, that the rejection of the objective of disarmament by the arms control community was a serious error. As Desmond Ball pointed out in one major recent review;

> . . . Vast expenditures on new weapon systems and capabilities have been justified in arms control negotiations on the grounds that modernisation would enhance stability. More importantly, the explicit distinction between arms control and disarmament in the classic studies led to the intellectual neglect of disarmament. The conditions for stability at greatly reduced weapons levels . . . have been essentially ignored.[5]

Thus, an overall assessment of arms control up to the mid-1980s would have produced, on balance, a somewhat mixed verdict.

As a set of intellectual ideas for dealing with the problems of security in the nuclear age, arms control at this stage was perhaps too concentrated on military-technical issues of crisis stability, to the exclusion of the political problems that were producing the various possibilities for crises arising. Even within its own technical area there was probably too much confusion over damage limitation and counterforce capabilities, and good reason to believe that the ideas were too limited because of their failure to address disarmament. In terms of implementation of their ideas, arms controllers certainly could claim some major successes – ABM and NPT remain the cornerstones of such arms control regime as we have – but it does appear that they had little to contribute in restricting the arms build-up of the mid- to late 1970s which, in part, was responsible for the increasing antagonism and second Cold War between the superpowers in the 1980s.

In another sense, a rounded verdict on the West's 'new thinking' on arms control in the late-1950s and early 1960s and its implementation in the period of détente should surely be more benign. Given the competing pressures, for example, of the old-fashioned search for superiority, and the view that national security must greatly restrict verification on national soil, it remains remarkable that the new ideas on co-operation with a distrusted antagonist could be put forward intellectually, and even implemented in major treaties. If a history of the latter part of this war-torn century is written from the perspective of a much more secure age, arms control as it was practised in the first period of détente will certainly have an important place in the development of means of coming to terms with our increasingly powerful science and technology.

The Gorbachev Peace Offensive, 1985–91

Given the weight of experience over the preceding 40 years, few analysts expected massive changes in Soviet arms control and disarmament policy when Gorbachev came to power in 1985. Since then we have seen three major treaties signed amidst a flurry of policy changes and initiatives. Before we can assess what might happen over the next decade, and what more might need to be done, we must try to grasp what has happened – and why it has happened – over the last six years.

The first significant arms control measure that (with hindsight) showed something very different about to happen was the agreement on Confidence and Security-Building Measures, signed in Stockholm in September 1986. This agreement was set within the overall framework of the Conference on Security and Co-operation in Europe (CSCE) and built upon the limited measures in the original Helsinki Agreement of 1975. Advance notification of military exercises and routine observation of such exercises – including limited on-site inspection – were aimed at increasing confidence about the nature of military movements.

The first major treaty was the Elimination of Intermediate-range Nuclear Forces (INF) signed by the United States and the USSR in December 1987. This Treaty consists of a short Preamble, 17 Articles, a Protocol on Elimination, a Protocol on Inspections and a Memorandum of Understanding which contains the very extensive database for the Treaty. In total, the Soviet Union agreed to destroy 1,836 missiles and the United States 867, over a three-year period. While critics pointed out that destruction of the nuclear warheads and guidance systems was not required, the really remarkable aspects of the Treaty – apart from its successful agreement after all the acrimony over SS-20, cruise and Pershing 2 missiles during the 1980s – were the verification conditions agreed by the USSR.

Previously the two parties had, in September 1987, made a separate agreement to establish Nuclear Risk Reduction Centers, to handle the massive data exchanges needed to operate the verification of the INF Treaty. A Special Verification Commission was also set up to assist in the implementation of the Treaty and to help resolve differences between the parties. Crucially, and in contradiction of previous Soviet policy, verification of the Treaty involved major on-site inspection. Inspections even included continuous monitoring of the output of some production facilities which was agreed should continue for many years.

The details of the INF Treaty were carefully crafted and precise, with the result that, despite some minor difficulties which were obviously to be expected in such a complex new arrangement, there have been no major problems in its implementation.

The second major treaty of the Gorbachev era was that on Conventional Forces in Europe (CFE) signed by the parties in November 1990. In many ways, this was even more remarkable than the INF Treaty, given the huge investment in such forces that had been made by both East and West in the preceding decades, and the fruitless 16 years spent on Mutual and Balanced Force Reduction negotiations since 1973!

In simple terms the balance of forces existing in Europe at the time can be described as investment by the Warsaw Pact in quantity and by NATO in quality. Thus the Pact had more men and weapons available, but NATO had better trained men and superior equipment. CFE defined five treaty-limited items – main battle tanks, artillery, armoured combat vehicles, combat aircraft and combat helicopters. It then set ceilings on the numbers and distribution of these items and required that the specified items were reduced to these levels. Clearly, the overall effect was to remove hugely asymmetric amounts of Soviet–Warsaw Pact forces (*eg* tanks) in reaching the new quantitative limits. Verification conditions were again strict and detailed. Effectively, NATO's fears of short-warning attack from the East were removed.

The final major treaty was signed in July 1991. This was the START agreement dealing with the superpowers' strategic nuclear arms. This massively complex treaty had taken most of the 1980s to negotiate, following on the failed SALT 2 negotiations of the 1970s. The Treaty dictates a cut of about 30 per cent in the numbers of strategic nuclear warheads on both sides and again involves massively intrusive verification conditions.

Perhaps the most important feature of the Treaty is the way that it specifically addresses US concerns. Thus the widely-advertised 50 per cent cuts, for example, really do apply to the SS-18 Soviet heavy ICBM which caused so many 'first-strike' fears in the USA; and the bomber-counting rule specifically discounts weapons in the bomber arm of the triad of forces – where the United States has traditionally been stronger.

The three major treaties have been accompanied by numerous

smaller agreements and waves of Soviet initiatives – such as
Gorbachev's initial Nuclear Testing Moratorium – over the last six
years. The evidence leaves little doubt that the driving force for
this renaissance in arms control and disarmament has come from
the Soviet Union. But what does it signify? In order to tackle that
question we need to understand a little more of what had gone
before Gorbachev.

Before Gorbachev

It is clear that the Soviet military has subjected the evolution of
military technology and its operational implications to very careful
analysis during the nuclear age, and that their views on the significance of these weapons has been subject to substantial change over
the years.

American analysts[6] suggest that immediately after the Second
World War Soviet military planning did not give prominence to
nuclear weapons, but continued to plan for operations similar to
those employed during the war, based on the assumption that the
available nuclear weapons were not numerous enough to have
significant effect. But the continued expansion of nuclear arsenals,
and the development of delivery systems, led to a dramatic change
in this view. In particular, Soviet plans for the crucial European
theatre were threatened in the early 1950s as NATO began to
introduce nuclear weapons there, and it became clear that the
Soviet techniques for conventional operations, so successful in the
Second World War, were increasingly in danger. A major theme in
Soviet war-planning was, therefore, a concern to deal with that
problem. Studies in the later 1950s led to a completely new strategy, announced by Khrushchev in 1960, which gave predominant
emphasis to nuclear forces and suggested that these would be used
massively and decisively from the start of a superpower war. Yet
this unbalanced viewpoint did not survive for long.

The new US President, John Kennedy, was drastically increasing the gap between the size of US and Soviet forces, and building
up US military capabilities overall. Khrushchev's attempt to redress the strategic balance by putting shorter-range missiles into
Cuba failed and, soon after his removal, the Soviet military moved
back to a more balanced view of the use of nuclear and conventional forces. They concluded that they had to be able, if necessary,

to fight many different kinds of wars. They decided that all-out nuclear war was not the only possibility and, most importantly, that there was a real chance of avoiding nuclear attacks on the Soviet Union. Indeed, they thought that this might be possible even if limited nuclear war broke out in Europe. Such conclusions had far reaching implications for the crucial problem of dealing with NATO theatre nuclear forces.

The assessment implied that the Soviet Union needed to try to defeat NATO conventionally and to deter NATO nuclear use by at least matching NATO nuclear forces; the problem caused by the introduction of NATO theatre nuclear forces would then be solved.

By the early 1980s the Soviet military appeared relatively happy with the situation that they had created. They appeared to believe that large-scale and protracted warfare was possible without general nuclear war breaking out. Yet Soviet planners have always been concerned over the impact of new military technology and they had clearly become worried over several new trends by the mid-1980s. At one level they were concerned at Western military responses to perceived Soviet strength: US strategic modernisation, SDI, and the emplacement of new and threatening nuclear systems in Europe. More fundamentally, they appeared to be concerned over the possibility of losing out in a new scientific-technical revolution in military affairs. Some important Soviet experts like Marshal Ogarkov believed that a new generation of conventional weapons with greatly enhanced capabilities was about to appear, and that these would be followed up by another generation of weapons based on newly-discovered physical principles. Soviet planners were not sanguine about being able to keep up with Western technology in these areas. They also appeared to believe that the new weapons could alter the balance in military operations in favour of the defence. Thus some authors believe that Soviet considerations of ideas such as 'defensive defence' may not have had a totally benign origin. In their view the Soviet military may have been prepared to take current cutbacks and accept a less offensive strategy in order to move necessary resources into military R & D and production of new systems.

It has to be understood, however, that until nuclear weapons in large numbers no longer exist, the worst case – general nuclear war – will still be planned for. William Lee states the issue that then arises quite clearly:

. . . In all cases, the bottom line is how each superpower proposes to employ . . . its weapons: What targets are to be attacked? What degree of damage is to be inflicted? What are the politico-military objectives, if any, of strategic nuclear strikes once deterrence has failed for whatever reason?[7]

Lee emphasises the Soviet dislike of the excesses of US and British strategic bombing in the Second World War and notes that they would have sought to avoid unnecessary destruction. Nevertheless, he believes that they had a nuclear war-fighting strategy for the worst-case contingency. If nuclear war came their aim would be, in this view, to defeat the enemy's armed forces:

. . . the principal targets of the SRF (Strategic Rocket Forces) would be the enemy's delivery systems, weapons storage, and fabrication sites; military installations; military industries; and centres of politico-military administration, command and control.

Such principles have been applied to different objectives in different theatres of operation. In Europe the aim was to defeat and disarm NATO with as little collateral damage as possible. However, as they would not occupy North America, targeting there would be heavier in order to prevent reconstitution and recovery.

According to Lee, in 1983 there were 900–1,100 targets in the Eurasian theatre, about 15 per cent of which were hardened. There had been an ability to cover these since the mid-1960s. There were many more targets to be covered in the United States, and Lee argues that it was only after a considerable struggle, over many years, that the Soviet Union achieved the targeting requirements in the United States. In short, before Gorbachev came to power the Soviet military basically believed – as did the military in the West – that security lay in maintaining as much 'parity' as possible at both the nuclear and conventional force levels. While hard-liners on the Soviet side undoubtedly thought – as did their counterparts in the West – that superiority would be better, the consensus hammered out in the Brezhnev years mirrored that of the arms controllers in the West.

Brezhnev's 'dual-track' policy has been described by Bruce Parrott as having a number of significant features:

. . . a nearly reflexive conviction that the continuous expansion of Soviet military power would automatically enhance Soviet security: a belief that diplomatic negotiations, particularly arms control negotiations, were a valuable complementary means of managing the competition with the

United States; a vigorous determination to expand Soviet influence in the Third World: and a desire to draw on Western economic inputs while simultaneously insulating the Soviet domestic system from Western political and cultural influences . . .[8]

Parrott also describes how this 'dual-track' policy was under threat from the hard-line Soviet conservatives in the early 1980s. They felt that the US military build-up under Carter and Reagan and the refusal to ratify SALT 2 raised doubts about negotiations with the West. They argued instead for an increase in the Soviet defence budget.

Change Under Gorbachev

Gorbachev came to power in all probability as a supporter of the 'dual-track' policy. This view was confirmed by the heavy support he received initially from Foreign Minister Gromyko. It is fair to suggest, however, that Gorbachev's increasingly large and daring deviations from this policy were motivated, first and foremost, by his growing awareness of the crisis throughout the whole Soviet system. In these conditions, Gorbachev and his colleagues had to attend to domestic – particularly economic – issues. Foreign policy had to be directed to providing favourable conditions for domestic revitalisation. The question is: Was that all that was involved?

In short, as happened in the 1960s and 1970s, new ideas on arms control have been influential during a period of negotiation. The question is: What was the extent of change in the foreign policy context within which arms control was taking place? Were we dealing with short-term alterations in forms or long-range redefinitions of goals? Or were we, perhaps, dealing with a complex mixture of parties and policies in the USSR?

While Gorbachev may have begun as a supporter of the old 'dual-track' policy, in foreign affairs he clearly surrounded himself with people such as Shevardnadze, Dobrynin and Yakovlev who held radically different ideas. He also increasingly reorganised his foreign policy-making apparatus to give radical civilian analysts much more opportunity to air very different ideas from those traditionally held by the military. It goes almost unremarked today that Gorbachev carried out a huge change in the presentation of Soviet policies. Gone are the grey days of the 1970s and early 1980s. During Gorbachev's early years the élites in the West were frequently surprised at the scale and speed with which the Soviet system was able to act. Moreover, a series of very able spokesmen – Gerasimov being a prime example – were produced to present Soviet policies in a way acceptable to Western audiences.

There can be no doubt either that the Soviet Union made adjustments in its policy direction in regard to arms control. The use of unilateral initiatives, asymmetric reductions, and acceptance of severe verification regimes signalled large changes in military doctrine and force structures towards more 'defensive defence' and 'reasonable sufficiency' in the intermediate term. The question is whether conservatives in the West were correct in thinking that all of this would have changed if the Soviet economy began to pick up?

Clearly, Soviet arms control policy was part of a huge change in Soviet foreign policy overall. The removal of forces from Afghanistan, the settlement of conflicts in Southern Africa the rapprochement with China, the new attitude to the role of the UN, and particularly the Security Council, surely suggested that deeper changes were underway in Gorbachev's Soviet Union. The release of Eastern Europe and the willingness to accept a reunited Germany after the devastation of the Second World War are but the most dramatic signs of this general change.

Within the realm of defence and security policy Gorbachev essentially allowed the development of a liberal rather than a conservative critique of Brezhnev's 'dual-track' policy. Rather than arguing that this line had been too soft towards the West, the liberal civilian analysts argued that it had been too hard. They suggested that the Soviet military build-up rather than being just a response to the West's actions, frequently caused the Western reaction. Furthermore these critics suggested that in the nuclear age security could not be obtained through military means. They rejected deterrence as a means of guaranteeing long-term security because it risked the outbreak of war in a crisis. In declaratory policy at least – for example Gorbachev's sweeping proposals of January 1986 – the Soviets even argued for rapid movement towards a denuclearised world.

Crucially, Gorbachev altered a fundamental principle of Soviet foreign policy. As noted by Parrott, shortly after the Reykjavik summit, Gorbachev suggested:

> . . . the Soviet pursuit of an international line based on 'class conflict' and the alleged interests of the working class **alone** should be moderated for the sake of more important common human values . . .
>
> (Our emphasis)

And as Parrott goes on to point out:

> . . . The main value Gorbachev seemed to have in mind was human survival in the face of potential nuclear war, but the slogan 'common human values' later came to symbolise the need for East-West co-operation across a wide spectrum of issues.

In short, arms control was not being carried out by the Soviet Union in the context of the acceptance of an unchanged political *status quo*.

The USSR, as we can see from the associated internal efforts at liberalisation and democratisation, was being driven by long-term redefinitions of goals and aspirations. In many ways we might argue that arms control – by opening up the possibility of initiating rapid change – was consciously used as a tool to help in the first stages of a profound political reorientation of the Soviet Union towards the West and its values.

In that sense then, the Soviet 'new thinkers' of the 1980s went far beyond the American 'new thinkers' on arms control in the 1960s. They suggested that a system based on fundamental East–West ideological and political antagonism and a nuclear deterrence system must involve continued arms-building and the risk of devastating war. They therefore argued that ideological and political change was needed in order to bring the military machines under control. (Naturally, they also argued for the political changes in the Soviet Union for other reasons as well). Within a different political context, arms control might be used to effect substantial reductions and longer-term control regimes. The questions that Western supporters of disarmament suggested arms control had left aside – such as the minimum level of arms – could begin to be debated.

Resistance to Gorbachev

If this liberal agenda had continued to hold centre stage in the Soviet Union many more remarkable proposals might reasonably have been expected. Unfortunately, as could surely have been expected, the liberals' agenda ran into increasing opposition from military and military-industrial interests.

The Soviet military certainly had, at its higher levels, a strong tradition of intellectual analysis. The impact of the new technology, based on the Third Industrial Revolution in electronics, was well understood and argued by people such as Marshal Ogarkov in the early 1980s. That is why they wanted more money spent on defence and would presumably also have supported some of Gorbachev's initial stress on industrial renewal. In a militarised society such as the Soviet Union, however, the military-industrial complex was a huge barrier to such renewal. For example, the privileges enjoyed by military industry necessarily were at the expense of civilian industry.

For the Soviet military hierarchy itself the scale of change from 1985 to 1991 must have been practically unimaginable, after years of endeavouring to build up their 'position of strength'. Giving up their new intermediate-range forces in Europe would have been as nothing compared to the reduction of their forces under the CFE Treaty and their control of Eastern Europe, and that was followed by cuts at the strategic nuclear level along lines suggested by the US. Moreover, the standing of the military in the Soviet Union had been under assault, opponents had had access to policy-makers, and the USSR was clearly disintegrating.

Resistance to the liberals and their agenda has been well documented and culminated in the loss at the centre not only of Shevardnadze but also of Yakovlev, and finally Gorbachev himself. Both these extremely important aides have openly complained of the danger of a right-wing reaction in the Soviet Union. Thus, while the demilitarisation of the Soviet system has been substantial and, following the failed coup of August 1991, should be resumed, the future direction of policy is uncertain, and perhaps ever more dependent on the West.

Western Reaction to Gorbachev

What, then, are we to make of the West's actions in arms control in the period of Gorbachev's rule? For many in the Western peace movements Soviet actions were both understandable and acceptable; much of the policy was, after all, what they had been urging on both East and West. For the Western élites in positions of long-term power within the Cold War system, the changes appear to have been difficult to understand and accept. Indeed, it might be argued that, while the West was willing to accept what Gorbachev offered, it has been no more forthcoming than that in its dealings with the Soviet Union.

If the West led the breakthrough in arms control in the 1960s and the Soviet Union was too slow to respond, the reverse is surely true for the period since 1985. There is no better indicator of Western élites' inability properly to understand the reality of the nuclear age than their determined clinging to the notion of nuclear deterrence – illustrated all too clearly by their refusal to consider negotiation of a comprehensive nuclear test ban. They stuck to deterrence and testing, for example, even when it wrecked the Non-Proliferation Treaty Review in the autumn of 1990 (because Third World countries would not agree to ignore testing). Even more clearly, the US and UK prevented the attempt in early 1991 to amend the Limited Test Ban Treaty to a Comprehensive Ban.

On the other hand, the West and the Soviet Union were able to make some progress on the further control of proliferation. Despite enormous technical difficulties, considerable progress has been made in the negotiation of a Chemical Weapons Convention and some improvements in the viability of the Biological Weapons Convention have been agreed. Additionally, the so-called Australia Group has improved co-ordination of controls on the export of materials connected with chemical and biological weapons pro-duction. The increasing information on what Iraq was able to import and produce during the 1980s will certainly lead to greater attention being paid to proliferation control.

A final indicator of what may be needed in the way of future developments is the Missile Technology Control Regime (MTCR). Rather than an international agreement, this is an identical set of national export policies. These were originally agreed in secret by seven Western countries and have been gradually extended to other participants since their open announcement in 1987. The basic idea is to prevent the development by more countries of longer-range missiles capable of carrying nuclear warheads. Despite their belief in deterrence for the West, our representatives clearly do not believe that the spread of such weaponry is sensible.

In short then, we may have seen half a breakthrough in arms control since 1985 (for which two cheers!). For a period, powerful policy-makers in the Soviet Union appeared to grasp the reality of the problems of controlling military technology in the nuclear age. They then appeared to be, at least temporarily, in retreat, and the present situation is very uncertain. In the West the élites in power cling to the notion of deterrence for themselves, but show increas-ing – and wholly reasonable – concern about the spread of military

capabilities across the world, though they appear unable to offer
rational solutions to the consequent dangers.

4

Military Momentum in the 1990s

Conventional wisdom would suggest that the achievements of the INF Treaty and the CFE agreement between 1987 and 1991, and the signing of the START agreement in 1991, together marked the end of the superpower arms race – that conspicuous feature of the second Cold War during the 1980s. That arms race took many forms, including strategic, intermediate and tactical nuclear weapons, SDI, and developments in C^3I, reconnaissance systems, strike aircraft, tanks, warships and all manner of weapons systems.

Even so, the breakthrough of the late 1980s is hailed as a turning point and it is certainly true that some cuts were started by the end of the decade, with more to come in the early 1990s. These include the elimination of ground-launched intermediate-range US and Soviet nuclear missiles in Europe, major cuts in conventional forces in Europe, unilateral cuts by both sides in naval tactical nuclear weapons and a curbing of defence budgets within NATO and the former Warsaw Pact countries.

Against this, there is, sadly, a sense in which 'we have been here before'. Experience of arms control negotiations in the 1970s certainly suggests we have, as mentioned in Chapter 3. From 1972–79, US and Soviet negotiators were involved in the second series of Strategic Arms Limitation Treaty (SALT 2) talks, intended to set upper limits to the numbers of strategic warheads held by each side. During these negotiations, the two superpowers nearly doubled the numbers of strategic warheads which they were deploying: US strategic arsenals rose from 5,600 to 8,900 and Soviet arsenals from 2,400 to 5,200.

In the event, SALT 2 was never ratified by the US Congress, although both powers informally abided by the agreement as long as it did not greatly hinder their strategic development plans, but it was a clear example of what Alva Myrdal has called 'the game of disarmament'. By this she meant that arms control negotiators might, to an extent, be serious in their intent, but their political leaders were far more likely to have their strategic policies dictated by military-industrial lobbies, and pay little more than lip service to the needs of arms control and disarmament.

Many analysts would argue that circumstances have changed drastically, that the fundamental reforms in the Soviet Union, the democratisation of much of Eastern Europe, the dissolution of the Warsaw Pact and the cuts in defence budgets across the industrialised world all foretell a period of genuine demilitarisation.

Against this, the massive investment in military research and development in the 1980s has given an impressive new momentum to military developments in many areas, the most significant being strategic nuclear weapons.[1] While this Chapter will touch on other areas of military development, it will concentrate on this, the most devastating form of military power, and will examine whether the optimism is really justified or whether a destabilising weapons dynamic is, in reality, continuing. An appropriate starting place is the recently-completed START agreement which appears, at first sight, to confirm the optimistic view that the strategic nuclear arms race is now firmly under control.

START Negotiations

As has been seen (Chapter 3), the START Treaty goes further than SALT 2 in agreeing substantial cuts in the size of strategic nuclear arsenals. In theory, the cuts could be as great as 50 percent but, in practice, the arcane counting rules ensure cuts of no more than 30 percent. Even here, though, there are two major problems with START, one of which being that it could have little perceptible effect on strategic nuclear rivalry.

The first point is to place START within the context of strategic nuclear developments. Negotiations on START commenced in 1982 and continued intermittently for nine years. Agreement should result in the strategic arms cuts being achieved within about seven years, probably by 1999.

Because of the rapid MIRVing of strategic missiles in the early 1980s, US and Soviet nuclear arsenals were already up to some 16,000 warheads by the start of the negotiations in 1982. Many new systems coming on stream during the 1980s took that figure up to about 24,000 by the end of the decade, when the rate of increase slowed down. Under the START Treaty, the totals will fall to about 16,000 warheads by the turn of the century, about the same level as in 1982. In other words, all that the implementation of the START agreement will do is to return us to the strategic *status quo* of the early 1980s.

In reality, it does not even do this, since it refers only to the crude numbers of warheads. START does virtually nothing about qualitative changes in strategic arsenals – indeed its primary effect will simply be to remove the more obsolete components of those arsenals. Completion of the START process will therefore result in smaller strategic nuclear forces but they will be far more advanced than those of the past two decades, where state-of-the-art and obsolete weapons have been deployed together. Given the trend towards production of more precise and usable weapons, with their first strike potential, this means that a post-START strategic environment could actually be less stable than before.

Against this, it can be argued that the easing of East–West tensions in the past three years has already led to considerable defence budget cuts and this alone will retard future strategic modernisation. Moreover, there is every prospect of further arms control negotiations leading to a second START agreement, which would bring in even deeper cuts in strategic arsenals and might even affect the more modern systems.

The reality appears to be somewhat different. Unless there is a greatly increased commitment by the United States to further strategic arms talks, there seems little prospect of a START 2 Treaty being agreed during the present decade. Moreover, there are clear indications that the continuing strategic modernisation will result in an unstable strategic environment and will also have dangerous side-effects in other areas of military activity.

We will explore these trends initially by examining recent, current and planned developments in US and Soviet strategic weapons, before moving on to look at their implications for other aspects of military strategy.

US Strategic Modernisation – 1985–2000

As they had developed by the mid-1980s, US strategic weapons continued to comprise a triad of land-based intercontinental missiles, submarine-launched missiles and manned bombers. Numerically, the land-based missile forces were the smallest, although they included the most accurate weapons.

The re-arming of the US under the Reagan administration gave a remarkable boost to strategic nuclear developments and included the rescue of the B-1 strategic bomber programme, which had been cancelled by Reagan's predecessor, Jimmy Carter. Early in the Reagan period, a modernisation programme for the mainstay of the ICBM force, the Minuteman III missile, was completed with an upgrade which involved a doubling of warhead yield and considerable improvements in accuracy, resulting in a force of 300 missiles with the most advanced counter-silo capability available in any US or Soviet system.

This strategic potential was superseded by the deployment of the M-X ('Missile-Experimental') Peacekeeper ICBM, a 10-MIRV missile, from December 1986 onwards. This has an accuracy of 120 metres CEP, giving it a considerable counter-silo and counter-bunker capability. Only 50 were installed in silos by the end of 1988; a further 50 were to be installed in a rail-mobile system but this has now been cancelled.

Similar problems have occurred with the newest US land-based ICBM, the small ICBM or Midgetman. This concept was originally promoted by Boeing in 1981, the idea being to produce a small ICBM to be carried by a toughened launch vehicle with some cross-country capability, thus making it virtually invulnerable to a disarming first strike. Martin Marietta won the development contract in 1985, the missile was first test-fired in May 1989 and development continues.

The US Navy has deployed three generations of SLBM over the past three decades, the most recent being the Trident C-4 missile carrying eight 100kt warheads with an accuracy of 450 metres CEP. During the 1980s, a fleet of 10 new *Ohio*-class submarines were deployed, each carrying 24 missiles. These were originally the Trident C-4 missile, but from the end of 1989, a new version was deployed, the Trident D-5.

The name Trident D-5 implies a minor development of the current Trident C-4 missile, but D-5 is an entirely new and much larger missile with two significant features. The first is that it is designed to carry a much larger warhead than the C-4, the W-87, with a destructive force of 300–475 kt. Secondly, a combination of inertial and stellar guidance will give the missile an accuracy of 120 metres CEP, matching that of the M-X ICBM. Although there is some slippage in the Trident D-5 programme, current indications are that up to 312 missiles may be deployed on at least 14 *Ohio*-class boats, with around 4,000 highly accurate warheads, by the tail-end of the decade, giving the United States a very considerable counter-silo and counter-bunker capability.

The bomber 'leg' of the US strategic triad has undergone comprehensive upgrading during the 1980s and this will continue through the next decade with a combination of new aircraft and stand-off missiles.

A four-part programme started with the development and deployment of the air-launched cruise missile (ALCM) on B-52 strategic bombers from 1982 onwards, the production line closing in 1986 after 1,715 missiles had been delivered. Each low-flying 880kph missile carries a W-80-1 variable-yield warhead ranging from 5–150 kt and its TERCOM (terrain contour-matching) guidance gives an accuracy better than 50 metres CEP.

The B-1 strategic bomber was originally developed in the 1970s and after its resuscitation by the Reagan administration, was redesigned with stealth anti-radar features and entered service in 1987. Within two years, 97 were deployed, each able to carry a mix of up to 36 nuclear bombs and stand-off missiles such as the ALCM. A follow-on to the ALCM, the stealthy advanced cruise missile (ACM) commenced development in 1983 and entered service in 1990 on B-1B bombers. The ACM has a similar warhead to its ALCM predecessor but is very difficult to detect, has a longer range and a greater accuracy, reported to be under 30 metres CEP. Up to 1,500 will be deployed in the 1990s.

Finally, a large stealthy bomber, the Advanced Technology Bomber (ATB) or B-2, was developed at great cost during the 1980s and was first test-flown early in 1989. This flying-wing design is intended to fly low, and virtually at will, over hostile territory, seeking out and destroying high-value targets, especially mobile ICBMs. The project has proved to be prohibitively expensive, each plane possibly costing over half-a-billion dollars, and the original plans for 132 planes have been cut back severely. Even so, the project survives and will give the USAF a remarkable if very expensive capability to project air power.

In summary, budgetary pressures are having their effect on US strategic programmes, but the momentum became so great during the high-spending years of the 1980s that there is a pronounced carry-over effect which is allowing substantial modernisation through the current decade. This is virtually unaffected by the START agreement or Bush's unilateral cuts announced in October 1991 which both mostly involve withdrawal of older obsolete systems that will, in any case, result in substantial cost savings.

Those high-spending years also led to a veritable surge in spending on research and development of nuclear weapons and their delivery systems, especially at the strategic level. This, too, is yielding significant results in the 1990s in four distinct areas. A number of programmes are concerned with improving missile accuracy. They include new inertial systems, stellar mid-course updates and terminal guidance, all aiming to achieve accuracies for fast ballistic missiles of 30 metres CEP or less. Other programmes involve the development of manoeuvrable re-entry vehicles which can change course repeatedly to avoid anti-missile defences.

Thirdly, a major development in warhead technology is now under way – the development of earth-penetrating warheads which burrow at least 20 metres underground before detonating. This increases their yield effectiveness up to 25-fold and makes them especially effective against silos and bunkers.

Finally, there is a continuing programme of research into destroying mobile targets such as rail- and road-mobile ICBMs. This can involve a combination of stealth bombers linked to the new TR-3A Manta stealthy reconnaissance plane, but may also involve ICBM or SLBM warheads which can be re-targeted using data from real-time satellite or aircraft-based observation of mobile targets.

All these programmes are linked in to missiles and aircraft already deployed or in production. In the longer term, there are further programmes under way. One is the so-called Boost Glide system, where an ICBM-launched vehicle glides through the upper atmosphere at around Mach 15 and is able to manoeuvre to cover a wide potential target area before homing onto one target. The Boost Glide proposal is in its very early stages, but a much more advanced programme is the Transatmospheric Hypersonic Vehicle (TAV), originally announced by Reagan in February 1986 and misleadingly suggested to be an intercontinental civilian transport to be called the Orient Express. In reality, the TAV, now known as the National Aerospace Plane (NASP) or X-30A, is a programme almost entirely financed from defence sources which aims to produce a hybrid aircraft/spacecraft which will use runways for take-off and landing but will transfer to space at speeds of up to Mach 25. NASP itself may have a reconnaissance rather than a strike role but will provide a range of technologies which will be applicable to other military projects.

This description of some of the advanced strategic projects now being funded does not imply that all will be deployed. What it does show is that a massive R&D effort is in progress, boosted by the budgets of the past decade. Some projects will collapse or be curtailed; others which are currently 'black' secret programmes will surface. But the trend throughout is towards more sophisticated systems, with at least some of the projects initiated in the 1980s coming to fruition in the current decade.

Soviet Strategic Modernisation – 1985–2000

Until the 1960s, the United States had a dominant lead over the Soviet Union in strategic nuclear weapons. By the mid-1970s, the Soviet Union had deployed substantial numbers of very powerful strategic systems. Although they could not match the reliability or accuracy of the US systems, they tended to carry much heavier warheads and, as a crude threat, they counterbalanced the numerically superior US systems.

By the 1970s, the US was moving rapidly ahead again as it produced large numbers of multiple-warhead missiles, both MRV and MIRV systems; but this technology was also developed by the Soviet Union and its effects began to be apparent at the end of the 1970s when the first MIRVed Soviet ICBMs were deployed.

By 1985, the Soviet Union was deploying at least 500 additional warheads each year, a momentum which has largely persisted since. Moreover, its strategic modernisation programme, unlike most areas of Soviet military expenditure, has shown little sign of levelling off. Taken with the momentum of the US strategic developments, this suggests a continuing process of mutual competition through the 1990s. It is not easy to explain why strategic systems are being given such special treatment in the current circumstances of economic crisis in the Soviet Union, and it is possible that the comprehensive political changes during the latter part of 1991 may have an effect in due course; even so, a description of the programmes gives some indications of the extent of the modernisation and, possibly, the reasoning behind this policy.

During the 1980s, the mainstay of the Soviet ICBM force was a trio of missiles, the heavy SS-18 and the light SS-17 and SS-19. Four versions of the SS-18 were deployed in the late 1970s and early 1980s, two with very large single warheads and two with MIRVed systems. After a lull in further developments, a Mod-5 version carrying ten 750kt warheads was deployed from 1989 and half of the 308 SS-18s are likely to be retro-fitted with this version. The combination of warhead size with a CEP of around 250 metres makes this a particularly destabilising first-strike missile.

A new missile, the SS-24, commenced test-firing in 1982, was first deployed in 1987 and continues in production. It has been deployed both in silos and in a rail-mobile form, carries 10 MIRV warheads rated at 100kt and has a CEP of perhaps 200 metres. Several hundred are expected to be deployed.

A further ICBM, the SS-25, is much smaller and is analogous to the US Midgetman. Deployed initially in 1986, production continues and up to 500 may be produced by the early 1990s. It is a single-warhead road-mobile missile, less accurate than the SS-24 or SS-18 but indicative of the Soviet concern with producing mobile ICBMs which can avoid destruction by the large numbers of highly accurate ICBM and SLBM warheads progressively being deployed by the United States. This commitment to mobile land-based missiles is, in turn, a prime reason for the heavy US investment in strategic systems to destroy relocatable targets.

There have been frequent reports of further Soviet ICBM development programmes, but these are probably additional variants of existing systems, although advanced ICBM programmes are likely to be under way.

The Soviet strategic submarine missile programme continues to receive heavy investment, although some aspects experienced technical difficulties in the late 1980s. Whereas the United States has relied on relatively small numbers of missile submarines with up to 60 percent on patrol at any one time, the Soviet Union has typically had at least twice as many, but with much lower reliability and as few as 15 percent on patrol.

Following a number of single-warhead SLBMs, especially the numerous SS-N-8, the Soviet Union first deployed a MIRVed SLBM, the SS-N-18, in 1978, although its accuracy, at nearly 1,000 metres CEP, was grossly inferior to the US Navy's Poseidon SLBM, which was first deployed seven years earlier. In 1981, the USSR deployed a large new SLBM, the SS-N-20, on the world's largest submarine, the 25,000 ton *Typhoon*-class boat, each boat carrying 20 missiles. This new class proved exceptionally expensive to build but, even so, six were constructed and deployed by the end of the decade. Over the same period, another SLBM, the SS-N-23 was developed for installation in the *Delta IV*-class submarine. Deployment was delayed nearly two years until 1989 because of problems with the missile, but five boats were deployed by the end of the decade, with possibly three more under construction. Yet another submarine is now being developed and is reported to be undergoing sea trials prior to deployment within two years. It may carry an improved version of the SS-N-20, and indicates a very active and continuing Soviet interest in modernising the ballistic missile submarine force.

Finally, Soviet long-range aviation has been modernised by the introduction of a new strategic bomber and at least two major stand-off missiles. The first missile, the AS-15, is analogous to the US Air Force's ALCM, with a broadly similar range and carrying a 250kt warhead. It has been fitted initially to a new version of the old turboprop Tu-95 Bear bomber, known as the Bear-H. Deployment of the plane commenced in 1984 and continued through the decade, possibly as an interim launch platform for the AS-15, pending the deployment of the large new supersonic bomber then under development. By the end of the decade, AS-15 production was reported to be continuing at the rate of 100 per year.

The new bomber is the Tu-160 Blackjack, larger than, but broadly similar in configuration to, the US B-1B. Development of the Blackjack was protracted and it was not deployed in squadron service until 1989. Up to 100 may now have been produced, and the Blackjack can carry 12 AS-15 cruise missiles or up to 24 defence-suppression missiles such as the new AS-16.

Yet another stand-off missile is reported to be under development, designated the AS-X-19. This is believed to be a large supersonic 3,200km-range weapon which would survive more by virtue of its speed than any stealth characteristics, an area of technology where the United States has a significant lead. The large size of the AS-X-19 may mean the Blackjack can carry only two missiles, one in each of the internal bomb bays. It will probably enter service in the mid-1990s.

In analysing the current and future development of Soviet strategic nuclear weapons, it is reasonable to draw three conclusions, the last of which being somewhat tentative. Firstly, some of these programmes have experienced technical difficulties, including the SS-24 ICBM, the SS-N-23 SLBM and the Tu-160 Blackjack bomber. Secondly, the range of strategic weapons systems now being developed provides for a considerable qualitative upgrading of the strategic inventory during the 1990s, even if the START agreement is in force.

Finally, there are few signs so far of budgetary pressures affecting these programmes. This contrasts with deep cuts to the army and quite substantial cuts in the naval ship-building programme. There are two possible explanations for this. One is that these strategic systems are regarded by the military as well-nigh sacrosanct, providing for final protection in an uncertain world. If this is the case, then for the political leadership to cut spending on strategic weapons would be so unacceptable to the military as to occasion a major crisis for that leadership, even despite the reduced standing of the military in the wake of the abortive coup in August 1991. The other is that the Soviet leadership, likely now to be dominated by Russian interests, regards maintenance of a substantial and modern strategic arsenal as a means of holding on to superpower status. The political and economic problems facing the Soviet republics are already leading to a marked decline in living standards and a widespread belief in many countries that the United States is the only remaining superpower. The state of the economy makes it impossible to maintain defence expenditure at anything remotely approaching the level of the 1980s, but if the savage cuts in many areas are balanced by the preservation and enhancement of strategic nuclear forces, this may be considered to provide Russia in particular with some remaining claim to world status.

Even though the old Soviet Union is changing into a much looser federation, and individual republics may argue for nuclear-free status, there is little firm evidence that the political leadership, either in the main republics such as Russia and the Ukraine, or within the transformed federal leadership, will move rapidly to curb nuclear modernisation. Such a move would most certainly be welcome and could prove an embarrassment to Western states, but the short-term indications are that future policy will favour maintenance and modernisation of strategic nuclear forces. Even Gorbachev's unilateral cuts announced in October 1991 were primarily directed at obsolete systems.

The end result of the overall process, whatever the precise

motivations, is that it will ensure a continuing environment of strategic competition. Even if a second series of START negotiations can be developed, recent experience suggests a protracted process lasting most of the decade. That alone will be long enough to provide more impetus for many new developments in military technology, especially, but not only, in the United States.

Strategic Defence and its Implications

The main argument in this Chapter has been that the momentum developed during the Cold War in the 1980s will not lightly be controlled and is likely to continue for many years to come. Furthermore, this means that a wide range of developments in military technology will occur, resulting in far more effective weapons.[2] This will not just be limited to strategic systems, for military R&D was boosted during the 1980s in most sectors of defence equipment, not least in the projection of conventional military forces (*see* Chapter 6). Moreover, innovations in one aspect of the strategic environment may have fundamental implications for military strategy across the board.

When the Reagan administration embarked on the Strategic Defense Initiative in the early 1980s, it was a process supposedly designed to protect the United States from strategic nuclear attack. Only its most compulsive addicts believed that a comprehensive protection against nuclear missiles could be achieved, but the essence of SDI was to attempt to get as close as possible to the perfect weapon system.

A weapon is primarily a device for delivering energy from a source to a target in order to destroy or neutralise that target. An 'ideal' weapon is, in theory, one which delivers an adequate quantity of energy to a target very rapidly and accurately and can do so over a long range. Possibly the most difficult target to hit is a distant ballistic missile accelerating rapidly to Mach 25, yet this was the express purpose of the SDI programme.

Over the past decade that programme has undergone many changes. Technical difficulties and budgetary pressures have curbed some of the early excessive expectations. Yet the essence of the programme remains – protection against fast ballistic missiles. The expenditure of tens of billions of dollars has already led to a wide variety of directed-energy research programmes, hypersonic interceptor missile programmes and attempts to produce third generation nuclear warheads with directional capabilities.

Many of the technologies will have applications in other military systems, whether nuclear or non-nuclear, naval, army or air force, tactical or strategic. The ultimate outcome of these programmes is almost impossible to predict, save that the massive boost given to military R&D by the SDI programme in the United States is likely to give that country an even greater lead in many spheres of military technology in the mid- and late-1990s. It may well be a fear of this technological prowess which contributes to the continuing Soviet commitment to strategic nuclear forces, however much the Soviet federation cuts back on conventional forces.

The ramifications of SDI and its long-term effects are likely to be the cutting edge of the more general momentum given to military technology in the 1980s. The end results of that momentum, clearly continuing into the 1990s as new threats are perceived, constitute a key factor in the kind of world order now likely to be created over the next few decades.

Implications of Military Momentum

The break-up of the Soviet Union at the end of 1991 is likely to lead to a period of several years of strategic uncertainty within the Soviet sphere, but the basic economic problems facing the republics will entail further defence cuts and withdrawal of forces from peripheral states. This, in turn, could lead to further defence budget cuts in the West, although there will be intensive arguments put forward in favour of 'keeping up the guard' in a period of uncertainty as well as responding to new threats from the Third World.

If defence cuts do prevail, this may be seen by some commentators as proof of a trend towards demilitarisation, but this would be a faulty analysis. Any cuts in Western defence budgets will lag well behind those of the Soviets, leaving the West in general, and the United States in particular, with massive military forces relative to any potential threat from the Soviet states. These, combined with the technological momentum boosted by the Cold War years, will provide military forces in search of a role, all too ready to represent a world polarised on a North–South axis as a legitimate reason for maintaining and enhancing those very defence budgets.

To this must be added the impetus likely to be given to the arms trade from the Northern industrialised countries. As local defence markets decline in these countries, a much greater urgency will attach to increasing exports. This will be aided by links between the major arms manufacturers of these countries and companies throughout the Third World, as attempts are made to co-develop and co-produce weapons systems for local and regional sale.

In short, the military momentum of the Cold War years has given us a legacy of global militarisation which will long outlast that era. It will mean that the Northern industrialised countries will be militarily powerful, but also that a technological momentum will continue to affect the rest of the world. In the next two Chapters we will examine the process of proliferation of weapons of mass destruction across the world, and look at the main motivations and capabilities for the projection of military force.

5

Proliferation: Nuclear, Biological, Chemical and Conventional

As the changes in the Soviet Union under Gorbachev started to have an effect on East–West relations, so, from the mid-1980s, prospects for arms control between the superpowers seemed to improve. The signing of the INF Treaty in 1987 was welcomed by most analysts in spite of its flaws, and the unilateral withdrawal of most Soviet military forces from Eastern Europe was accompanied by rapid progress on multilateral conventional arms control. Even the START negotiations on strategic weapons came to a successful conclusion in mid-1991.

None of this had any direct effect on the proliferation of weapons of mass destruction in other parts of the world, but there were hopes that the changed climate between the superpowers would have an effect on other countries, even though the agreed cuts represented a small proportion of their total nuclear weapons. By 1991 there was some evidence to support this hope, but only with regard to nuclear proliferation. In other areas, the dangerous trends which had become apparent in the 1970s and 1980s looked set to continue, if not accelerate, in the 1990s.[1]

Nuclear Proliferation

In the mid-1980s, the two superpowers and the three middle-ranking nuclear-weapons states, Britain, France and China, were all still engaged in expanding their nuclear arsenals. Three other states were regarded as having a nuclear capability.

Israel was believed to have an arsenal of at least 100 nuclear warheads, principally for delivery by strike aircraft and by the Jericho ballistic missile. It was thought to be developing thermonuclear weapons and, possibly, enhanced radiation weapons as well. South Africa was widely believed to have developed nuclear weapons during the 1970s, when it regarded its main security threat as coming from Black African countries to the north. By the mid-1980s it was reckoned to have a handful of nuclear weapons, probably free-fall bombs, although there had been suggestions of a joint programme with Israel for producing nuclear artillery. India had tested a nuclear device in 1974. By the mid-1980s its nuclear weapon status was uncertain as the government gave the impression of supporting control of proliferation only if it was matched by progressive superpower nuclear disarmament. Most analysts believed that India either had a small nuclear arsenal or could assemble one quickly.

Three states, Argentina, Brazil and Pakistan, were considered to be near-nuclear states, and it was widely believed that determined efforts by any of these could ensure a nuclear capability by the early 1990s. Two other states, Iraq and North Korea, were considered to have very active nuclear aspirations. Finally, a number of other states were believed to have longer term nuclear weapons plans, but the status of these was often unclear. These included South Korea, Taiwan, Iran, Egypt, Libya and Syria.

By mid-1991, it was possible to report some progress as well as set-backs in the control of proliferation. On the positive side, the most significant development was the greatly improved relations between Argentina and Brazil which included much more openness on their respective nuclear weapons programmes, together with strong indications that the programmes themselves had been severely curbed. While both governments faced considerable economic problems on the domestic front, it was hoped that civil rule would be maintained and that a regional nuclear arms race would be delayed, if not avoided.

Similarly, there was some optimism concerning the position of South Africa. The race reforms brought in by the de clerk administration, the easing of relations with neighbouring Black states, and the announcement, in June 1991, of a willingness to sign the Non-Proliferation Treaty were all indications that any South African nuclear weapons capability will be less of a cause for instability during the 1990s than had previously been feared.

There were also indications that pressure from the United States on South Korea and Taiwan was serving to hinder, at least to an extent, any nuclear aspirations. South Korea apparently had a nuclear weapons programme in the 1970s but this was largely wound down and the country had ratified the Non-Proliferation Treaty in 1976. Taiwan was less susceptible to US influence but, even here, there were indications that any nuclear weapons programme was proceeding only slowly.

Although North Korea had ratified the Non-Proliferation Treaty in 1985, there was continuing concern in the following years that it retained nuclear aspirations. Even Soviet influence and the improving relations with South Korea failed to convince most analysts that North Korea had dismantled its nuclear weapons development programme.

A more worrying focus for nuclear proliferation was South and South-West Asia. Pakistan appears to have started a large-scale nuclear weapons programme in the mid-1970s. This was, in part, in response to developments in India, even though India's own motives related much more to its rivalry with China. By the end of the 1980s, Pakistan was either on the verge of having a limited nuclear capability or had already managed to construct some devices. It appeared unlikely to test a device, not least because of the harmful effect this would have on US aid, but the technical assistance it had received from China in the 1980s had been of great value, and Pakistan's nuclear potential looks set to be realised in the 1990s and, in turn, to cause India to make public its own nuclear capabilities.

In the Middle East, the presence of a major nuclear weapons state, Israel, continued to act as a spur to a number of other states. Iran's programme, quite advanced under the Shah, had atrophied after the revolution and during the Iran–Iraq war, and there were few indications that it would be quickly revived as the country devoted most of its resources to civil reconstruction. The same could not be said of Iraq, where the Saddam Hussein regime, having concentrated more on chemical weapons developments during the early war years, turned its attention and plentiful resources to accelerating the development of nuclear weapons. By the time of the invasion of Kuwait, Iraq was probably still five years from a usable nuclear arsenal of any size, and the programme was severely damaged, though not destroyed, during the 1991 war.

Libya was considered to have strong nuclear aspirations but lacked the technical capability to realise them, though there were suggestions that it was helping to finance Pakistan's programme. Egypt was probably the most technically advanced Arab state, with a well-developed indigenous armaments industry but while some nuclear weapons research may be in progress, the consensus is that Egypt has refrained from taking the political decision to commit large resources to such a programme.

The most difficult country to analyse is Syria. There is virtually no direct evidence of a nuclear weapons programme, yet the country has committed considerable resources to the development and deployment of other weapons of mass destruction, especially chemical weapons and ballistic missiles. It also regards itself as a major regional power, especially in view of its influence in Lebanon and the damage done in the 1991 war to its rival, Iraq. A Syrian nuclear weapons programme reaching fruition in the late 1990s cannot be ruled out.

One of the central problems in proliferation control was the failure to exert firm control of technology transfer, with Iraq being a notable example of the leakage that is possible. While the outcome of the Coalition's war with Iraq included the destruction of its immediate nuclear ambitions, the inspections of its facilities conducted by UN personnel during 1991 revealed just how far Iraq had been able to go in developing nuclear weapons.

Three aspects of this were significant: Iraq had developed considerable scientific and technical expertise among its own nationals; it had bought in a wide range of technology through the open market without great difficulty; and, where there were problems with imports, it had set up a remarkable network of agencies and companies in industrialised countries for the purpose of bypassing regulatory channels. In a sense, Iraq demonstrated how small was the concern of the major nuclear powers seriously to control the export of nuclear technology.

Limiting the proliferation of nuclear weapons in the 1990s therefore remains a major requirement, although some progress has been made. Argentina, Brazil and South Africa are all countries where progress in proliferation control has occurred, and there is little evidence of imminent nuclear aspirations in Egypt, Iran, South Korea and possibly Taiwan. Against this, Pakistan is clearly on the verge of being the ninth nuclear-capable state, there is concern over North Korea's ambitions, the Iraqi regime appears to maintain its nuclear ambitions even after the 1991 war, and there is longer term concern over the intentions of Syria.

All the nuclear arms control negotiations of the 1980s involving the superpowers have, in practice, resulted in the withdrawal of very few nuclear weapons. Others continue to be produced in large numbers and there are major qualitative improvements under way, especially for strategic nuclear weapons. Similarly, the limited progress in proliferation control has been welcome, but there remain major areas of concern.

In South Asia and the Middle East, in particular, control of proliferation is difficult to envisage. India and Pakistan are major countries with considerable indigenous technical competence, the capability of producing nuclear weapons and, from their own viewpoint, justifiable strategic reasons for doing so. For the moment, the immediate tensions in Indo-Pakistan security provide the main motive, but it is worth remembering that India has a second motive, the perceived need to counter the strategic power of China.

In South-East Asia, the nuclear ambitions of North Korea are not at all easy to assess. While Taiwan and South Korea have, not least as a result of heavy US pressure, reined in their nuclear prospects, North Korea could all too easily do the opposite. Although links with South Korea are slowly developing, Russian pressures on the country to control proliferation are likely to diminish. It is all too possible for North Korea to develop as a maverick nuclear weapons state, going its own way and setting up new proliferation pressures in the region.

In spite of Iraq's defeat in early 1991, and the large-scale destruction of its widespread nuclear facilities, the Middle East as a whole remains the region with the greatest potential for nuclear proliferation. Without a truly comprehensive peace agreement between Israel and its Arab neighbours, there is no chance of Israel giving up its substantial nuclear weapons arsenal. On the contrary, it is a programme which is still very much under development, the main current aim being to develop a thermonuclear missile capability that can target states throughout the Middle East and North Africa.

With Iraq's (possibly temporary) demise, the most likely candidate for an Arab nuclear power is Syria, but other states, including Egypt and ultimately even Libya, cannot be ruled out; nor can a link between one or more of the oil-rich Gulf states and Pakistan.

In short, the 1990s cannot be said to offer prospects for the comprehensive control of nuclear weapons proliferation. Indeed, in the Middle East and South Asia, two of the world's most tense regions, prospects are bleak. Nuclear weapons may comprise just one category of weapons of mass destruction, and the great majority of states may show little interest in acquiring them, yet they remain attractive to some key states – hardly surprising in view of the lack of interest shown by the nuclear powers in rapid and effective nuclear disarmament.

Chemical Weapons

With the improvements in East–West relations of the late 1980s, there was an acceleration in negotiations on chemical weapons, principally between the United States and the Soviet Union. By early 1991, it seemed probable that both countries would progressively cut back their chemical weapons stocks and refrain from deploying new systems. Even as these positive signs became apparent though, there were other concerns arising as chemical weapons appeared likely to proliferate to a number of countries.

Modern chemical weapons are much more effective than conventional high explosive munitions when used against unprotected military and civilian targets. They can be employed in different ways – lethal or incapacitant, persistent or non-persistent – to suit particular objectives, and they can have a considerable psychological effect on potential or actual enemies. Against this, their effectiveness is heavily dependent on weather conditions, they can be difficult to store and handle and their effects can be countered by cumbersome but effective protective equipment.

While chemical weapons are thus of limited military value when used against armed forces which have CW protection, they can be effective against poorly equipped troops in static battlefields. They can also be used to devastating effect against civilians.

The large arsenals of chemical weapons developed by the superpowers comprise bombs, missile warheads, artillery shells and mortar rounds, and include blister agents such as mustard gas and nerve agents such as sarin and VX. Most US and Soviet stocks are expected to be destroyed during the next decade, but both countries are likely to retain small arsenals as long as other states possess chemical weapons.

There was a window of opportunity for controlling CW proliferation at the end of the 1970s, when there were signs of progress at the UN Committee on Disarmament negotiations on chemical weapons in Geneva. If the progress had extended into the early 1980s and had resulted in a comprehensive treaty, this could have curbed, if not eliminated, the spread of these weapons. In the event, prospects for progress were destroyed by the onset of the new Cold War from 1979 onwards, and a precious opportunity was lost.

Prospects for worldwide chemical disarmament now have to be considered poor. The heavy commitment of the superpowers to chemical weapons in the 1960s and 1970s helped to set in motion a process of proliferation which now involves a number of countries, especially in Asia and the Middle East, the most notable CW states being Iraq, Israel, North Korea and Syria.

The well-developed Iraqi programme originated in the 1960s but was given a considerable boost after the 1973 Arab–Israeli War, when several years of high oil prices boosted the level of investment Iraq could make in its CW programme. By the late 1980s, Iraq was reported to be producing 50 tons of nerve agent and 700 tons of blister agent a year, with delivery systems including free-fall bombs, missile warheads and artillery shells. Chemical weapons were extensively used against Iranian troops during the early 1980s and Kurdish towns were also attacked with devastating effect in early 1988, including a series of raids over a two-day period on the town of Halabjah, during which up to 5,000 people were killed.

While chemical weapons were not used in the 1991 Gulf War, Coalition troops were fully prepared to fight in a CW environment. After the war, the cease-fire agreement included the strict inspection and ultimately destruction of Iraq's CW capability, but this is expected to take several years.

Elsewhere in the Middle East, Egypt is considered to have a substantial CW arsenal and is reliably reported to have used chemical weapons during its intervention in North Yemen in 1963–67. Iran may now have a small CW development and production programme and Libya, too, has work in progress and may already have deployable weapons.

With the demise of the Iraqi programme, the leading Arab nation is probably now Syria. It appears to have sought aid from Eastern bloc countries in producing chemical weapons, but this was not forthcoming. During the 1970s Syria, therefore, developed an indigenous capability, using commercially acquired equipment and developing its own expertise. Its main CW plant is near Homs, 140km north of Damascus, and there appears to have been a production plant for nerve agents operating since 1986. Syria has also invested heavily in delivery systems, almost certainly including missiles with CW warheads, and has adopted a strategy of opposing Israel's nuclear capability with its own CW programme.

Israel itself, apart from being a major nuclear weapons state, initiated a CW programme in the late 1960s and is reported to have had an operational capability by 1973. CW agents include blister agents such as mustard gas and nerve agents such as VX. Apart from spray bombs, Israel is likely to have CW warheads for its Jericho missile, recent versions of which can reach targets throughout the Middle East.

Away from the Middle East, countries such as Pakistan and India have CW research programmes, as do Chile and Brazil. The R&D programmes in Pakistan and India are believed to be quite advanced and may be connected with their ballistic missile developments. South Africa is credited with CW stocks, made up mainly of incapacitants and intended primarily for internal control.

China is widely considered to have a range of chemical weapons, but details are surprisingly sparse, especially when one appreciates the extensive information available on China's nuclear and conventional weapons. It is known to have invested heavily in CW protection equipment and has the full range of delivery systems which could be used for CW projection, including missiles, strike aircraft and artillery.

North Korea has, over the past 20 years, developed a CW arsenal believed to amount to many hundreds of tons of agent, including blister agents such as lewisite and nerve agents such as sarin and tabun. Delivery systems are believed to include artillery, strike aircraft, battlefield missiles such as the FROG 5 and longer-range Scud B tactical missiles.

Many other states are believed to have chemical weapons or to be developing them, including Iran, Burma, Vietnam, Taiwan and South Korea. The CW status of these countries is not clear and most data is unreliable, a situation made more complex by the overlap between non-lethal CW agents used essentially for public order control and more truly military CW systems.

Assessing the potential for the proliferation of chemical weapons thus presents us with an apparent contradiction. At the superpower level, there are clear indications of a willingness to cut back on the massive CW arsenals by a very substantial amount. There is also hope that a more general multilateral CW agreement can be reached. At the same time, the reality is that CW proliferation has proceeded far further than nuclear proliferation. At least a dozen countries, principally in the Middle East and Asia, have substantial CW programmes which involve a wide variety of delivery systems. The easing of superpower tensions may make a general CW treaty more likely, but it has to be admitted that a number of key countries are unlikely to agree to it in the near future.

Chemical weapons have little military utility on the high-tech battlefield where armies are heavily protected, but most recent wars have not been fought on such battlefields, nor will they always be in the future. Consequently, enough countries see CW systems as having value, albeit often for political rather than military reasons.

A great opportunity for CW control was lost at the end of the 1970s and since then more than a decade has been largely wasted. The opportunity could be grasped once more in the 1990s, but it will be more difficult to achieve and will require a far greater effort of political will than might have been necessary before.

Biological Weapons

Shortly before the Gulf War of 1991, US and UK military personnel were reportedly being vaccinated against BW agents, probably anthrax and possibly cholera. This led to speculation that Iraq was well on the way to having deployable BW systems, a suspicion which deepened when the US Air Force claimed to have attacked and destroyed BW production and storage sites during the war. If this was so, then Iraq had gone much further along the road towards biological warfare than almost all independent analysts had expected.

Until recently, biological weapons proliferation was conditioned by two linked factors. One was that the 1972 Biological Weapons Convention prohibited the production, deployment and use of biological weapons, although not research into defensive measures. The second was that it was widely thought that biological weapons had little military utility. Although there are many pathogenic organisms which can devastate human populations in epidemic circumstances, it has rarely been considered possible to use them to any great military effect in time of conflict. The circumstances which lead to major natural epidemics usually arise in conditions of poverty, overcrowding or civil disorder; they rarely apply to modern armies on the battlefield.

Moreover, most pathogenic organisms are difficult to introduce into human populations in such a way as to cause immediate and widespread disease. To be a successful BW agent, a pathogenic organism must produce the disease when present in low concentrations, must be highly contagious so that it will spread rapidly through the target population and must not be quickly treatable either through vaccines, chemotherapy or other means, although an attacker must be able to protect its own forces.

Furthermore, it should be easy to produce in bulk, stable in storage, able to survive delivery by bomb or missile warhead, and should even diminish in effect once the target population has succumbed. These requirements rule out virtually all known human pathogens, although anthrax and tularemia partially fulfil the requirements.

Because of these limitations, biological warfare has not, as yet, become a widely deployed military phenomenon. Many would argue that the 1972 Biological Weapons Convention was agreed precisely because biological weapons were difficult to develop. Against this, though, there are three aspects of biological warfare that cause concern, the third of which suggests that current limitations may not last.

The first is agricultural warfare. While the use of BW agents against crops and domestic animals is forbidden by the Convention, it is a form of biological warfare which has greater immediate potential than use against human populations.

Secondly, a number of toxins or poisons produced by living organisms have been isolated which might have potential in warfare. They include botulin, ricin and a group of toxins produced by fungi termed mycotoxins. They would be used rather like CW agents but, because of their much greater toxicity, could be considerably more effective. Their use would be in contravention of the BW Convention, but research on toxins is permitted.

Finally, and most seriously, developments in genetic engineering since the early 1970s allow the prospect of 'tailored' micro-organisms which could be engineered to give characteristics making them more suitable for use in warfare. These might include increased infectivity, rate of spread of infection and resistance to treatment and improved survivability in the non-host environment. It might even be possible to produce organisms which attenuate in their effects within days of use, and even allow attackers to have vaccines which are precisely specific to the organism and not available to the defenders.

One has to stress that there is much speculation and controversy over BW potential in an era of genetic engineering, but new techniques clearly exist which could, in theory, revolutionise the use of BW agents. Furthermore, the 1972 Convention does not seem in any way adequate to police such developments, not least because it was written before the full significance of the new developments was clear. It is especially open-ended in allowing research into defensive measures, for such research can all too easily be used as a cover for developing offensive systems.

Few countries currently have the necessary expertise to conduct substantial genetic engineering research, and even fewer of these have a direct interest in BW agents. The United States has accused the Soviet Union of working in this area, while claiming its own programmes are purely defensive. There were also claims in the late 1980s that Libya and Iraq were among a number of countries working to develop usable BW agents.

It is at least possible that biological weapons will be given a new lease of life (or perhaps death) in the mid- to late-1990s, as genetic engineering techniques become available in more countries. It is also possible that technologically advanced countries which are signatories of the Convention may still develop usable BW agents. From being a form of military technology that has been dismissed as largely irrelevant, biological warfare may shortly have to be taken far more seriously.

Conventional Weapons of Mass Destruction

As discussed in Chapter 2, most attention concerning conventional weapons of mass destruction has recently been focused on the proliferation of ballistic missiles, especially those with a range of over 150 km. This interest was given a particular boost by Iraq's use of Scud missiles in the 1991 Gulf War, but this only added to an existing concern about the spread of such weapons in the Third World.

We would argue that this concentration on ballistic missiles is misplaced, and that it is the revolution in area-impact munitions (AIM) such as cluster bombs which is much more significant in increasing firepower and, thereby, the sheer destructiveness of conventional war. This is not to say that missile proliferation should be ignored, especially as it is likely to encompass the use of AIM warheads in the coming decade.

Missile Proliferation

In practical terms, the types of ballistic missile currently available have little immediate military value. The throw-weights of the missiles are seldom above two tons, they are not sufficiently accurate to threaten precise military targets and the ranges involved are not, as yet, inter-continental, so they are only available for regional conflicts.

For the possessors, there are four main reasons for acquiring ballistic missiles. One immediate military rationale is that they are very difficult to intercept. Even though they can only deliver conventional high-explosive warheads, in the longer term they will have the potential to deliver chemical or nuclear warheads. While the damage that they can currently cause is small, they can have a significant psychological effect, giving rise to feelings of vulnerability, especially in cities, which would not otherwise exist. More generally, they have come to be seen as symbols of military status, as with Saudi Arabia's decision to purchase obsolete Chinese CSS-2 missiles in the late 1980s.

Ballistic missiles may be purchased abroad, either from Soviet, Western or other sources; they may be modifications of imported missiles, or they may be produced indigenously, albeit usually with foreign technical assistance. Argentina, Brazil, India and Pakistan are examples of countries which have indigenous ballistic missile programmes; Syria, Libya and Saudi Arabia have imported missiles of Soviet or Chinese origin; Israel deploys the US Lance missile but has a highlysignificant indigenous programme; and Iraq has developed a range of indigenous missiles using the Soviet Scud as the basic system.

Argentina produced the Condor in the mid-1980s, but the longer-range Condor 2 programme, which involved collaboration with Egypt and Iraq, was halted, principally on economic grounds, at the end of the decade. Brazil has the Orbita and Avribas missiles with ranges of up to 1,000 km and it is likely that such missiles will be available for export or co-production during the present decade.

India's extensive space programme was developed initially with Soviet help and has been accompanied by a ballistic missile development programme resulting in the Prithvi and Agni missiles with ranges of 240 km and 2,000 km respectively; both are likely to be deployed during the 1990s and lead on to larger systems. Pakistan's programme is at an earlier stage. The Haft-2 missile can carry a 500 kg payload over a 240 km range, will be deployed during the decade and forms part of a larger programme.

Importers of Scud missiles include Syria, Libya, Yemen, Egypt, Iran and Iraq. Most have originated in the Soviet Union, but a recent development has been the entry of North Korea into the supplier market, producing not just the Scud B but also longer-range versions. Saudi Arabia has purchased and deployed Chinese CSS-2 intermediate-range ballistic missiles. These were deployed by China with nuclear warheads but have been sold with conventional warheads. They have been re-designated DF-3A in Saudi Arabia and are not at all accurate, with a CEP poorer than 1,800 m, but they have a range of some 3,200 km, making them the longest, range missiles deployed in the Middle East.

Israel's indigenous capability, focused on the 900-mile range Jericho 2 missile, has also resulted in a satellite launcher and is expected to lead to a 2,400+ km missile capability during the 1990s. Unconfirmed reports indicate an interest in medium-range missile development by South Africa, Taiwan and South Korea, any of which may link in with Israel.

Apart from those of Israel and possibly India, none of the missiles mentioned carries nuclear warheads and only those of Syria, Israel, North Korea and formerly Iraq may be capable of taking CW munitions. Thus, in most cases, the effectiveness of the missiles is against large targets, principally cities, where the impact may be primarily political.

During the coming decade, though, it is likely that a number of missile systems will be fitted with substantial cluster warheads, able to scatter sub-munitions over areas of many acres rather than confining damage to limited areas. Such area-impact warheads are already being developed in Argentina and Brazil and probably other countries. They will, at least in part, overcome the inaccuracy of conventionally-armed ballistic missiles and hugely increase their destructive potential. Such systems have, of course, already been deployed by countries such as the United States and the Soviet Union.

Area-Impact Munitions

Area-impact munitions (AIMs) are specifically designed to cause destruction over a wide area but in a controlled manner. They may include delayed-action mines, anti-armour munitions or other specific weapons, but the most significant forms of area-impact munition in terms of increased conventional firepower are those systems which dispense large numbers of high explosive fragmentation sub-munitions, grenade-sized 'bomblets'.

Such AIMs are most commonly delivered in one of two ways, either by air-dropped cluster bombs or by surface-to-surface missiles, usually launched from multiple-rocket-launchers. As mentioned earlier (Chapter 2), the development of AIMs was given a considerable boost during the Vietnam War, and most industrialised military powers deploy a wide range of systems.

A specialised type of area-impact munition is the fuel–air explosive (FAE) in which a high energy fuel such as butane or propadiene is dispersed from air-delivered cannisters to produce an aerosol which is then detonated to produce explosive combustion. As the oxidant for the explosive is atmospheric oxygen, an FAE is innately more efficient than a conventional high explosive, with much higher blast overpressures being produced than equivalent weights of conventional high explosive. FAEs have been used for mine clearance and against bunkers but are also highly effective anti-personnel weapons, especially against troops sheltering in trenches.

The significant development in the late 1980s and into the 1990s has been the proliferation of AIMs throughout the world. This has involved three routes of proliferation. One, obviously, is the conventional arms trade, with arms industries in developed industrialised countries willing to export AIM systems throughout the world. The second is the development of co-production agreements where such companies set up schemes in conjunction with arms industries in intermediate and Third World countries. Finally, such countries may themselves develop an indigenous capability to produce AIMs.

A number of countries in Latin America, Africa, the Middle East and Asia are now significant producers of AIMs. Brazil produces a number of multiple-rocket-launchers as well as the SBAT-70 helicopter-borne 19-round system. Versions of the latter can carry multiple fragmentation grenades or flechette dispensers, the latter designed to penetrate deep into the human body.

Chile is a major producer of cluster munitions, the most significant company being Cardoen SA which has a range of cluster bombs of up to 250kg. The largest can spread high-velocity shrapnel fragments over an area of nearly five hectares. The Chilean army is working with the Royal Ordnance division of British Aerospace to develop a multiple-rocket-launch system. Chile exported an estimated 20,000 cluster bombs to Iraq during the 1980s and also helped Iraq build its own cluster bomb factory.

Israel produces the TAL and ATAP cluster bomb series which are available for export and also manufactures a range of multiple-rocket-launchers. South Africa produces the remarkable CBU 470 system which comprises 40 spherical bomblets which are activated when they hit the ground after dispersal from the cannister. As they bounce back up from the ground, they detonate at a height of about four metres, to produce a hail of high-velocity shrapnel fragments.

In Asia, China produces several types of AIMs, including a new range of fuel–air explosives, India is now producing an indigenous 250kg cluster bomb and North Korea, South Korea and Pakistan are believed to have similar plans.

Area-impact munitions are routine instruments of war for industrialised countries and are now exported worldwide. There is no arms control regime currently concerned in any way with their control, and the proposed UN arms transfer register will not involve controls. Even if industrialised countries were to seek to control AIMs proliferation in a systematic way, this would not have too great an impact unless exports from intermediate and Third World producers were controlled. This is highly unlikely to happen.

It follows that one of the major trends in the proliferation of weapons of mass destruction is the spread of AIMs, and it can certainly be argued that this is far more important in terms of casualties in future wars than conventionally-armed ballistic missiles.

Trends and Implications

This Chapter has examined the trends in the proliferation of weapons of mass destruction and we must conclude that problems exist in every category. While the rate of spread of nuclear weapons has not fulfilled the worst fears of 25 years ago, and in Latin

America there has been a curbing of nuclear ambitions, in the Middle East, South Asia and, possibly, East Asia, there are heavy pressures promoting nuclear proliferation.

There may be a prospect of considerable cuts in superpower CW arsenals, but there is no sign that many countries in the Middle East and Asia are likely to cut back on their CW programmes. Biological weapons may be technically insignificant at present, but developments in biotechnology, especially genetic engineering, open up new possibilities, and these may be taken up during the coming decade.

Ballistic missile proliferation is a subject for fashionable concern, even though the military value of most of the current inaccurate systems is limited. Improvements in range and accuracy are in progress in several Third World countries, and this, combined with the likely development of area-impact warheads, will make these weapons highly significant before the end of the decade.

Finally, area-impact munitions such as cluster bombs are becoming much more widely deployed throughout the world. They, and some of the other systems described, will certainly make wars much more dangerous and damaging.

The INF, CFE and START agreements all give an impression of major cuts in the military deployments of the superpowers and their immediate allies. It is not entirely an illusion, for some cuts are being made and defence budgets are falling across the board, for the first time in a generation. Yet the very arms races of the 1970s and 1980s have spawned new types of weapons, and these are now proliferating across the world.

The limited arms control progress of the late 1980s can all too easily disguise some disturbing global trends. If, as we would argue, a potential North-South axis of conflict is now developing, this process of proliferation could make that axis of conflict all the more dangerous. One of the worst legacies of the 40-odd years of the Cold War is, therefore, the enhancement of militarisation, carrying with it the risk that future North-South conflict may exact a terrible toll.[2]

6

Military Force Projection and the New World Order

Send a Gunboat

The mercantile empires of Western Europe were essentially based upon the ability to project military power. The colonisation of Latin America by Spain and Portugal, of South and South-East Asia by the British, French and Dutch, and of Africa by many European powers, all depended, at root, on naval power. Frequently this was used to compete against other colonising powers, and local militias were often adequate to impose and maintain colonial order; but the ultimate power was military, and the means of deploying it was almost invariably naval.

In the latter part of the colonial period, especially in the late 19th Century, 'gunboat diplomacy' was widely practised, and it was not just the province of the European powers. Japan was to deploy military power in the early part of the 20th Century, leading eventually to the plans for the 'Greater East-Asia Co-Prosperity Sphere' in the 1920s and 1930s, one of the more interesting euphemisms for colonial conquest.

Even earlier, the United States was able to demonstrate that the absence of direct colonies (excepting a few territories such as the Philippines) was no reason to avoid the use of military force in the pursuit of economic power. As the influence of Spain and Portugal in Latin America declined, so the United States moved in. Under the Monroe Doctrine, from 1823, the United States considered that future interference by European powers in the economic and political structures of the emerging Latin American countries would be contrary to US interests.

US expansionism of the mid-19th Century resulted in the eviction of Mexico from nearly half its territory, California, Texas and New Mexico, and by the end of the Century US economic power was becoming dominant in Central America, backed up by the frequent use of military force. The main instrument of force projection was the US Marine Corps, and the first 40 years of the 20th Century saw interventions in Cuba, Honduras, Panama, Nicaragua, Haiti, the Dominican Republic and El Salvador.

This process was best described by General Smedley Butler of the Marine Corps, who was involved in many of these actions. Writing in 1935, he recalled:

> I spent thirty-three years and four months in active service as a member of our country's most agile military force – the Marine Corps. I served in all commissioned ranks from a second Lieutenant to Major-General. And during that time I spent most of my time being a high-class muscle man for Big Business for Wall Street and, for the bankers. In short, I was a racketeer for capitalism . . . Thus I helped make Mexico and especially Tampico safe for American oil interests in 1914. I helped make Haiti and Cuba a decent place for the National City Bank to collect revenues in . . . I helped purify Nicaragua for the international banking house of Brown Brothers in 1909–1912. I brought light to the Dominican Republic for American sugar interests in 1916. I helped make Honduras 'right' for American fruit companies in 1903.[1]

The Monroe Doctrine and its consequent projection of US power in Latin America continued through the inter-war isolationist years, but it was the experience of the Second World War which changed US force-projection capabilities from a regional to a global potential.

Projecting Global Power

During the Second World War, US involvement in the European theatre was massive, but operated from European and North African bases, especially from Britain. In the Pacific, though, the conflict with Japan was fought over thousands of miles of oceans and hundreds of islands, large and small. During more than three years of intense conflict, the war industries of the United States were used to create a capability to project maritime force in a manner never before achieved by any state. Aircraft-carriers, troop-carriers and especially the assault ships assigned to the Marine Corps collectively produced a capability for force projection which progressively turned the tide of the war against Japan.

By the end of the Second World War, the US Navy was the world's foremost maritime force. Although Britain, France and the lesser European colonial powers conducted wars against insurgents in their colonies, these were small-scale and essentially wars of retreat. Meanwhile, the United States, in its rise to globalism, was being transformed into the world's strongest military power, with the greatest capability to project force in pursuit of foreign policy objectives.

The Korean War and, in a sense, the Berlin Airlift, were early examples of this, but for most of the 1950s and early 1960s the primary policy was one of containment – surrounding the perceived Communist axis of the Warsaw Pact and China, principally with ground and air forces in Europe and maritime forces in the Mediterranean and the Pacific.

The continuing threat from Communism was seen to take two main forms. One was the control of Eastern Europe, met by NATO and the deployment of substantial US forces in Western Europe; the second was Soviet and, to a lesser extent, Chinese influence in the Third World. This took the form not so much of direct military force projection but arms transfers, training schemes and the use of military advisers. The US response was in kind, but extended to a worldwide network of bases, including key facilities in such places as Panama, South Korea, Guam, the Philippines and Diego Garcia, together with force-projection potential based principally on aircraft-carriers and amphibious assault ships.

The policy of containment went badly wrong during the Vietnam War and a consequence of this was a certain reluctance to project military power during much of the 1970s. As we have seen (Chapter 3), the decade of the 1970s was a period of relative détente and even of negotiations on arms control, although it was also a period in which the United States maintained forces and overseas bases throughout the world, and training missions, arms transfers and the use of special forces all had their role. While Vietnam had an effect, it did not greatly limit US deployments worldwide – only the political will to use them. Thus the United States had, by the mid-1970s, effectively taken over most global military roles from Britain and France.

With the coming of the Reagan era, the start of the new Cold War and the re-arming of America, US military force projection capabilities received a huge boost. This was, in practice, the second and less well understood aspect of Reagan's 're-arming of America'. While most attention was focused on the escalation of the nuclear arms race with the Soviet Union, an expansion of conventional force-projection capabilities was under way which was, in its own way, almost as significant. Indeed, in the long term, it may have left the United States with a much more usable form of military power for the post-Cold War era.

Reagan, Resurgence and Resources

The rise of US force-projection capabilities in the 1980s was complicated by two different motives which interacted in a complex manner, one of which survives the ending of the Cold War. These factors were concern over resource supplies and the policy of containing Soviet expansionism.

Even during the early 1970s, the first factor was rising up the political agenda, helped in particular by the oil crisis of 1973–74 and the huge price increases which followed the action of Arab members of the Organisation of Petroleum Exporting Countries (OPEC) during the Yom Kippur/Ramadan War of October 1973. Their action involved a cut in production, an embargo on exports to the US and a substantial increase of over 70 per cent in crude oil prices. This is covered in more detail in Chapter 7, but suffice to say here that the disruption to Gulf oil supplies occasioned by the Arab action had a traumatic and long-lasting effect on US perceptions of security.

During the 1973–74 oil crisis, the use of military force to secure Western oil supplies was considered, but it became apparent that, even if such a move were politically feasible, it would be militarily impossible. The central problem was that the Western nations in general, and the United States in particular, did not have forces at their disposal which could be deployed sufficiently quickly and effectively to make the take-over of key Middle East oilfields a viable proposition. The time necessary to achieve such an objective was far greater than the time required to render the oilfields inoperable by sabotage, and the several months required for reinstatement would have been catastrophic for oil supplies to the West.

Although the oil crisis was instigated by Arab oil producers, a second effect of the crisis was to reinforce the view that the Soviet Union could threaten Middle East oil supplies and thereby greatly damage the Western economies in time of East–West crisis or conflict.

An immediate outcome of the oil crisis was a reassessment of military strategy towards resource supplies and this became part of a much larger process of analysis which placed issues of world resource supplies in the context of East–West competition. Furthermore, this occurred in the context of an increasing recognition of the steady shift in 'resource balance' in favour of the non-industrialised countries.

Europe had experienced such a shift long ago. In the early 19th Century, for example, Britain had been a major producer of metals such as copper, lead and tin from its own mineral reserves. These had long since come close to depletion and by the early 20th Century Britain, like most of Western Europe, was dependent on overseas supplies. Indeed, one of the driving forces of European colonial expansion had been the huge requirements for raw materials fuelled by the process of industrialisation spreading across Europe.

For the initially resource-rich United States, however, large-scale importing of raw materials was a much more recent phenomenon and was only recognised as important by military and foreign policy analysts after 1974. Consequently, within a few years, maintenance of the resource base of the United States came to be considered a major objective of military strategy. This was expressed forcibly in the Pentagon's Military Posture Statement for Fiscal Year 1982, the first statement of the Reagan administration's period in office:

> The dependency of the United States on foreign sources of non-fuels, minerals and metals has increased sharply over the last two decades. Taking a list of the top 25 such imported commodities, in 1960 our dependency averaged 54 percent. In fact, our dependency is 75 percent or more on foreign countries where war could, in the foreseeable future, deny us our supplies of bauxite, chromite, cobalt, columbium, manganese, nickel and tantalum. These metals and minerals figure in the manufacture of aircraft, motor vehicles, appliances, high–strength or stainless steels, magnets, jet engine parts, cryogenic devices, gyroscopes, superconduc-

tors, capacitors, vacuum tubes, electro-optics, printed circuits, contacts, connectors, armour plate and instrumentation, among other things.

The Posture Statement went on to give a detailed account of the importance of Middle East oil supplies, before stressing the Soviet position of near self-sufficiency of resource supplies in comparison with US vulnerability.

The comparison here is interesting. Western European states and Japan are relatively poorly endowed with fuel and mineral resources – even North Sea oil deposits are small by global standards. Consequently, they import most raw materials from overseas, a natural consequence of the West European colonial expansion and the more recent Japanese economic expansion into much of Eastern Asia and the Pacific. The expansion of the Russian Empire into Siberia and the consolidation of more than a dozen states into the Soviet Union provided the USSR with a wealth of natural resources. Though the exploitation of these was frequently inefficient, it left the Soviet Union with little need to import from elsewhere.

Initially, the United States was in a similar position to the Soviet Union, the mineral wealth of the country and the oil resources of Texas, Oklahoma, Louisiana and California providing the raw materials for the immense industrial expansion of early and mid-20th Century America. The resource shift worked against the United States 50 to 100 years after it had worked against Western Europe and, by the 1970s, depletion of domestic reserves was rapidly altering the resource security of the country.

It was the contrast with the Soviet Union, and its potential for destabilising Third World sources of US resource supplies which so concerned the Pentagon in the early Reagan years. As the 1982 Military Posture Statement put it:

The Soviet Union's self-sufficiency in fossil fuels – oil, natural gas and coal – is mirrored by virtual self-sufficiency in other minerals. The Soviet Union must import only six minerals critical to its defence industry, and only two of these are brought in for as much as 50 percent of its requirements. In contrast, the United States relies on foreign sources to supply amounts in excess of 50 percent of its needs for some 32 minerals essential for our military and industrial base. Particularly important mineral imports (for example, diamonds, cobalt, platinum, chromium and manganese) come from southern Africa, where the Soviet Union and its surrogates have established substantial influence, and where US access, given the inherent instabilities within the region, is by no means assured.

Thus, an emphasis on the security of resource supplies developed during the early years of the Reagan administration and, while primarily concerned with Third World resources, it was clearly perceived in an East–West context. The Soviet Union and its perceived surrogates were seen as constituting the ultimate problem for US interests.

Development of the Maritime Strategy

During the early years of the Reagan administration, the Pentagon developed a strategy which could be applied to safeguarding US economic interests worldwide and also winning a war with the Soviet Union, a war which was confidently expected by hawkish analysts in the tense Cold War environment of the early 1980s.

While the US Army concentrated principally on preparing for conventional (and nuclear) war in Europe, and the US Air Force expended most of its efforts on strategic nuclear programmes, the US Navy and Marine Corps sought to develop a 'Maritime Strategy', a doctrine concerned simultaneously with constraining the Soviets, safeguarding resources and other US interests in the Third World and, in the final analysis, contributing to victory in a global conflict with the Soviet Union.[2] The strategy was developed in the early 1980s and made public early in 1986.

In the worst-case scenario, war with the Soviet Union, it was assumed that if deterrence broke down, there would be three broad stages of confrontation short of nuclear exchange: *transition to war*, comprising mobilisation and forward deployment of forces; *seizing the initiative*, including initial attacks on Soviet strategic ballistic missile submarines, 'bottling up' the Soviet naval forces, and preservation of the lines of communication; and *carrying the war to the enemy* or favourable war execution and termination.

This final phase was described succinctly by the then Chief of Naval Operations, Admiral James D. Watkins, writing in a supplement to the *Proceedings of the US Naval Institute on the Maritime Strategy*, published in January 1986:

> The tasks in this phase are similar to those in earlier phases, but must be more aggressively applied as we seek war termination on terms favourable to the United States and its allies. Our goal would be to complete the destruction of all the Soviet fleets begun in Phase II. This destruction allows us to threaten the bases and support structures of the Soviet navy in all theatres with both air and amphibious power. Such threats are quite

credible to the Soviets. At the same time, anti-submarine warfare forces would continue to destroy Soviet submarines, including ballistic missile submarines, thus reducing the attractiveness of nuclear escalation by changing the nuclear balance in our favour.

During this final phase, the US and its allies would press home the initiative worldwide, while continuing to support air and land campaigns, maintaining sealift, and keeping sea lines of communication open. Amphibious forces, up to the size of a full Marine Amphibious Force, would be used to regain territory. In addition, the full weight of the carrier battle forces could continue to 'roll up' the Soviets on the flanks, contribute to the battle on the Central Front, or carry the war to the Soviets. These tough operations, close to the Soviet motherland, could even come earlier than the last phase.

Keeping the Violent Peace

The expansion of US conventional forces in the early 1980s may have been primarily to execute the new Maritime Strategy against the Soviet Union, but it led to a worldwide enhancement of military readiness. As Admiral Watkins remarked in 1986:

> We now maintain a continual presence in the Indian Ocean, Persian Gulf and Caribbean, as well as our more traditional forward deployments to the Mediterranean and Western Pacific. Although we are not at war today, our operating tempo has been about 20 percent higher than during the Vietnam War.

This military readiness could just as easily be applied to other conflicts and proxy conflicts with perceived Soviet surrogates or other forces which were considered to threaten US security interests. This second aspect of the Maritime Strategy was termed 'keeping the violent peace' in the Third World, and naval forces such as aircraft-carrier battle groups and amphibious warfare ships were essential for such a strategy. According to two US navy commanders, Robinson and Benkert, it differed from the requirements for global war with the Soviet Union in three broad ways. First, a wartime strategy, in their view, concentrates on countering overt Soviet aggression while:

> peacetime strategy objectives are more diffuse and perhaps best characterised as furthering an ill-defined set of interests of which countering the Soviets is only part, although a very important part.

Second, a violent peace strategy is inherently less structured and clear-cut in its objectives and processes. Finally, political and diplomatic considerations may dominate or circumscribe military considerations, at least in the early stages of a particular crisis. Within this context, the major aims of a violent peace strategy are:

— protecting sea lines of communication and transit rights;
— allowing the United States continued access to resources and markets; and
— demonstrating US interests overseas.

Throughout the early 1980s, the build-up of US force projection capabilities went hand-in-hand with an increasingly aggressive maritime strategy and a belief by the Reagan administration that US interests, especially in South-West Asia and the Caribbean, were directly at risk.

The US Force Projection Expansion

There were six main areas of interest in the expansion of force projection capabilities: carrier battle groups, battleships, amphibious forces, logistic support, rapid deployment forces and special forces.[3] Each will be described briefly in terms of the forces deployed by the mid-1980s, and the capabilities being developed for the 1990s will then be assessed.

1. Carrier Battle Groups By 1986, the United States had 14 operational aircraft-carriers, and several in reserve. Each operational carrier could be deployed in a carrier battle group (CBG) along with escorts of cruisers, destroyers, frigates and submarines, together with supply ships. No other country had forces which were remotely comparable. Indeed, as *Table 1* shows, just three US carrier battle groups could deploy more fixed-wing aircraft than all the carrier-borne forces of the remaining countries of the world.

Each CBG provides a mobile strike capability comprising interceptors, strike aircraft, electronic warfare and maritime reconnaissance aircraft, and airborne early-warning planes. A protective screen of 800 km radius is possible around the CBG and the strike aircraft can operate out to an even wider combat radius and are nuclear capable. CBGs are routinely equipped with a range of tactical nuclear weapons, including land attack ordnance and anti-submarine depth bombs.

The 14 carrier battle groups that had formed by 1987 represented the most powerful form of US naval force projection.

Table 1
Fixed-wing carrier-borne aircraft (early 1987)

Country	Carriers	Aircraft per Carrier[+]	Total Aircraft
Argentina	1	15	15
Brazil	1	8	8
France	2	29	58
India[*]	2	16[**]	32
Spain	1	5[**]	5
USSR	4	12[**]	48
UK	3	5[**]	15
USA	12	80	} 1100[***]
	2	70	

Notes: [+] Numbers likely to be higher in wartime
[*] Figures for late 1987
[**] STOVL aircraft of limited range (Harrier/Forger)
[***] Excluding STOVL planes on amphibious warfare ships

2. Battleship Surface Action Groups Apart from the use of a battleship for a short period during the Vietnam War, the United States did not maintain operational battleships for a quarter of a century after the mid-1950s. This was changed with the 1981 decision to reactivate and modernise the four *Iowa*-class battleships then in reserve as dedicated land-attack platforms. Three were deployed by 1987 and the fourth a year later.

The ships retained their massive 16-inch main armament, but eight of the 20 secondary 5-inch guns were replaced with 32 Tomahawk land-attack cruise missiles and 16 Harpoon anti-ship missiles. The main armament enables a ship to fire nine one-tonne high explosive shells over a 15-mile range simultaneously. The *New Jersey* used its guns in this manner against shore targets in Lebanon on several occasions in December 1984.

Because of the very heavy armour of this class of battleship, it would require multiple mine strikes or torpedo hits or intensive aerial bombing to destroy such a ship. The armour would, for example, offer virtually complete protection against anti-ship missiles such as the Exocet or Otomat. It is therefore extremely well suited for operations against relatively weak countries which cannot mount sustained large-scale anti-ship attacks, and would survive a threat environment, which a frigate, destroyer or even cruiser could not.

No other nation possesses the naval bombardment potential of the *Iowa*-class battleship or anything remotely approaching it. It was thus quickly recognised that the battleship reactivation programme greatly strengthened potential fire support for marine amphibious landings.

3. Amphibious Forces With 190,000 personnel, the US Marine Corps is far larger than the entire British Army and around an order of magnitude ten times larger than its Soviet equivalent of 20,000. It has some 40 amphibious warfare ships of above 10,000 tons displacement, compared with seven for all other countries. The Corps maintains its own integral air support and a wide range of specialised equipment including tactical nuclear weapons, and is deployed for combat at one of three levels – unit, brigade or force.

The basic marine component, the Marine Amphibious Unit, is fully equipped with tanks, armoured personnel carriers and artillery and up to 25 medium- and heavy-lift helicopters. Moreover, the larger ships such as the *Tarawa*-class amphibious assault ships are specifically designed to allow battalion-sized troop groups to remain on board for long periods in some comfort.

While the Marine Corps was not being enlarged to any great extent during the mid-1980s, important qualitative improvements were made. These included the deployment of over 300 advanced AV8B Harrier jump-jets, all nuclear-capable, the purchase of Piranha light-attack vehicles and the development of an entirely new class of large amphibious assault ships, the *Wasp*-class, which entered service by the end of the decade. In the early 1990s, the deployment of large numbers of armed air-cushion vehicles will greatly extend the ability of the Corps to conduct amphibious assaults, increasing the proportion of coastlines over which assaults can be conducted at least three-fold.

Table 2 indicates the make-up of the three levels of Marine Corps organisation. The intention, by the early 1990s, is for the Corps to be able to field a complete Marine Amphibious Force and a Marine Amphibious Brigade simultaneously in time of war.

Table 2
US Marine Corps Air-Ground Task Forces

Structure	Marine Personnel	Navy Personnel	Amphibious Shipping
Marine Amphibious Unit (MAU)	2,350	156	4–6
Marine Amphibious Brigade (MAB)	15,000	670	21–26
Marine Amphibious Force (MAF)	48,200	2,400	c.50

More important in the context of force projection and keeping the violent peace, however, is the development of permanent basing backed up by logistical pre-positioning. By the mid-1980s this involved two MAUs in the West Pacific and Indian Ocean and one in the Mediterranean, but such routine force levels were being upgraded substantially by the development of logistical pre-positioning and of integrated rapid deployment forces involving army as well as marine units, with much of the emphasis on South-West Asia and the Eastern Mediterranean.

4. Logistic Support Unless army or marine forces are fully supplied with food, fuel, munitions and other stores, their capabilities in combat decline rapidly. US military strategy under the Reagan build-up called for the capacity to act with force virtually anywhere in the world, often many thousands of miles from US territory or even from standing deployments of US forces in, for example, Europe and South-East Asia.

The primary service providing such support is Military Sealift Command and, during the 1980s, it invested heavily in improving its capabilities. Eight large container ships were converted into Fast Sealift Support ships. These were, for example, capable of transporting most of the equipment for a complete armoured division to the Gulf via the Suez Canal in two weeks.

The technique of pre-positioning supplies was developed, the aim being to be able to ship supplies to a crisis area, not from the continental United States but from a regional centre, the supplies then being married up with the troops who would be flown in from the US or Europe. As an interim measure, a force of 17 ships was established, known as the Near Term Pre-positioning Force. These were hastily-adapted commercial vessels rather than custom-built and many were based either in the Mediterranean or at the Indian Ocean island of Diego Garcia. This force was able to maintain a complete Marine Amphibious Brigade of 12,000 troops and its supporting personnel, over 15,000 in all, for 30 days without re-supply.

The Near Term Pre-positioning Force was a temporary measure established during the early 1980s and was progressively replaced by the permanent Maritime Pre-positioning Force (MPF) of 13 ships of up to 46,000 tons laden weight. Eight were converted merchant vessels and five were custom-built for the MPF. All were in service by 1986 with most based at Diego Garcia or at Guam, the latter base being regarded as in a 'swing-zone', able to support deployments throughout the West Pacific, southern Asia and the Middle East.

While not widely recognised, this revolution in logistic support was probably more significant in terms of increased force-projection capabilities than the expansion of the carrier battle groups or the reactivation of battleships. The developing logistic policy of the 1980s was tailored largely, though not entirely, to South-West Asia, including the Middle East, but could be used elsewhere. The island of Diego Garcia, a British possession in the Indian Ocean from which the Ilois inhabitants had been evicted to Mauritius, was leased to the United States and was an essential component of this strategy, giving the US a capability for inter-vention in the Middle East which was notably absent during the oil crisis of the early 1970s.

5. The Rapid Deployment Force and CENTCOM After the traumas of the mid-1970s, one of President Carter's early actions on security was to order a study on force projection. Presidential Directive 18 in 1977 ordered the Department of Defense to identify existing forces which might be tasked for operations in remote areas. After a considerable amount of service in-fighting, the Joint Chiefs of Staff responded in 1979 with a plan for a pool of forces from the four branches of the armed services, based in the continental

United Status but trained, equipped and provided with transport for action worldwide. This became the Joint Rapid Deployment Task Force (JRDTF), created in 1980 and known more popularly as the Rapid Deployment Force.

Although it was theoretically available for deployment anywhere in the world, from the start the JRDTF concentrated on South-West Asia and the Middle East, and its planning and training formed part of the substantial build-up of force projection capabilities of the early Reagan years. Indeed, in 1983 the JRDTF was elevated to the status of an entirely new unified military command, to be known as US Central Command (CENTCOM). Just as Pacific Command was responsible for US security interests in the Pacific, and Southern Command 'looked after' Latin America, so CENTCOM had a particular zone of responsibility. This was the maintenance of US interests in North-East Africa and South-West Asia, comprising 19 countries stretching in an arc from Kenya through the Middle East to Pakistan.

By late 1984, the forces available to CENTCOM included four army divisions and one brigade and a marine division and a brigade, together with comprehensive air and sea support. A key concept was rapid deployment, with elements of the army's 82nd Airborne Division being kept at a high state of readiness. Thus a complete army brigade of over 4,000 troops with comprehensive air-mobile artillery and air defences was available for air transport at 20 hours' notice.

By the late 1980s CENTCOM had been further expanded and had some 300,000 personnel from all four services assigned to it. It comprised the Third Army, the Ninth Air Force, three carrier battle groups and a marine amphibious force together with elements of Strategic Air Command and substantial intelligence, reconnaissance and special forces units. While most of the forces and the HQ of CENTCOM were located in the United States, the forces were trained and equipped for rapid movement to, and deployment in, the Middle East and surrounding areas. The logistical pre-positioning already described was integral to this strategy. At the end of the 1980s, the head of CENTCOM was a General Norman Schwarzkopf of the US Army.

6. Special Forces and Tactics One of the areas of most rapid expansion in the early Reagan years was that of special forces. A Unified Command for Special Forces was set up, covering units such as the Green Berets, Navy SEAL (Sea-Air-Land) forces, Air Force Special Operations Squadrons, Rangers and Delta Force. All were particularly concerned with low-intensity operations and most of their experience in recent years has been in the Third World. Special Operations Force (SOF) active duty personnel increased by 30 per cent, from 1981–85, to 14,000 and, together with reserves, totalled about 32,000 with further expansion coming in the latter part of the decade. A wide range of new weaponry and tactics were developed, including a three-fold increase in USAF specialised aircraft to support SOF activities, as well as greatly improved communications equipment.

New Technology for Long-range Intervention

Even with this expansion in numbers and improvements in weapons, a major drawback in Third World intervention is the risk of casualties and the political consequences in terms of domestic opinion. Although the US armed forces no longer operate a draft, one legacy of Vietnam has been a reluctance to risk American lives in small wars in far-off places. This has provided a motive in the development of some weapon systems which avoid this risk, even though the main motive for their development may have been potential conflict with the Soviet Union.

One example is the application of 'stealth' radar-avoidance technology to strike aircraft such as the F-117A. Though developed to avoid concentrated Soviet air defences, the secondary value of such planes is their ability to fly through less well developed Third World air defence systems almost at will.

A second, widely deployed, system is the long-range 'smart' land-attack missile launched from ships or submarines at sea. The main example is the land-attack version of the Tomahawk sea-launched cruise missile, progressively being deployed in some 200 ships and submarines and produced throughout the mid- and late-1980s at the rate of some 400 missiles per year. Some 2,600 such missiles will eventually be deployed, with a range of up to 700 miles, carrying either a single high-explosive warhead or a package of area-impact sub-munitions.

The use of inertial and 'scene-matching' guidance systems gives such missiles an accuracy of under 100 feet. Thus, a submarine patrolling 100 miles off a Third World country can fire a salvo of missiles at targets 600 miles inland, using these missiles to destroy barracks, air-fields, guerrilla concentrations and similar targets. Such attacks are possible with no risk to US combatants.

Force Projection – Recent Use

In summary, the expansion of US force-projection capabilities during the early and mid-1980s was a second string to the bow of US military power. It received far less attention from analysts or, indeed, from the media, than the nuclear expansion, yet may well have much greater long-term significance in the post-Cold War world.

US capabilities are hugely greater than those of any other country. Although, at the height of the Cold War, the Soviet Navy was a powerful force, its prime capability was the defence of the Soviet homeland rather than long-range power projection. Lacking sophisticated carrier air capability, power projection was critically dependent on land-based air power. Although some major overseas bases were expanded briefly in the 1980s, Cam Ranh Bay in Vietnam being the most notable example, the Soviet Navy lacked the logistic support forces necessary to maintain power projection away from bases. The policy was essentially defence against US containment rather than taking a war to the enemy.

Britain and France have limited force-projection capabilities, as both countries have some carrier air power and assault ships, but these are tiny in comparison to US forces. The Falklands War strained British naval forces to the limit, whereas the United States could have mounted a task force at least five times the size of Britain's.

During the Reagan years, force projection was used increasingly as an instrument of foreign policy, not always with the expected results. The use of special forces, the mining of harbours and deploying a battleship in a show of strength all failed to ensure the overthrow of the Sandinista government of Nicaragua. The Marines' deployment in Lebanon resulted in over 200 soldiers dying in a suicide car-bomb attack, and the shore bombardment by a battleship surface action group killed many civilians and led to an increase in anti-American tensions.

In Grenada, though, the overthrow of the Left-wing government, ostensibly to protect American medical students, was judged a great success by the administration, as were actions against Libya which culminated in the bombing of targets in Tripoli and

Benghazi in 1986. On a much larger scale was the intervention in Panama at the end of 1989 which resulted in the capture of General Noriega, sometime CIA employee and close ally of the US, who had come to be regarded as unfit to rule and a threat to US security in Central America.

By far the largest example of force projection to date has been Central Command's involvement in the Gulf. This initially took the form of protecting 're-flagged' US shipping against Iranian action but amounted to considerable military support for Iraq in its war with Iran. Later, paradoxically, it was Iraq that became the threat to US interests and the target for the much larger military operations of Desert Shield and Desert Storm. The context and implications of these operations will be examined in subsequent Chapters.

Force Projection – Future Potential

The future potential of US military force-projection capabilities is complicated by two separate factors, the easing of Cold War tensions and the experience of the Gulf War. A major effect of improved East–West relations has already been a series of cuts in the defence budget, and there is no doubt that these cuts will be applied to force-projection capabilities as well as to other areas.

Thus, it is highly unlikely that the target of 15 operational aircraft-carriers will be reached; the four battleships are being put back into reserve although an improved naval gunfire programme has been started; fewer of the *Wasp*-class amphibious warfare ships will be ordered; the Clark Field air base in the Philippines will be closed and there will be cuts in personnel in many areas.

At the same time, proportionately the greatest area of cuts is likely to be in the US armed forces in Europe, especially the US Army, and, in relative terms, CENTCOM and similar forces will remain largely intact. Yet the purpose of military force-projection was always two-fold – to contain the Soviet Union in the Middle East and elsewhere, and to safeguard US interests throughout the world. Given the collapse of the Soviet threat, this actually leaves a much greater capability to counter non-Soviet security threats elsewhere in the world.

Furthermore, throughout the defence community in the United States, the tendency is to accentuate conventional power projection. Thus the US Navy and Marine Corps points to the operations in Libya. Grenada and the Gulf as evidence of a need for its continued role in the post-Cold War world. The US Army, similarly, argues that the Gulf War demonstrated the need, in the final analysis, to be able to commit armoured ground troops in a conflict overseas. The US Air Force, in particular, has concentrated on conventional air power as an essential means of maintaining security throughout the world. It even sees the prohibitively – expensive B-2 'stealth' bomber as acquiring a new saliency in conventional air-power projection rather than as a strategic nuclear bomber.

What *is* clear is that the expansion of US force projection in the 1980s leaves the United States with a very powerful legacy which stretches far beyond the end of the Cold War. If, as we will argue, the world really is moving towards a period of North-South tensions, based at least in part on the North's increasing need of the South's resources, force projection provides the military answer to the problem of securing those supplies. Nowhere is this demonstrated more clearly than in the case of the oil resources of the Persian Gulf.

7

Oil and US Security

As relations between the United States and the Soviet Union improved towards the end of the 1980s, so some analysts began to suggest that a new, and more peaceful, world order might be created. The easing of Cold War tensions made it seem highly unlikely that a major war would be fought by either of the superpowers. However, in early 1991, the Gulf War shattered that optimistic view. During the six weeks of the war, over 100,000 people were killed, two countries were physically crippled and two more were badly damaged economically.

The crisis originated on 2 August 1990, when armed forces of Iraq invaded and over-ran the state of Kuwait. Following strong international condemnation of this action, a coalition of UN member states, led by the United States, built up massive military forces in the neighbouring Gulf states and also sought to use diplomatic measures and economic sanctions to force Iraq to withdraw.

In early November, the UN Security Council set the Iraqi government a deadline of 15 January 1991 to withdraw from Kuwait. Over the following two months, the diplomatic and economic pressures continued while very large military forces were built up, dominated by the forces of US Central Command. Following the expiry of the deadline, military operations commenced against Iraq, initially by means of a series of massive air strikes at targets throughout the country. After five weeks of air assault, a four-day ground war ensued as Iraqi forces tried to withdraw from Kuwait.

A temporary cease-fire was later made permanent but the end result was far from restoring peace and security to the region. In Iraq, an uprising against the regime, by Kurds in the north and

Shi'ite rebels in the south, was put down by the Iraqi government with great severity, leading to a mass exodus of refugees into neighbouring countries, especially in the north. This culminated in Coalition troops occupying a part of northern Iraq for four months to protect the refugees.

Following the war, there was considerable disorder in Kuwait, where the ruling Al-Sabah family had great difficulty in providing leadership and restoring order. Kuwait's difficult situation was compounded by Iraq's sabotage and firing of most of Kuwait's oil wells, a process resulting in serious environmental and economic damage.

Operation Desert Storm, as the US-led military operation was called, was hailed as a great victory in the United States, an example of how US leadership and military strength could counter the actions of a brutal dictatorial regime. In Europe, though, there were misgivings, and in much of the Third World the conflict was seen as demonstrating US dominance of a new world order, especially when Western economic interests were under threat.

The United States and its allies also regarded the Gulf War as an example of effective action by the UN, in that the Coalition forces, while not directly under UN command, were acting in support of UN Security Council resolutions. This view was not shared by many UN member states, and the action was widely regarded, in many parts of the Third World in particular, as an abuse of the UN system.

Thus, there is a marked dichotomy of views on this, the first large-scale multinational military operation since the Korean War. Western ethnocentrism causes most Western analysts to see the war as a large-scale and fully legitimate policing action, but this is far from the prevailing view elsewhere. More generally, the Gulf War is already seen as a marked extension of US force projection activities, 'keeping the violent peace' on a massive scale.

We would argue that it was also significant for two other major reasons. It was a remarkable example of a conflict which, at root, was concerned with control of global resources – in this case, oil. It also demonstrated the effects of using the new generations of area-impact munitions which had been under development for two decades. Far from being a precise 'war against real estate', it demonstrated the effectiveness of area-impact munitions at a level of intensity not seen since the Second World War.

There are, therefore, four good reasons for examining the context and consequences of the Gulf War in a book concerning future global security. The war itself was fought, to a considerable extent, because Iraq's actions threatened a key Western resource. While it was viewed by leading Western states as a successful use of the UN system in resolving conflict, this was decidedly not the view in most of the world. It was, instead, seen as an extension of US force projection activities. Finally, it demonstrated new forms of warfare which are already proliferating across much of the world and indicated that, if we are indeed moving into an era of potential North–South conflict, such conflict could be immensely costly to the human community.

This Chapter will examine the historical context to the development of the crisis[1] and will also discuss the strategic significance of Middle East oil. The following Chapter will analyse the development of the crisis, with particular reference to the role of the major participant countries and of the UN. Finally, we will examine the conduct of the war itself, its aftermath, and its implications for the creation of a new world order.

The Context of the War

Following the defeat of the Ottoman Empire of Turkey in the First World War, a number of Middle East states which had formerly been under Turkish rule were administered by Britain and France under mandates from the League of Nations. Britain assumed responsibility for Iraq, Transjordan and Palestine, and France for Lebanon and Syria. The mandates comprised quasi-colonial administrations but the territories concerned were not regarded as strategically or economically important. Oil-prospecting was on a small-scale and gave little indication of the huge reserves to be discovered later.

Iraq was a disparate country with 80 percent Arabic speakers, 15 percent Kurds and the remainder Turkomans and Persian speakers. Ninety percent of the total population was Muslim, of which about 60 percent were Shi'ite and 40 percent Sunni. British policy in Iraq involved progressive devolution of administrative responsibility to a locally established government, formalised in the Anglo-Iraqi Treaty of 1922, but involving continuing British control of foreign and defence policy. Iraq gained independence in 1932.

After the First World War, Kuwait was one of a number of small city states on the Persian Gulf. The town itself had a population of just 35,000 in 1920, and the principal income was from pearling and fishing. Kuwait, along with most other Gulf sheikhdoms and emirates, had treaty obligations with Britain dating from the 19th Century, but these were seen by Britain as constituting *de facto* protectorates, maintaining British influence in Gulf waters while involving little cost or interference in internal affairs. This began to change with the exploitation of oil reserves in Bahrein from 1934, but only in the late 1940s did Kuwait become a significant oil producer.

The oil potential of Saudi Arabia became apparent rather earlier, but here British influence was overshadowed by the US presence during the Second World War, consolidated after the war into a large-scale US commercial presence. East of the Gulf, Iran was already clearly set to become a major oil-rich state. It was also a much more heavily populated country than the western Gulf states and was strategically important in the new Cold War context because of its common borders with the Soviet Union, Afghanistan and Pakistan. Under the Shah it was seen, first by Britain and later by the United States, as a crucial bulwark of Western security interests in the region.

Until the early 1950s, Britain had considerable commercial control over the production of oil in Iran, Iraq, Kuwait and Bahrein, but this diminished as American companies moved in to exploit newly-discovered reserves. This coincided with a more general loss of British influence in the Middle East, due in part to increasing Arab antagonism to British bases in the area, especially in Egypt and Iraq, but also to an increasing US interest in the strategic importance of the Middle East, exemplified by an increasingly close alliance with Iran from 1954.

Pre-war fears in the US that European powers would monopolise the newly-significant Middle East oil reserves had resulted in acquisition of oil concessions by US companies, the most significant being those in Saudi Arabia, later developed by ARAMCO, a consortium of five large US oil companies. During the 1950s, US government policy towards the Gulf states changed slowly from merely a desire to keep the Soviet Union out, to a commitment to be the major strategic power in the region. This change was greatly boosted by the failure of British and French foreign policy in the Middle East during the Suez crisis in 1956 and led to the issue of the Eisenhower Doctrine on 9 March 1957, which involved a US commitment to economic and military assistance for any Middle East state threatened by Communism.

Britain retained significant political influence over the small Gulf states until the 1960s, during which decade most of the states gained independence. Kuwait was the first, in 1961, but independence was immediately followed by threats from Iraq, based on disputed claims that Kuwait was, in the Iraqi view, merely a province of Iraq. Britain deployed troops to deter Iraqi military action and Iraq subsequently backed down, recognising Kuwait's independent status in 1963. Over the next decade and a half, Kuwait and the other Gulf states developed rapidly as major oil producers.

Iraq, to the north, had been ruled by a Hashemite monarchy until the coup of July 1958. There followed a period of 10 years during which the political power of major landowners declined, a degree of land reform was introduced and a state-centred bureaucracy acquired power. There was considerable political disturbance, with a number of coups and coup-attempts, but the period was also characterised by the slow increase in power of the Ba'ath Party, which combined a degree of social and economic reform with nationalism and a firmly defined power structure.

The Ba'ath Party finally acquired power in Iraq in July 1968, and during the 1970s, oversaw its rapid development as a result of the exploitation of oil reserves in the north and south-east of the country. Over the same period, the Ba'ath Party successively curbed the political power of the Iraqi armed forces and developed its own system of rigorous, even brutal, social and political control through internal security forces.

The core of the party was provided by people from Takrit, a town on the Tigris River, 100 miles north of Baghdad. Hasan al-Bakr, from Takrit, was leader of Iraq until 1979, but the much younger Saddam Hussein, his deputy in the Ba'ath Party and also from Takrit, was primarily responsible for the Ba'athist consolidation of power in the 1970s. He also ensured that power within the party was concentrated in his own hands and those of his Takrit clan. Saddam Hussein took power in Iraq in 1979 when al-Bakr stepped down.

The Iran–Iraq War

In 1975, Iran and Iraq settled historic differences over the control of the strategically important Shatt al'Arab waterway, the confluence of the Tigris and Euphrates rivers entering the Gulf. The agreement also curbed Iranian support for Iraqi Kurds, but did not involve settlement of some minor territorial differences.

After the overthrow of the Shah of Iran in the revolution of 1979, Iran's new theocracy under Ayatollah Khomeini developed a bitter opposition to the Iraqi regime, such an essentially secular regime ruling over many millions of Shi'ite Muslims being anathema to Iranian Shi'ites. Following a rapid increase in tension, Iraq renounced previous agreements and invaded Iran on 20 September 1980, hoping to use its superior military power to defeat an Iranian army seriously weakened by revolutionary disruption. After initial gains, Iraqi forces became bogged down and built comprehensive fortifications which were maintained until 1982.

After a rapid process of rearmament and mobilisation, Iran took the offensive and regained lost territory from the Iraqis but its forces, in turn, were halted by Iraqi defensive positions on their own borders. For four years the ground war remained largely static, despite massive offensives and bombardments and the loss of tens of thousands of lives.

Iraq was seen by the Gulf states as providing a protection against militant Iran and much of its war was funded by Kuwait and Saudi Arabia. Although the United States and Britain remained technically neutral in the war, they too regarded Iraq as a buffer, protecting their Western Gulf oil interests from Iranian excesses. For the United States, the Iranian regime was particularly reviled because of its seizure of US diplomats as hostages, early in the revolution.

The US and Britain maintained an official arms embargo against both countries but, apart from the Irangate anomaly, it was Iraq that received the greatest unofficial help. Iraq armed itself primarily with Soviet and French equipment, but used many other sources of supply, including Egypt and Brazil, and its more general industrial development was greatly aided by technical assistance from many Western countries. Israel, on the other hand, regarded Iraq as a potential threat to its security and gave aid to Iran.

Sporadic attempts, by both sides, to disrupt oil exports from the Gulf escalated into the 'tanker war' of the mid-1980s, with the United States and other Western countries becoming heavily involved in protecting shipping. Although Iraq instigated most of the attacks, US naval efforts were directed almost entirely against Iran, a clear 'tilt' in favour of the Iraqi regime. This policy of support for Iraq involved major attacks on Iranian warships and off-shore oil installations being used as military facilities during 1987–88, culminating in a major naval action in April 1988, when US warships and planes sank an Iranian frigate, a corvette and several patrol craft and crippled a second frigate, with the loss of around 200 Iranians. Coupled with renewed ground offensives by Iraq early in 1988, this turned the tide of the war against Iran, which eventually accepted a UN Security Council resolution dating from July 1987 calling for a cease-fire. This took effect, under UN supervision, on 20 August 1988.

In the later phases of the ground war, Iraq used chemical weapons on the battlefield, both mustard gas and nerve agents. They made relatively little difference to the course of the war, but were also used in the suppression of Kurdish revolt within Iraq, the most notable example being an attack on the town of Halabjah early in 1988, when some 5,000 inhabitants were killed.

After the war, Iran steadily moderated its policies and, after the death of Ayatollah Khomeini, the more pragmatic government of President Rafsanjani concentrated its efforts on post-war economic reconstruction and development. Iraq, by contrast, commenced a major rearmament programme, involving the acquisition of advanced aircraft and tanks, primarily from French and Soviet sources. Although the United States and Britain maintained an official embargo on arms sales to Iraq, relations were good and there was considerable involvement in the economic development of the country.

Thus, a regime which was denounced by human rights activists as brutal, repressive and capable of using chemical warfare on a large scale against its own population, was regarded as an ally by Western countries. In part this was due to the enormous potential of the country, given its large oil reserves, but it was also seen as a continuing counter to the potential power of Iran, even after the damage it had sustained during the eight-year war. In both senses, though, Middle East oil resources lay at the heart of Western policy towards the region.

Strategic Significance of Middle East Oil

The Organisation of Petroleum Exporting Countries (OPEC) was founded at a meeting in Baghdad in September 1960. Founder members were Venezuela, Iran, Iraq, Saudi Arabia and Kuwait. Further states joined the organisation during the 1960s, including Algeria, Nigeria, Libya and Indonesia, so that even as early as 1970 OPEC member states controlled some 60 percent of world crude oil reserves.

OPEC grew in power partly because it maintained unity on the matter of oil policy, but also because oil increased hugely in importance to the industrial economies of the West. By the early 1970s, all the major Western industrial powers, even the United States, were importing substantial quantities of oil from OPEC states. In turn, individual member states of OPEC and, to an extent, the organisation as a whole, were starting to use their economic power to bargain with major oil consumers. This reached a peak in Gaddafi's takeover of Western oil interests in Libya in September 1973, but was followed, a month later, by an even more spectacular action by the Arab members of OPEC acting together.

Dismayed by the lack of progress of the Egyptian/Syrian offensive in the Yom Kippur/Ramadan War, the members of OAPEC (Organisation of Arab Petroleum Exporting Countries) decided on 17 October 1973, in the middle of the war, to use oil as a weapon against Israel and its main backer, the United States. Oil production by OAPEC members was cut by 15 per cent to engineer a scarcity, all oil exports to the United States and The Netherlands (location of the key Rotterdam oil market) were embargoed, and the price of oil was increased by an average 71 percent. Subsequent action from October 1973 to May 1974 led to a quadrupling of world oil prices, setting in motion the most fundamental shake-up in Western economies since the 1930s, exacerbating the 1974 world food crisis and leading ultimately to the Third World debt crisis of the 1980s.

Apart from the major impact on US security perceptions (*see* Chapter 8), the 1973–74 oil price increases led to a massive search for alternative oil supplies, especially outside of OPEC member states. During the late 1970s and early 1980s, major oil fields in Alaska, Mexico and the North Sea were discovered and exploited. Against expectations, though, the largest new oil reserves were actually found in the Middle East, especially in the Gulf states, and by 1989 this was the dominant region for world oil reserves, a position made even more significant by the slow but steady depletion of oil reserves in the United States, Canada, the Soviet Union and north-west Europe.

The pattern established by the end of the 1970s was of world oil *production* predominantly outside the Middle East but *reserves* located primarily within that region. Thus, *Table 3* shows world oil production for 1989, with the Soviet Union as the largest producer, followed by the United States, with the United Kingdom and Canada also in the top 10.

Table 3
World Oil Production – Top 10 Countries

(1989 – million barrels per day)

1	Soviet Union	12.475
2	United States	9.175
3	Saudi Arabia	5.260
4	Mexico	2.875
5	Iran	2.865
6	Iraq	2.825
7	China	2.790
8	Venezuela	1.980
9	United Kingdom	1.905
10	Canada	1.725

Source: Adapted from *Middle East and North Africa Yearbook, 1991*.

A very different picture emerges when this is compared to the distribution of oil reserves. *Table 4* shows world oil reserves for early 1990, with the Soviet Union and the United States numbers 7 and 9 respectively, and the table dominated by Gulf states. On these figures, the oil reserves of Iraq and Kuwait combined were nearly six times as great as those of the entire United States including the Alaskan deposits. Iraq, Kuwait and Saudi Arabia together controlled 449.5 billion barrels of proven oil reserves, representing almost 45 percent of the world total reserves of 1,011 billion barrels.

The pattern was therefore established of countries such as the Soviet Union, the United States, Canada and Britain producing oil heavily from a relatively low reserve base, but with oil strategically located primarily in the Gulf states. Furthermore, the United States was becoming increasingly dependent on imported oil.

The strategic significance of this was recognised by the United

Table 4
World Oil Reserves – Top 10 Countries

(January 1, 1990 – billion barrels)

1	Saudi Arabia	255.0
2	Iraq	100.0
3	Kuwait	94.5
4	Iran	92.9
5	UAE – Abu Dhabi	92.2
6	Venezuela	58.5
7	Soviet Union	58.4
8	Mexico	56.4
9	United States	34.1
10	China	24.0

Items 1–3 bracketed: 449.5

Source: As *Table 3*

States in the late 1970s and led to the establishment of the Joint Rapid Deployment Task Force, the prime function of which was to safeguard Middle East oil in the event of any future security threat.[2] The Task Force was, in turn, developed in the 1980s into a unified military command, US Central Command (CENTCOM), with responsibility for securing US strategic interests in an arc of 19 countries stretching from Kenya in East Africa throughout the Middle East to Pakistan in South-West Asia.

CENTCOM had already seen considerable military action in the Gulf prior to 1990, especially in its destruction of Iranian warships in 1988. As the Kuwait crisis developed in mid-1990, CENTCOM's very existence, and the forces available to it, gave the United States a remarkable instrument of foreign policy with which to respond to Iraq's aggression. That response had little to do with the illegal and brutal invasion of a smaller state, even though the international community was rightly appalled at the Iraqi action. The US action was much more concerned with the takeover of Kuwait's oil reserves and the threat to the even larger reserves located on Saudi territory to the immediate south of Kuwait.

Iraq under Saddam Hussein may have been a highly acceptable counter to militant Iran during the Gulf War, but the prospect of the Iraqi regime controlling one-fifth of the world's oil reserves and threatening another quarter was totally unacceptable. Some analysts have regarded this factor as of limited importance, pointing to the relatively small role of Gulf oil *production* in world oil markets. This is to miss the point. The strategic value of Gulf oil lies in its utter dominance of world oil *reserves* – 65 per cent of total world reserves coming from Iraq, Iran and the Gulf states. From being an ally of the West, a buffer against the perceived threat from a militant Iran, Iraq was transformed rapidly into a real threat to Middle East oil supplies and, therefore, to Western economic security.

8

The Gulf – Crisis Into War

By 1990, Iraq's rearmament programme had placed it at the forefront of Middle East states. It had a standing army of 500,000 and a modern airforce, it was producing and had used ballistic missiles and chemical weapons, and was developing nuclear weapons. The regime seemed intent on taking on a leadership role within the Arab world and was increasingly antagonistic towards Israel.

The United States and Western European countries were keen to improve their trade links with this oil-rich country and paid little attention to the rhetoric coming out of Baghdad, or to the persistent reports of gross human rights abuses within Iraq. Even the persistent and large-scale use of chemical weapons against Kurdish civilians received little more than ritual condemnation from the West.

Israel was becoming increasingly concerned at Iraq's growing military strength. It was itself under pressure from Western public opinion because of its treatment of the Palestinians in the occupied territories as the 'intifada' uprising continued, and attempted repeatedly to draw attention to Iraq's aggressive intent, partly through genuine fear of the expansionist regime but also to divert international attention away from its own problem.

The Soviet Union, though preoccupied with momentous internal change, regarded Iraq as a close ally in the Middle East, keeping several thousand technicians in Iraq, many of them maintaining Soviet-made military equipment.

The Gulf Arab states were increasingly ambivalent in their attitude to Saddam Hussein and Iraq. They had regarded Iraq as a hugely beneficial buffer against Iranian power in the region, but with the war now over and Iraq clearly developing into a major military power, they were becoming suspicious of its motives, especially as Baghdad was calling repeatedly for higher oil prices to finance its further development.

The crisis itself developed in the summer of 1990 as a result of a direct conflict of economic interests between Iraq and Kuwait.[1] Iraq's massive programme of economic development and military enhancement could not be supported by its oil revenues because of the low price of oil on world markets. It was therefore running into debt at a time when the belligerent tone of its foreign policy was starting to cause concern to Western states.

Kuwait, by contrast, had long had very high oil revenues, proportional to the needs of its population, and had reinvested much of its earnings overseas, especially in industrialised countries. By 1990, about half of its entire income came from revenues from overseas investments and it therefore had a considerable interest in ensuring economic growth overseas, for which low oil prices were important.

Early in 1990, Iraq accused Kuwait and the United Arab Emirates (UAE) of deliberately overproducing oil, against OPEC recommendations, thereby keeping oil prices low and damaging the Iraqi economy, even though Iraq had, in its view, protected them for much of the previous decade against the threat from Iran. Iraq concentrated its pressures on Kuwait and extended the dispute to include control of the strategically important Kuwaiti islands of Bubiyan and Warba and a claim that Kuwait was overproducing oil from its part of the Rumaila oil field, which straddles the Iraq/Kuwait border but was mainly beneath Iraqi territory.

With the Brent crude 'marker' price of oil falling from $19.60 a barrel in February to $15.60 in June, Iraq's financial position worsened markedly, and in July Saddam Hussein fiercely attacked the Gulf states for overproduction. Although Iraq and the Gulf oil states had agreed measures to curb overproduction at a meeting in Jeddah, Saudi Arabia, on 10–11 July Saddam Hussein subsequently started a sustained diplomatic offensive against Kuwait, beginning with a speech on 17 July, stating that 'if words fail to protect Iraqis, something must be done to return things to their natural course'. Kuwait placed its army on alert on 18 July and its Foreign Ministry began an intensive diplomatic counter-offensive among Arab League member states.

The Arab League and Egypt's President Mubarak attempted to calm the crisis, with Mubarak visiting Iraq, Kuwait and Saudi

Arabia on 24 July; but the anti-Kuwait campaign in the Iraqi media intensified, and US sources reported that Iraq had moved two armoured divisions totalling 30,000 troops towards the Kuwait border. Although US forces in the Gulf quickly arranged joint exercises with UAE units, Washington's view was that Baghdad was sabre-rattling as a means of pressuring Kuwait for further concessions.

OPEC oil ministers met in Geneva on 26–27 July and agreed new oil production quotas aimed at getting an oil price of $21 a barrel by the end of the year, ($4 a barrel less than Iraq's demands), and talks between Iraq and Kuwait, scheduled for 28–29 July, were delayed three days.

Meanwhile, tensions rose rapidly, despite mediation attempts by the Saudis, King Hussein of Jordan and Yasser Arafat. By 31 July, US sources indicated six Iraqi army divisions numbering 100,000 troops were massed on the Kuwaiti border, but talks between the two states finally commenced on that day in Jeddah.

The talks collapsed after a single two-hour session, with the Iraqi delegation returning to Baghdad claiming that the Kuwaitis had refused serious negotiations. Unofficial sources said that Iraqi claims included a write-off of $10 billion of debts owed to Kuwait, a further $10 billion of aid from Kuwait, $2.4 billion compensation for excessive Kuwaiti extraction of oil from the Rumaila field and a long-term lease of Bubiyan and Warba Islands to Iraq.

The Invasion of Kuwait

An initial contingent of 30,000 Iraqi troops, including units of the élite Republican Guard, crossed into Kuwait at 2.00 am on 2 August, 1990, and quickly advanced towards Kuwait City, meeting little opposition and entering the capital at about 7.00 am. The small Kuwaiti army was caught largely by surprise in spite of having been on alert for the previous two weeks. This, coupled with extensive air support from the Iraqi air force, ensured rapid progress, although ground forces met opposition later on 2 August in the vicinity of the Amir's palace and the Shuwaikh Barracks.

The Amir and the Crown Prince were evacuated to Saudi Arabia by helicopter early in the Iraqi attack and by the end of 2 August there was only scattered resistance to the Iraqi forces. A number of Kuwaiti army and air force units, including A-4 strike aircraft, were able to escape to Saudi Arabia, but the Iraqis captured large quantities of equipment including advanced anti-aircraft and anti-tank missiles. Casualties during the fighting were variously estimated at 200–1,000 killed.

The successful invasion was greeted with enthusiastic demonstrations in Baghdad, although there were unconfirmed reports of disagreements within the Iraqi army over the value of the invasion. Baghdad claimed that its forces had been invited into Kuwait by opposition groups and a pro-Iraqi Provisional Free Kuwaiti Government (PFKG) began broadcasting from Kuwait City late on 2 August. The deposed Kuwait Government moved to the Saudi mountain resort of Taif and established a government-in-exile.

Initial Iraqi policy towards Kuwait implied a withdrawal of most forces, to start on 5 August, once a pro-Iraqi government had been established, but Western sources indicated a build-up of Iraqi forces towards the Kuwait/Saudi Arabia border, suggesting a threat to Saudi Arabia itself, or at least its strategically significant north-eastern oil-fields. In the event, Iraq formally annexed Kuwait on 8 August, 1990.

Responses to the Invasion

Within the Arab world, opinion on the Iraqi invasion of Kuwait polarised. Egypt, Saudi Arabia, Syria and the smaller Gulf states sought an unconditional withdrawal. Jordan, Yemen and Sudan supported a negotiated settlement within Arab ranks, a stance also adopted by the Palestine Liberation Organisation (PLO). The Arab League met in Cairo on 3 August but a resolution calling for immediate withdrawal was opposed by six of the 21 members.

Among the international community, there was general and wide-ranging condemnation. Within the UN organisation there was particularly strong feeling among professional diplomats that the forceful takeover of one member state by another could not be tolerated.

Israel sought to gain the maximum support for its previous antagonism to Iraq, and was quick to point out that the Iraqi action merely confirmed the aggressive nature of the regime and Israel's repeated warnings of its danger to regional security. The Israeli government also emphasised the support of the PLO for Iraq as evidence of the extremist nature of that organisation.

Although there was intense activity at the UN Security Council, the more significant developments occurred in Washington where, within three days of the invasion, the decision had been taken to commit substantial military forces to Saudi Arabia. This required the agreement of the Saudis, but they were persuaded of the necessity of US military aid by information from US intelligence sources apparently showing a direct Iraqi military threat to their northern oil fields which lay close to the Kuwait and Iraq borders.

Thus, while the United States sought to operate in support of UN resolutions, it succeeded, by 7 August, in obtaining Saudi agreement to station substantial military forces there. The build-up was rapid and followed well-rehearsed CENTCOM contingency plans. Aircraft started arriving on 8 August, six days after the Iraqi invasion of Kuwait and two days after the US decision to intervene. Elements of the 82nd Airborne Division were dispatched from the US. The *Independence* carrier battle group was directed to the Gulf, followed later in August by the *Eisenhower* and *Saratoga* carrier battle groups and a naval surface action group led by the battleship *Wisconsin*.

The stated aim of these deployments was to protect Saudi Arabia from Iraqi attack, with economic sanctions being used to secure the unconditional withdrawal of Iraq from Kuwait and the restoration of legitimate government. President Bush made clear on 8 August that further aims were the protection of US citizens and the establishment of stability in the region, and it became clear that, even at this early stage in the crisis, the US government did not rule out the direct use of force.[2]

During the latter part of August, the Pentagon continued building up to a force level of about 250,000 troops in Saudi Arabia and neighbouring countries, utilising long-established CENTCOM procedures, and also making use of Saudi Arabia's very impressive network of air bases, ports and army facilities, many of them constructed with US help in previous decades. While Saudi Arabia had been reluctant to have any direct Western military presence on its territory, its willingness to allow a dormant military infrastructure to be in place made the US military build-up a relatively straightforward process.

The US was joined in its deployments by Britain, France, Egypt and Syria, and eventually by a Coalition of over 20 countries, although over 80 per cent of all foreign forces deployed to the region remained American. West Germany and Japan responded with much greater caution, with Japan constitutionally handicapped in any endeavour to deploy military forces overseas. In addition to trade sanctions imposed on Iraq, the United States and several major European countries froze Iraqi financial assets in their countries.

As the Western military build-up continued, still dominated by the US but including several Arab states, so Arab public opinion slowly gravitated towards Iraq. Arab governments were divided: key supporters of the US included Egypt, Syria and, obviously, Saudi Arabia, whereas Jordan and Yemen were greatly concerned by the build-up of forces. Even in Syria and Egypt, though, there was considerable support for the Iraqi position, and this was much stronger in the North African states, especially Algeria.

The attitude was not one of supporting Saddam Hussein in all his policies – the brutal nature of the Iraqi regime was well-known – but three factors undermined support for the Western response to the invasion. One was a widespread dislike of the Gulf Arab states and their sheer wealth, especially their refusal to distribute their 'accidental' oil wealth across the Middle East. A second was the scale of the US military response, which showed all the signs of a Western superpower gaining a major military presence in the heart of the Arab world. Finally, there was the persistent refusal of the US and its allies to put pressure on Israel to negotiate on the Palestinian issue. This last factor was used continually and effectively by Saddam Hussein to gain public support for his action, as he sought to link Iraqi withdrawal from Kuwait to progress on the Palestinian question.

The Soviet Union, in spite of its close links with Iraq, was broadly supportive of the actions agreed by the UN Security Council during August (see below) and also suspended all arms shipments on 2 August. At the same time, it made efforts to keep diplomatic links with Baghdad functioning smoothly. China, seeking international respectability after the events of two years earlier, was also willing to support the strong position on the crisis.

For the United States, all this meant that it was in a remarkably strong position within the UN Security Council, where all five permanent member states with a power of veto were broadly supportive of its firm policy against Iraq.

Immediately after the invasion of Kuwait, there were fears that the crisis would lead to massive increases in the price of oil. In the event, there were significant temporary increases to over $30 a barrel by 22 August. Subsequent reports that Saudi Arabia would substantially boost production to make up for the shortfall caused by the crisis began to calm oil markets later in the month.

The UN Response to the Invasion

The UN Security Council met on 2 August, shortly after the invasion, and passed Resolution 660 demanding unconditional withdrawal, followed later by a negotiated settlement of their disputes by Kuwait and Iraq. On 6 August, Resolution 661 was passed 13 to 0 (Yemen and Cuba abstaining) calling for mandatory trade sanctions against Iraq. These included a ban on all oil exports, followed by the closing of Iraqi oil pipelines through Saudi Arabia and Turkey.

Resolution 662 of 9 August, passed unanimously, condemned Iraq's annexation of Kuwait and Resolution 664 of 18 August demanded safe conduct for foreign nationals from Kuwait and Iraq and that Iraq rescind its order closing diplomatic missions in Kuwait. Resolution 665 was passed by 13 to 0 on 25 August, with Yemen and Cuba abstaining, and authorised the use of force by warships in the enforcement of Resolution 662.

While support for sanctions was widespread among UN member states, there was also concern that the deployment of military forces by the United States and its Coalition allies would lead to military action under UN auspices. There were widely differing opinions on the validity of this, with the UN bureaucracy broadly opposed to such action. Thus the military Coalition was not a UN force and military action in excess of Resolution 665 would not be justified by the states involved, under Article 51 of the UN Charter on self-defence.

The series of debates and motions within the Security Council demonstrated the coalition of support which the United States could maintain from among the five permanent members, but it did not reflect opinions throughout the organisation. While there was almost universal condemnation of the Iraqi invasion of Kuwait, there was a strong feeling, particularly among Third World member states, that a 'rush to war' could get out of control. The UN bureaucracy was reflecting this caution in its opposition to a formally-established UN military force.

It is also fair to say that neither the United States nor its key allies were convinced that a formal UN force was for the best, as there was always a risk that it could constrain options which might be sought by the leading members of the anti-Iraq coalition.

Iraqi Strategies after the Invasion

From an initial position that it would withdraw from Kuwait leaving behind a new government, Baghdad had quickly moved to annex Kuwait as the 19th province of Iraq, claiming historical precedence for this. During August 1990, Iraqi forces consolidated their control of Kuwait. There was sporadic resistance which was suppressed vigorously, and there was systematic looting of industrial and domestic goods.

Hundreds of thousands of Asian and North African 'guest workers' attempted to flee from Kuwait and Iraq, and by 6 September, 470,000 refugees had crossed into Jordan, causing huge problems for relief agencies. Western residents of Kuwait and Iraq became, effectively, hostages, as almost all were denied exit permits and many were grouped together in hotels under government control. Women and children were given permission to depart early in September, but some 5,000 men were kept behind, mainly in Baghdad, several hundred of them apparently being moved to military installations to act as 'human shields'.

Earlier, on 15 August, Saddam Hussein had concluded a surprising peace deal with Iran, accepting all Iranian demands for a final end to the Iran–Iraq War, and thereby releasing substantial numbers of troops from duty on the Iranian border. This was a significant addition to Iraqi capabilities which could be moved to face the coalition build-up of military forces in Saudi Arabia.

Throughout September and October, the Iraqi government attempted to link the annexation of Kuwait with wider Middle East issues, particularly a Palestinian settlement, but also stressing the need for a Holy War (*Jihad*) against Western forces which, it claimed, were occupying Saudi Arabia and threatening Islamic holy places. This, in turn, was linked with calls to the populations of coalition Arab partners, especially Egypt and Syria, to overthrow their governments. While there were tensions in several countries, this did not extend to major disorder, though the support which Saddam Hussein had sought from ordinary Arab opinion was largely maintained in many countries.

It is probable that Saddam Hussein had originally calculated that Western reaction to his invasion of Kuwait would be muted, and that he could play off his old ally, the Soviet Union, against the United States. He was wrong for two reasons. The first was that the easing of East–West relations, coupled with the severe domestic problems facing the Soviet Union, ensured that Moscow would not respond as he expected. Secondly, the United States was quite unable to countenance Iraqi control over one-fifth of the world's oil reserves, with the further risk of the Saddam Hussein regime threatening the further quarter of world oil reserves located in Saudi Arabia.

Given this fundamental miscalculation, Iraq was quickly faced with a formidable Coalition military build-up, and it is remarkable how quickly Saddam Hussein was able to move to a peace agreement with Iran, thereby freeing substantial military forces. It is also indicative of his powerful position within Iraq that he was able to agree what amounted to a capitulation to Iranian demands at the end of a brutal eight-year war without himself being deposed or even substantially under threat.

From August through to the end of October, Iraq moved progressively to develop military defences in Kuwait and south-east Iraq. Progressive mobilisation took the armed forces from their core strength of 500,000 to 900,000, of whom 300,000 were already based in the potential war zone by the end of August. As forces were redeployed from the Iranian frontier, though, large numbers were sent to the Turkish and Syrian borders, and substantial reserves of the élite forces such as the Republican Guard were maintained in central Iraq.

Initial International Reaction

Throughout the crisis, the US was the lead actor among the Coalition partners. By 25 August 1990 it already had 40,000 troops, some 200 aircraft and three carrier battle groups in the area, and the military build-up continued through September to a level exceeding 200,000 by the end of that month. Over the first three months, the United States military continued to state that the deployments were essentially defensive, although in mid-September, the US Air Force Chief of Staff, General Michael Dugan, told journalists that if war broke out, targets throughout Iraq, including Baghdad, would be attacked. He was dismissed on 17 September.

US foreign policy towards Iraq, aimed at maximising economic and diplomatic pressure while building up military forces, was somewhat constrained by the presence of US hostages within Iraq, although the administration was at pains to point out that this would not limit US military action in the event of war. Indeed, Washington maintained pressure on UN member states to adopt an increasingly tough stance while building and extending the coalition of states prepared to commit forces.

The strongest support for the US came from Britain, under Margaret Thatcher, motivated in part by the opportunity to enhance Anglo-American relations. Britain committed strike aircraft, interceptors and an armoured brigade to the Gulf and reinforced Britain's existing naval forces. The British attitude contrasted with the relative caution of other major West European states. While President Mitterrand's government made major force commitments to the region, France, along with Italy, Germany and the Netherlands, was stronger in its support for continuing diplomatic initiatives, with the European Community seen as playing a potentially intermediary role.

Germany and Japan, both reluctant to be directly involved in military confrontation, were persuaded to aid in financing military operations, and the United States succeeded in gaining cautious acceptance from the Soviet Union and China that it should maintain its leadership of the Coalition. The role of Moscow was pivotal, and a hastily-arranged superpower summit in Helsinki on 9 September was devoted almost entirely to the crisis. Once again, it became clear that its almost total preoccupation with internal difficulties would ensure that the Soviet Union did not hinder the development of Washington's policy towards Iraq.

Within the Middle East, the Syrian and Egyptian governments became increasingly committed to the possible use of force and, during September, increased their ground forces in Saudi Arabia to 14,000 and 20,000 respectively. Jordan, Yemen and the PLO continued to call for an Arab solution to the crisis. Jordan suffered major economic losses due to the effects of the blockade of Iraq, as much of the latter's trade had gone through the Jordanian port of Aqaba. Yemen and Egypt suffered from the loss of earnings of 'guest workers' previously in Iraq, and Yemen also suffered from a withdrawal of some US aid programmes.

In Israel and the occupied territories tension rose during September, culminating in the killing of 17 unarmed Palestinians by Israeli border police on the Temple Mount in Jerusalem on 8

October. This led to widespread international denunciation of the Israeli action and resulted in UN Security Council Resolution 672 condemning the shootings and welcoming a peace mission to Israel to be sent by the Secretary-General. This, in turn, formed part of wider diplomatic activities by the Secretary-General's office, which included meetings with Iraqi, European and US diplomats.

Crisis Into War

During October 1990, tensions increased steadily as further US forces reached the Gulf. On 2 October, the aircraft carrier *Independence* entered Gulf waters for a brief period, placing its aircraft within range of Kuwait and Iraq without refuelling, although it was primarily a symbolic move.

During the course of the month, reports of Iraqi mistreatment of Kuwaiti civilians increased, and there was growing concern over the Western hostages in Iraq. In a move probably intended to weaken Western unity, Iraq progressively released all French hostages, and Saddam Hussein received visits from former British Prime Minister Edward Heath and other Western figures, releasing small numbers of hostages in response.

On 29 October, the UN Security Council passed Resolution 674 by 13 to 0, with Cuba and Yemen abstaining, condemning the continued Iraqi occupation of Kuwait and ill-treatment of residents.

By the end of the month, US impatience at lack of a solution was expressed forcefully by President Bush, who compared Saddam Hussein with Hitler and warned the US public of the likelihood of war. Bush's attitude to Saddam Hussein was in marked contrast to previous US support for the regime, especially during the latter stages of its war with Iran. While some analysts suggested his forceful posturing was merely a part of the electioneering for the mid-term Congressional elections, it followed a visit to the Gulf by the Chairman of the US Joint Chiefs of Staff, General Colin Powell. His assessment was that offensive action to eject Iraqi forces from Kuwait required a major reinforcement of the coalition forces. This was, in part, due to Iraq's earlier peace deal with Iran and the release of Iraqi military forces which that allowed. On 9 November, President Bush announced a near-doubling of US forces to be completed by January 1991.

This was a key decision, taking US forces from the 230,000

already in place to over 400,000. The former level was judged more than sufficient for all defensive postures and the reinforcement was intended to ensure that an all-out war against Iraq would be short and complete. The build-up, under the continuing command of General Norman Schwarzkopf, C-in-C of CENTCOM, was well above that envisaged under CENTCOM planning and was a reflection of the size and power of the Iraqi forces being faced. It required the movement of armoured divisions from Europe and their adaptation to desert conditions, deployment of well over 1,000 air force planes, six carrier battle groups and two battleship surface action groups.

Within the United States, the armed forces were facing severe budgetary restraint as a result of the easing of East–West relations. Each branch of the armed forces – navy, army, air force and marines – was only too keen to demonstrate its potential value in this crisis, and these inter-service rivalries did much to heighten their commitment to the military build-up in the Gulf.

In addition to US forces, some Coalition states, notably Britain and France, announced further reinforcements. By early December these were estimated at 30,000 British, 11,700 French, 20,000 Egyptians, 20,000 Syrians, 6,200 Moroccans and 5,000 Pakistanis, together with 67,500 Saudi troops and smaller contingents from Gulf states and from exiled Kuwaiti units. In theory, the Saudis had ultimate command of forces in their territory, but they agreed to allow US command of forces operating forward into Kuwait and Iraq. In practice, the entire operation was commanded by the US under the immediate leadership of General Schwarzkopf.

As the Coalition forces expanded into a major offensive configuration, Iraq also reinforced its troops, announcing on 19 November that 150,000 troops would be added to the 450,000 troops reportedly in Kuwait and southern Iraq.

Washington's efforts to persuade the United Nations to endorse military action to force Iraq from Kuwait were finally successful on 29 November 1990 when the Security Council passed Resolution 678 by 12 to 2, with Cuba and Yemen voting against and China abstaining. Paragraph 2 authorised:

> member states co-operating with the government of Kuwait, unless Iraq on or before 15 January 1991 fully implements. . . . the foregoing resolutions, to use all necessary means to uphold and implement Security

Council Resolution 660 and all subsequent relevant resolutions and to
restore international peace and security to the area.

Thus the use of sanctions as the means of removing Iraqi forces
from Kuwait was replaced by an endorsement of other methods,
including the use of force.

This represented a fundamental shift in the approach to the
crisis. Once a deadline for withdrawal was set, the military option
was established as the prime approach to the crisis, and sanctions
were relegated to a peripheral role. While this change of policy
appears, on the surface, to have taken place in late November, the
build-up of military forces, together with a number of reports from
sources in Washington, indicates that the decision was probably
taken in September, within a few weeks of the invasion. This was,
though, a hidden agenda – the declared policy was pursuit of a
solution through sanctions, altogether more acceptable to world
public opinion.

This policy also involved systematic diplomatic action to maintain UN support for US action against Iraq, which in turn meant a
rapid reversal of previous US attitudes to the UN. During the
Reagan era, the UN had been viewed with suspicion; the United
States had withdrawn from UNESCO and had itself owed the UN
dues of up to $200 million. Now, the support of the UN Security
Council for military action against Iraq was considered essential.

In its efforts to maintain support, especially for Resolution 678,
the United States used promises as well as threats, and the former
involved direct US aid as well as assistance from organisations such
as the World Bank and IMF, where the US had considerable
influence. Both Ethiopia and Zaire were offered new aid packages
and improved access to World Bank/IMF assistance, and the US
offered direct assistance to Colombia. Yemen, on the other hand,
voted against Resolution 678 and, three days after the vote, the
United States cut its $70 million aid programme.

During November, the movement of US reinforcements to the
Gulf accelerated and it became clear that the aim was to complete
the process by the mid-January deadline. In Britain, Prime
Minister Margaret Thatcher was in the middle of a serious domestic political crisis and was eventually forced to resign, although
the Conservatives remained in power, committed to Coalition aims
under the new Prime Minister, John Major. Mrs Thatcher's last act
as Prime Minister was to order a further major increase in British

ground troops, aircraft and warships deployed to the Gulf, ultimately taking British forces to 45,000, third only to US and Saudi forces in the area.

During the last two months of 1990, the Iraqi armed forces commenced building major defensive fortifications along the coast of Kuwait and on the southern borders of Kuwait and Iraq with Saudi Arabia. These comprised deep minefields, anti-tank embankments and trenches, triangular fortifications and networks of bunkers as well as large numbers of artillery and tanks, mostly dug into defensive revetments.

The entire process benefited from Iraq's considerable skills in combat engineering, developed largely during the early 1980s in the war against Iran, and led Coalition military leaders to embark on extensive training of their troops in offensive action against such defences. By the end of the year there were reliable reports that Iraqi army engineers had laid demolition charges on Kuwaiti oil refineries, pipelines and a large proportion of the oil wells. Early in the New Year, environmentalists in Europe and the United States warned of an environmental catastrophe if these facilities were destroyed and set on fire.

As well as reinforcing their forward defences, the Iraqis moved major units of mobile reserve armour, including four divisions of the élite Republican Guard, to southern Iraq. They also suppressed remaining Kuwaiti resistance in Kuwait City, and moved substantial quantities of artillery and anti-aircraft defences into the city. At the same time, Baghdad was careful to station the Republican Guard units north of the border in Iraq rather than in Kuwait itself, and substantial reserves, including other Guard divisions, were kept in central and northern Iraq.

These preparations were accompanied by a mixture of political actions. Baghdad justified its continuing occupation of Kuwait in the face of UN Resolution 678 by continuing to claim an historic right to the territory, but its rhetoric extended to allegations of an anti-Islamic conspiracy by the United States and Israel. It also expressed strong support for the Palestinian cause and was aided in this by a number of visits from Yasser Arafat to Baghdad.

At the same time, Baghdad also decided to reduce tensions by announcing that remaining hostages, reported to number some 2,000, would be progressively released towards the end of December. This policy was duly implemented. The Iraqi policy thus appeared to be a combination of appealing to Arab public opinion over the heads of governments of countries such as Syria and Egypt, while suggesting to Western governments that there was a willingness to make compromises.

Unconfirmed reports from Iraq indicated that there was some opposition to the regime's policies towards Kuwait but there was also a general belief that war would be avoided. This attitude was also prevalent in most Western countries, including the United States, even though attempts to start discussions between Iraq's Foreign Minister, Tariq Aziz, and Secretary of State James Baker failed in mid-December. By the end of 1990, there was still a widespread belief that the Coalition could achieve a negotiated settlement, even though the deployment of forces in the Gulf was almost complete.

Public opinion in the United States was broadly in support of the government and in favour of a military solution if need be. In Britain, there was considerable apprehension about the possible casualties of a war and in most other Western European countries there was a widespread reluctance to support a war.

As the deadline approached, intensive mediation efforts were made, and a meeting took place between Tariq Aziz and James Baker in Geneva on 9 January 1991. France maintained links with Iraq and with Algeria, the Soviet Union and the PLO, all of whom attempted to mediate. The head of the French National Assembly Foreign Affairs Committee, Michel Vauzelle, visited Baghdad on 2–5 January, and European Community officials were also active prior to the Baker/Aziz meeting. In the United States, both houses of Congress produced votes in favour of the use of force, with 250 to 183 in the House of Representatives and 52 to 47 in the Senate.

The UN Secretary-General, Perez de Cuellar, visited Baghdad on 12 January for last-minute diplomacy, and had discussions with Saddam Hussein the following day, but failed to make progress towards Iraqi compliance with UN demands. Last-minute French initiatives on 14 January were similarly unsuccessful and the deadline expired the following day.

Parallel Processes

While there was considerable media coverage in the West of the Coalition military build-up, the major emphasis throughout the period August to December 1990 was on the political negotiations. Right through to the end of the year, most people believed that war would be avoided. In practice, the decision to set a deadline of 15 January was the turning point in the crisis as it meant the abandonment of the process of achieving a solution through sanctions and a reliance on either early Iraqi withdrawal or the large-scale use of military forces.

In this context, the key determining factor was that the Coalition states, and especially the United States, had the military means to go to war. The use of military force as an instrument of foreign policy is only practicable if the military capabilities are sufficient to achieve the aim. In the case of the Kuwait crisis, the United States had built up through CENTCOM, the military forces necessary to intervene in any dispute threatening oil supplies.

All the pre-planning, pre-positioning and reinforcement capabilities could be employed to prepare for military action, and this was proceeding in parallel with an apparent concentration on non-military solutions. Furthermore, the United States was able, by a combination of fortunate political circumstances and forceful diplomatic activity, to persuade the UN Security Council finally to support military action. The first major crisis after the Cold War would be settled by early recourse to war.

9

The Gulf Conflict and its Implications

By mid-January 1991, armed forces numbering more than one million were deployed in Kuwait, south-east Iraq and Saudi Arabia, and the war which followed was probably the most intensive since the closing stages of the Second World War.

The Balance of Forces

Total US forces numbered 395,000, comprising 315,000 army and marines, 45,000 air force and 35,000 navy. Equipment included over 2,000 tanks, 2,600 armoured vehicles and 1,700 helicopters. Naval forces comprised more than 70 warships with 400 combat aircraft including six aircraft-carriers and two battleships. Air forces in Saudi Arabia, the Gulf states and Turkey numbered 1,000, comprising 800 combat and 200 support aircraft. The former included F-4s, F-15s, F-16s, F-111s, F-117s, A-10s and B-52s. The Fifth Special Forces Group was operating in the area.

These US forces were larger than had been intended under CENTCOM planning, especially in terms of aircraft and warships, but also with additional heavy armoured divisions brought from Europe. This primarily reflected a determination to make any war a very swift affair, with minimal US casualties.

Apart from the 45,000 British ground troops and air and naval personnel, the other major contingents by mid-January comprised the following ground troops: 10,000 French, 6,000 Bangladeshi, 35,000 Egyptian, 20,000 Kuwaiti, 38,000 Saudi and 16,000 Syrian, (with 50,000 troops on the Syria/Iraq border).

Coalition air force deployments included 66 combat aircraft from Britain, 29 French, 18 Canadian, 8 Italian, 52 NATO (in Turkey) and 370 from Saudi Arabia and other Gulf states. Naval forces included four destroyers and frigates from Britain and four from France, together with numerous support ships from these countries and small naval deployments from 15 other countries. In all, it was estimated that Coalition forces numbered about 600,000 personnel rising to 700,000 by the end of January. They had over 2,500 tanks, 1,500 fixed-wing combat aircraft, well over 2,000 helicopters and about 100 warships.

Iraq had 55 army divisions with 550,000 regular troops and 480,000 mobilised reserves. Equipment included 5,000 tanks, 4,000 armoured vehicles and 3,000 artillery pieces.

In the Kuwait Theatre of Operations (KTO), comprising Kuwait and southern Iraq, there were 520,000 ground troops with 4,000 tanks, 2,500 armoured vehicles and 2,700 artillery pieces. Of these, 200,000 were forward-based, 210,000 were a mobile reserve, including four Republican Guard divisions comprising about 50,000 troops, and the remainder were in static positions within Iraq or were support troops. The four key Republican Guard divisions were deployed in Iraq, close to the Kuwaiti border. The troops in the defensive positions closest to Coalition forces in southern Kuwait were mainly peasant conscripts.

Away from Kuwait and southern Iraq, 250,000 to 300,000 troops were deployed close to the Syrian and Turkish borders, but these were relatively poorly equipped. Some 200,000 troops were based in central Iraq or on the Iranian border. This group included well-equipped troops, including as many as four Republican Guard divisions, in or close to Baghdad.

The Air Force was organised into two bomber squadrons, 17 fighter/ground attack squadrons and 16 interceptor squadrons, almost all of Soviet or French origin. While total aircraft numbered around 700, modern front-line aircraft were barely 300. Iraq had a comprehensive network of large air-bases equipped with hardened aircraft shelters, many with multiple runways, and also had around 50 dispersal fields. It had a chemical weapons capability estimated at some thousands of tons of agent, principally mustard gas but with smaller quantities of sarin and tabun nerve agent. Delivery systems included artillery, free-fall bombs and, possibly, ballistic missiles.

Missile forces included several hundred Scud-B and modified

Scud (Al-Hussayn and Al-Abbas) missiles, most launched from fixed sites but with up to 70 mobile launchers. The navy was a coastal patrol force of little consequence, apart from some anti-ship missiles and a mine-laying capability.

Comparisons of Quality

In terms of technical quality, the great majority of Coalition forces were superior to all but a small proportion of the Iraqi forces, only about 150 front-line aircraft and 500 tanks being on a par with Coalition equipment. One exception was the Iraqi artillery which was considered effective and generally well organised.

Coalition forces had comprehensive remote sensing reconnaissance capabilities comprising imaging and electronic surveillance satellites, high-flying TR-2 and the new TR-3A Manta spy-planes, airborne early-warning aircraft and ground- and ship-based electronic surveillance facilities. These provided real-time and near-real-time capabilities and by early January were overstretching analysis capabilities in the Gulf and in the United States.

By comparison, Iraq had limited reconnaissance and surveillance capabilities but was thought able to use human intelligence throughout the Gulf, though rarely in real time.

Strategic and Tactical Options

Iraq was expected to fight a largely defensive war, hoping to exact high casualties of Coalition forces, especially US ground forces, and stretch the war on into the Spring and Summer, when Coalition chemical warfare protection systems would become impracticable because of heat stress. Tactical withdrawal was thought possible with the aim of enticing Coalition forces firstly into costly urban warfare in Kuwait City and then into southern Iraq itself.

Coalition tactics were expected to involve a short but extremely intense air assault on Iraq aimed at destroying the air force, the command and control system, logistic support for ground troops in Kuwait and then the equipment of those troops, followed by a brief ground and amphibious assault into Kuwait. Analysts commonly predicted a 7–10 day air war followed by up to three weeks of ground combat.

The Air War

Operation Desert Storm began just before 3.00 am local time on 17 January 1991, with extensive Coalition air attacks on targets throughout Iraq and Kuwait, together with the launching of more than 50 Tomahawk cruise missiles from ships at sea. In the first 14 days of the conflict, Coalition sources said that 30,000 sorties were flown, about half of which were attack sorties against targets in Iraq and Kuwait and the remainder were combat air patrols, reconnaissance and tanker flights and other logistic support flights.

During this initial period, the main targets were Iraqi air defences, especially surface-to-air missile sites, air bases, the military command, control and communications system and munitions facilities, including chemical and nuclear weapons research and development plants. In addition, there was a policy of targeting civil facilities associated with Iraqi war capabilities, including electricity power plants, telephone exchanges and radio and TV transmitters.

Within 24 hours of the start of the conflict, reports from Washington suggested that the Iraqi military capabilities were being devastated and that the air assault might be sufficient to bring about a withdrawal from Kuwait. By the third day, though, it was clear that, while damage had been great, many of the Iraqi facilities were heavily protected and were not being destroyed. This included much of the command bunker system and the great majority of the air force, the latter having been dispersed to hardened shelters or to remote air strips.

At the same time, the Iraqi air force offered only the most sporadic resistance to the air assault, and Coalition air losses were far lighter than had been expected. In part this was due to the effective use of anti-radar air-to-surface missiles against Iraqi air defence radar, but also to the use of F-117 stealth strike aircraft against high-value heavily defended targets.

On 23 January, General Colin Powell claimed general air superiority over Iraq and reported that Iraqi air defence radar was 95 per cent destroyed and all but five of the 66 air bases were severely damaged, although only 41 planes were confirmed destroyed. Contrary to earlier predictions from analysts, he expected the air assault to continue for many days and to concentrate increasingly on Iraqi ground forces, the aim being to damage them severely before any ground assault, thus minimising Coalition casualties. Of the Iraqi army in Kuwait, he said, 'first we are going to cut it off, then we are going to kill it'.

As the air assault developed, the major problem facing Coalition aircraft was the use of concentrated anti-aircraft artillery fire rather than modern surface-to-air missiles. The British Royal Air Force, which specialised in low-level anti-runway attacks, suffered relatively high losses, losing six Tornado strike aircraft.

One of the rare Iraqi air counter-offensives occurred on 24 January when three Mirage F-1 strike aircraft, believed equipped with Exocet anti-ship missiles, attempted to launch an attack on Coalition shipping in the northern Gulf. The attack failed and two aircraft were intercepted by a Saudi F-15.

By the end of January, two weeks into the air war, there were reports of up to 100 Iraqi air force planes being flown to bases in neutral Iran, in an apparently pre-planned operation to safeguard them from attack. The Iranian government assured the Coalition that these planes would not be released until after the conflict.

On the second day of the war, Iraq launched seven Scud missiles against Israel and one against the Dhahran air base in Saudi Arabia. Two Scuds hit Tel Aviv and one hit Haifa, causing damage and some injuries. The missiles did not carry chemical warheads, and were of little military significance, but aroused great political concern in Israel.

Over the 14 days to 31 January, 57 Scuds were fired from Iraq, mostly at Tel Aviv, Haifa and Riyadh. Ten hit the cities, 17 landed in open country and 30 were intercepted, although debris from these frequently caused damage. Four people were killed in Israel and one in Saudi Arabia and there were 224 injuries. As the attacks continued, Patriot anti-aircraft missiles demonstrated an anti-Scud capability and, by late January, Patriot batteries had been flown to Israel to provide air defences. Coalition strike aircraft also made repeated efforts to find and destroy mobile Scud launchers and this, combined with occasional periods of poor weather, delayed the progress of the air assault towards the end of January.

On 29–30 January, Iraqi ground troops launched a number of offensives into Saudi Arabia, the largest involving nearly 2,000 troops who succeeded in capturing the coastal town of Khafji. This was retaken by 2 February after heavy fighting, involving the loss of 12 US marines, 15 Saudi troops and 30 Iraqi soldiers. Up to 500 Iraqi soldiers and 31 US troops were captured.

Although the Khafji attack failed, it was represented as a psychological victory for Iraq, and a probable attempt to incite an early ground war before the bombing campaign damaged Iraqi forces too much. General Schwarzkopf stated on 30 January that the air assault had cut off 90 per cent of supplies to Iraqi forces in Kuwait, and it was clear that the attack was moving into a second phase against Iraqi ground troops in southern Iraq and Kuwait.

At sea, there were a number of small naval actions, mostly involving Coalition planes and attack helicopters against Iraqi patrol craft. By early February, almost all available Iraqi naval units had been damaged or destroyed.

Throughout the early weeks of the war, reports from Coalition sources to the Western media concentrated on depicting the air war as being a precise war against military targets, involving precision-guided missiles and bombs and very low levels of collateral damage and civilian casualties. By mid-February, there were indications of considerable civilian casualties, particularly in the cities of Basra and Nasiriyah in southern Iraq and, on 13 February, an air raid shelter in Amarya, a western suburb of Baghdad, was destroyed, killing 300 people including at least 90 children. The Pentagon insisted that the shelter had a military function as a bunker, but the Iraqis denied this and the incident got extensive coverage in the international media.

During the latter part of the five-week air assault, targeting shifted to supply routes within Iraq, especially those linking Kuwait, and to Iraqi army units and facilities in Kuwait and southern Iraq. Protracted day and night bombing caused heavy damage and high casualties among the military. Even by 8 February, three weeks into the war, Coalition sources claimed 750 tanks, 600 armoured vehicles and 650 artillery pieces destroyed, but General Powell and Secretary of Defence Cheney told President Bush on 11 February that the air assault should continue.

At no time during the war did the Coalition authorities release estimates of Iraqi casualties, only equipment destroyed. This contrasts with the Vietnam War where the 'body count' was an important aspect of propaganda. In the Gulf War, the official line appears to have been to maintain the idea of a clean war – there appears to have been a fear that indications of high casualties within Iraq and Kuwait could have led to a loss of support for the war.

During February, Iraq continued to fire Scud missiles, but at a much lower rate than in the first two weeks of the war. Most were intercepted but one penetrated air defences on 26 February and hit a US Army reserve barracks near Dhahran, killing 28 people and injuring some 100 more.

Coalition warships continued to fire Tomahawk cruise missiles in the latter stages of the air war, and the 16-inch guns of the battleship *Missouri* were used in shore bombardment. Two US warships, the assault ship *Tripoli* and the cruiser *Princeton* were damaged by mines in the northern Gulf on 18 February.

By 23 February, Coalition air forces had conducted 94,000 sorties and the authorities estimated that 39 percent of Iraqi tanks, 32 percent of armoured vehicles and 48 percent of artillery in the Kuwait theatre of operations had been destroyed. Once again, no estimates were given for human casualties. A ground offensive into Kuwait seemed imminent.

Diplomatic Initiatives

During the early part of February, attempts were made to mediate between Iraq and the Coalition, so avoiding a costly ground war. On 4 February, Iranian President Rafsanjani sent a peace proposal to Baghdad after a visit to Tehran by the Iraqi Deputy Prime Minister, Sa'adoun Hammadi. This came to nothing but President Gorbachev announced a new initiative on 9 February, sending a personal envoy, Yevgeny Primakov, to Baghdad. After this visit on 12 February, the Iraqi government announced, on 15 February, an offer to withdraw, but on condition that Coalition forces withdrew from the region within one month and Israel withdrew from the West Bank and Gaza; this was entirely unacceptable to Washington, even though it did raise the issue of an Iraqi willingness to withdraw.

Iraqi Foreign Minister Tariq Aziz went to Moscow on 21 February and Iraq then accepted a Soviet peace plan which incorporated most, but not all, UN requirements. Washington responded on 22 February, demanding immediate Iraqi withdrawal commencing by noon New York time (8.00 pm Gulf time) on 23 February, justifying this response principally by pointing to Iraq's 'scorched earth' policy with 150 of Kuwait's 950 oil wells already on fire. President Gorbachev made repeated efforts on 23 February to obtain more time for negotiations, but the deadline passed and the Coalition forces commenced a ground offensive within eight hours.

The Ground War and Ceasefire

Contrary to expectations, the ground assault did not include major amphibious landings. US marines and Arab Coalition forces breached the Iraqi defensive positions in a land attack across the Kuwait/Saudi border; as a result of the bombing campaign, they met little resistance in moving forward towards Kuwait City.

The US 18th Corps, together with French units, moved deep into Iraq from a point well to the west of Kuwait, establishing a forward air base 'Cobra Base' towards the Euphrates river and then proceeding to cut the main road linking Baghdad and Kuwait near Nasiriyah on the Euphrates.

Meanwhile, the main Coalition ground attack, comprising the US 7th Corps along with the UK 1st Armoured Division, crossed the Iraqi border immediately west of Kuwait and moved rapidly north to surround Iraqi forces in Kuwait and attack the Republican Guard divisions north-west of Kuwait. The Iraqi military leadership had committed considerable forces to oppose the expected amphibious assault and was also expecting the other main Coalition attack to come directly into Kuwait. It appeared unprepared for the speed of the Coalition armoured movements west of Kuwait and was unable to bring mobile reserves to counter-attack, not least because of total Coalition air superiority.

Within 48 hours of the start of the assault, the Coalition claimed to have destroyed 270 tanks and taken 20,000 prisoners. Saddam Hussein broadcast an order for an immediate and total withdrawal from Kuwait on 26 February and this proceeded in a chaotic and disorganised way, with large convoys of army vehicles and commandeered civilian vehicles clogging the two highways into Iraq. These were caught in intensive Coalition air attacks, resulting in massive Iraqi casualties. Before they left the Kuwait oil fields, Iraqi army personnel destroyed and fired most of the 950 producing wells, although some 30 had previously been ignited by Coalition air attack.

By 27 February, Iraqi resistance was collapsing, with 2,000 tanks reported destroyed and 30,000 prisoners taken by Coalition forces, although Republican Guard units were still in combat in south-east Iraq, albeit taking very heavy casualties. Later in the day, President Bush announced a temporary ceasefire to start at midnight New York time (8.00 am Gulf time) on 28 February. That same evening, Iraq informed the UN that it accepted all 12

UN resolutions, and later agreed to allow its military commanders to meet Coalition counterparts within 48 hours.

Over the next three days, there were occasional clashes as opposing units disengaged, but a formal ceasefire was agreed between military commanders on 3 March. Coalition forces were in control of much of southern Iraq south of the Euphrates and east of Nasiriyah.

Aftermath

The ending of the war was represented as a massive military victory for the Coalition forces and it was widely assumed that the Saddam Hussein regime would not long survive the war. Within weeks of the end of the war, rebellions broke out against the Baghdad regime in Kurdish areas in the north and Shi'ite areas in the south. President Bush and others encouraged these rebellions but, to the surprise of many analysts, the Baghdad regime was able to regroup its military forces and repress both rebellions with great severity.

This repression led to the movement of millions of refugees away from the areas of fighting. In the north, over one million Kurds fled to the mountains, many of them crossing into Turkey and Iran. Their plight was widely publicised in the Western media and, as a result, a large force of Coalition troops moved into northern Iraq, creating a protective zone and then encouraging the refugees to return to their homes. By the end of June, the Coalition troops were withdrawn, leaving a reinforced 'rapid reaction' brigade in Turkey.

The plight of refugees in southern Iraq was not met with a similar response. Coalition forces quickly withdrew and the Saudi and Kuwaiti authorities tried to discourage the movement of refugees across their borders. Large numbers succeeded in entering Iran where the government struggled to provide relief, with little help from the West.

Within the newly-liberated Kuwait, there was widespread disorder for several months, with kidnappings, torture and murder of those thought to have collaborated with the Iraqi occupiers. The large Palestinian community in Kuwait came under particular threat and many thousands fled the country.

A month after the end of the war, some 600 Kuwaiti oil wells were on fire, including many large high-pressure well-heads. While the copious quantities of smoke, sulphur dioxide and other pollutants were not being driven into global atmospheric circulation on a large scale, there were fears of serious regional environmental and health effects from the pollution.

By August 1991, the Saddam Hussein regime appeared secure and in general control of Iraq, despite the massive destruction which had been visited on the country. In part, this was because a brutal regime can still control a country even if it is severely damaged. But it was also because Iraq still had its own energy sources even if sanctions were still largely working, and because the regime had always kept back some of its best forces from the fighting. The destruction of the Republican Guard, in particular, had not been anything like as complete as the Coalition authorities had sought to suggest at the end of the war.

Casualties of War

Immediately after the end of the war, and in marked contrast to the previous reports, Coalition sources at last began to indicate the extraordinarily high level of Iraqi casualties. Saudi military sources estimated the number of Iraqi military casualties at 65,000 to 100,000 killed. Later estimates varied between 100,000 and 200,000, although one Pentagon estimate suggested that desertions were responsible for a proportion of missing Iraqi troops. Even allowing for desertions, most analysts believed Iraqi military losses to exceed 100,000, although some believed they were substantially lower. Finally, and not until four months after the end of the war, a source in the US Defense Intelligence Agency revealed that the estimates were of the order of 100,000 killed and 300,000 injured.

Civilian casualties during the war were reported to be around 7,000 killed by early February, with no reliable estimates as to final numbers. Refugee reports from Basra and other parts of southern Iraq suggested substantial casualties later in the war, and figures in excess of 10,000 civilian dead have been suggested. The destruction of Iraq's health infrastructure was thought likely to lead to a huge increase in infant and child mortality during and after the war, with many tens of thousands of children being at risk. It is also believed that at least 10,000 Kurdish refugees died in the mountains, most of them children.

Total Coalition military casualties were believed to be around 250, of which 100 were killed in accidents. Civilian casualties in

Kuwait were estimated by resistance forces to number thousands, but indications after the war were that these were over-estimates, although at least several hundred Kuwaitis died through the period of Iraqi occupation, in addition to those killed during the original invasion.

Coalition matériel losses included 36 aircraft in combat. Losses of tanks, artillery and armoured vehicles were thought to number under 100. Iraqi matériel losses were estimated to number 3,500 tanks, 2,140 artillery pieces and 2,000 armoured vehicles, with 141 aircraft destroyed in the air or on the ground and up to 200 more in damaged shelters. About 200 aircraft survived the war in Iraq, together with 147 which had been moved to Iran, of which 121 were combat planes.

A picture therefore emerges of huge Iraqi matériel losses, as indicated from Coalition sources during the war, but also of massive human suffering and deaths. This contrasts strongly with the constantly reinforced image of a war fought against objects rather than people, but an examination of the munitions and tactics used offers an explanation for this anomaly, demolishes the myth of the clean war, and also gives a clue as to the likely future conduct of conventional war in the Middle East and elsewhere.

The Myth of the Clean War

Operation Desert Storm lasted six weeks, with almost the whole of that period comprising an air assault against targets in Iraq and Kuwait. When the ground war started, on 24 February, the Iraqi forces soon attempted to retreat, but many were destroyed in the process, especially on two roads leading north out of Kuwait City towards Iraq.

During the war itself, the Coalition forces gave few indications of Iraqi casualties. While detailed figures were given for the progressive destruction of tanks, artillery and other equipment, little was said about the loss of life. Indeed, one central feature of the reporting of the entire conflict was the effort made by the Coalition military to give an impression of a war being fought almost entirely against military targets, with the emphasis on equipment rather than people. Strenuous efforts were made to present a picture to the media of the use of high-technology precision-guided munitions which could hit individual missile sites, runways or other military targets but which caused little or no collateral damage. This reached its height with General Schwarzkopf's famous press conference when he showed a video of an attack on a bridge carried out just after a vehicle had crossed it, describing the driver as the luckiest person in Iraq.

Throughout the air war, extensive video footage was made available to the media by the military, showing the use of precision-guided weapons. Invariably these showed the blowing up of targets which appeared deserted; people were never to be seen. By the end of the air war, viewers in the United States and Britain had become convinced that precision-guided warfare was a new 'clean' and more civilised form of warfare. In reality, the footage released to the media was carefully selected to promote this view, presumably to ensure continuing public support for the war. If it had become known that Iraqis were being killed by the thousand each day, such support might well have waned.

On only two occasions during the air war were there well-publicised indications of the high level of casualties. One was the bombing of the Amarya bunker in Baghdad on 13 February when over 100 civilians were killed and the other was a report of a British raid on a bridge at the city of Fallujah, where a bomb missed its target and hit a market area. In the former case, the Pentagon made strenuous efforts to insist that the bunker had a military function, and in the latter case there was little publicity given in the United States.

Throughout the war, though, the emphasis was on the low level of casualties and only after it had ended were there indications that many tens of thousands of people had been killed and injured. While this had some impact in Europe, it was submerged in the euphoria and triumphalism that gripped the United States for several weeks.

What has now become clear is that, alongside the 'precision war' of the laser-guided bombs and pin-point missiles, there was a second type of war being fought, using munitions specifically designed to kill and injure people on the widest scale possible. There has been almost as great a revolution in these so-called 'area-impact munitions', the successors to napalm, as in precision-guided weapons. Their use was largely covered up during the war, but some details are now becoming clear, and it is also apparent that their further development and proliferation has huge implications for the future conduct of war.[1]

Use of Ordnance

While some of the casualties may have been caused by precision-guided ordnance, this made up a very small proportion of the total ordnance used. According to Air Force Chief of Staff General Merril McPeak, just 6,520 out of 88,500 tons of bombs dropped by US planes on Iraq and occupied Kuwait were precision-guided weapons, barely seven per cent of the total. Of these, 90 per cent hit their intended targets whereas only 25 per cent of the conventional bombs did so. Figures for the British forces show a rather higher proportion of precision-guided munitions. Some 3,000 tons of ordnance were dropped including 6,000 bombs of which 1,000 were laser-guided.

While most of the munitions used by Coalition troops comprised free-fall bombs, area-impact munitions were used on a far larger scale than in any previous conflict and were highly effective in an anti-personnel mode. Like napalm and the early cluster weapons, modern area-impact munitions are designed to spread their destructive force over a wide area rather than concentrate their energy on a precise target. This is normally achieved in one of two ways. It either involves producing a cloud or mist of explosive potential which is then detonated, such as a fuel–air explosive (FAE), or else it comprises large numbers of sub-munitions or 'bomblets' which are dispersed from a container prior to being detonated, as with a cluster bomb.

Although napalm and fuel–air explosives were used in the conflict, the main area-impact munitions were cluster bombs and multiple-launch rocket systems equipped with sub-munitions. A new form of the Tomahawk sea-launched cruise missile was also used, which was fitted with sub-munitions rather than a single high-explosive charge.

The dropping of napalm was reported right at the end of the war, as was the use of fuel–air explosives. FAEs were reported to have been used for detonating mines, although unofficial sources indicated that the production of aerosol clouds which could penetrate into trenches made them especially useful in killing infantry. Reports of use against troops included one by the US Marine Corps against an Iraqi army position.

As well as FAEs, US forces also dropped the massive 15,000lb BLU-82/B slurry bomb, known as 'Big Blue' or the 'Daisycutter'. This contains the specialised explosive DBA-22M, comprising ammonium nitrate, powdered aluminium and a polystyrene soap binding agent in an aqueous solution and can produce blast over-pressures of up to 1,000 psi, exceeded in force only by nuclear weapons.

Cluster Bombs and Missiles

Cluster bombs and missiles were much more widely used in the conflict than FAEs, the two main weapons being the US Rockeye and the British BL755. The standard US bomb is the Rockeye II Mk 20 which is a free-fall weapon weighing 222kg and dispensing 247 bomblets over an area of rather more than an acre and reported to produce a devastating hail of nearly 500,000 high-velocity shrapnel fragments.

The British BL755 cluster bomb, produced by British Aerospace, was used extensively in the Falklands War in 1982 as well as the Gulf War. This 277kg weapon dispenses 147 bomblets over slightly less than an acre, producing 300,000 anti-personnel fragments.

Cluster bombs are regarded as much more effective anti-personnel weapons than napalm even though they do not have the same negative overtones in the public mind. They produce effects which are on a larger scale yet are far more controlled than napalm which is now widely considered to be obsolete in most circumstances.

Full details of the US use of cluster bombs in the Gulf are not yet available, although the extent of their use is now becoming clear. F-16As were reported to carry four Rockeye cluster bombs per sortie. Those based at the A1 Kharg Air Base in Saudi Arabia as part of the 4th Tactical Fighter Wing (Provisional) were also reported to carry the CBU-52 cluster bomb unit and the more recent CBU-87 combined-effects cluster bomb, in which the sub-munitions have a combined effect against armour and people.

Cluster bombs were also used extensively by the most modern long-range strike aircraft in the USAF inventory, the F-15E Strike Eagle. A typical patrol pattern against Scud missile launchers and their support vehicles involved two F-15Es, one equipped with four GBU-10 laser-guided bombs and the second carrying either six CBU-87 cluster bombs or 12 Mk. 82 conventional high-explosive bombs. If vehicles were spotted, the first plane would attempt to hit them with the laser-guided bombs. If this failed, the second plane would saturate the target with cluster bombs or HE bombs. On other raids, F-15Es used three other types of cluster bomb, including the Rockeye Mk 20.

After the war, the Commander of the Marine Air Wing 3, Major General Royal N. Moore Jr., singled out 2,000lb conventional high-explosive bombs and Rockeye cluster bombs as being the ordnance which was of most value to the Wing during the war, rather than precision-guided munitions. 'I'm afraid [analysts] will concentrate on the smart weapons, but without question it was sustainability that won this one', he said, defining sustainability as the continuous accurate delivery by disciplined pilots of massive amounts of conventional, unguided 'green bombs'.

The experience of the US Navy would support this Marine Corps view. During the Gulf War, carrier-based planes dropped 21,254 bombs; of these, just 1,203 were laser-guided and 20,051 were unguided free-fall bombs, including 4,473 Rockeye cluster bombs. The British RAF also used cluster bombs, Jaguar strike aircraft dropping the BL755 cluster bomb repeatedly. Targets included anti-aircraft artillery, communications facilities, Republican Guard units and even patrol craft.

The cluster-munition version of the Tomahawk sea-launched cruise missile (TLAM-D) was used, carrying a total of 166 Aerojet BLU-97/B fragmentation sub-munitions which could be dispensed in three packages on different targets; 297 Tomahawks were fired during the war although most are believed to have been the non-cluster variant.

The Multiple-launch Rocket System

The area-impact weapon with the most devastating effect is the Multiple-Launch Rocket System (MLRS). It was deployed by the US and British armies and consists of a self-propelled launcher-loader, a tracked vehicle which carries two pods of six missiles. The entire load of 12 missiles can be ripple-fired in less than 60 seconds with the fire control system allowing re-targeting between launches at approximately five second intervals. The 227mm-calibre solid-fuel rocket has a length of nearly 13 feet and a maximum range of about 20 miles.

The most common warhead used in the Gulf War comprised the M77 sub-munition, a grenade-sized bomblet with an anti-personnel and anti-armour capability. One salvo of 12 missiles from a launcher can deliver nearly 8,000 of these fragmentation sub-munitions dispersed over an area of up to 60 acres. This system is the most devastating single conventional weapon in existence and was used in large numbers during the war.

A very recent variant is the Army Tactical Missile System (ATACMS), also fired from an MLRS launcher, but at a rate of just two much larger missiles per launcher. The two can deliver nearly 2,000 sub-munitions to a range of up to 80 miles.

During the war, the US army fired more than 10,000 MLRS rockets, almost entirely in the Kuwait area. The British fired a further 2,500 rockets. The ATACMS system had not been deployed prior to the crisis, but some were rushed to the Gulf and 30 were fired.

Unexploded Ordnance

A major problem which arose after the end of the war was the widespread distribution of unexploded cluster sub-munitions. Over eight million sub-munitions were delivered by bomb and missile during the war, and an estimated 20–30 percent failed to detonate, partly because the impact fuses frequently failed when they hit soft sand and mud. Around two million bomblets therefore remained as threats to future activity, and severely hampered operations to extinguish the oil-well fires in Kuwait.

According to Major Nick Moody of the British Royal Engineers' 49 Explosive Ordnance Unit, based at the Camp Freedom Allied base south of Kuwait City:

> Minefields are not such a problem because you know where they are, but bomblets could be almost anywhere and you need to kill them to save lives. They are fused to go off with the slightest pressure so when we find them we do not move them, we blow them up *in situ*. We have had a lot of fatalities among servicemen as well as civilians. Sub-munitions are turning up every day all over the country and they will be turning up in 50 years' time.[2]

A Higher Form of Killing

The extensive use of area-impact munitions was one of the less reported but militarily significant aspects of the Gulf War and contributed substantially to the very high level of Iraqi casualties. Although the public impression was of a war fought with great precision, primarily against 'real estate' rather than people, this was a distortion. Throughout the war there was systematic targeting of Iraqi personnel, frequently with dedicated anti-personnel weapons.

One of the major military lessons learnt will concern the use and effectiveness of these weapons in the Gulf and is likely to lead to a much greater deployment of them in the future. Within a few months of the end of the war, Saudi Arabia was seeking to buy over 2,000 US-made cluster bombs, and, as we have seen, there is considerable potential for the proliferation of these weapons throughout the world.

Reflections on the War

In the United States, the end of the war was marked by a surge of euphoria bordering on triumphalism. While a minority had opposed the war, the prevailing view was that it had finally demonstrated US power and its capacity to create a new world order. While earlier US interventions during the Reagan era, such as Grenada, Libya and Panama, had proved popular, the Gulf War can be said to have laid the ghost of Vietnam.

Some of the gloss was taken off the victory by subsequent events, notably the survival of Saddam Hussein and the treatment of the Kurds, and in Europe there was little feeling of a great victory, even immediately after the war. In Britain, quite unlike the aftermath of the Falklands War, politics returned to 'business as usual' within days of the war's end, with domestic issues such as the poll tax and the state of the economy again dominating the media.

Even so, most analysts in the United States and Britain tended to see the war as an indication of a changing world order.[3] In spite of the failure to oust Saddam Hussein, the established view was that a major military action had successfully evicted Iraqi forces from Kuwait, even if the aftermath had been uncertain. The Iraqis had flagrantly breached international law by invading Kuwait, and a hastily put-together Coalition force had brilliantly restored sovereignty.[4]

Viewed in terms of the aim of the key UN Resolution (678 of 29 November, 1990) '. . . to restore international peace and security to the area', it is difficult to be so sanguine. The war appears to have cost some $80 billion for the Coalition forces and certainly some tens of billions of dollars for the Iraqis in terms of direct military costs. The destruction to Kuwait and Iraq is well nigh impossible to estimate but is believed to exceed $100 billion by a considerable margin. Jordan and Yemen suffered crippling economic costs, and many other countries in the Middle East were affected, as labour markets dried up and trade was interrupted.

In human terms, military casualties were in the region of 100,000 killed and 300,000 injured. At least 10,000 civilians died directly during the war, some 10,000 Kurds died in the refugee camps and in the mountains and the destruction of Iraqi medical facilities and food shortages are likely to cause the deaths of some tens of thousands of people, mostly children. Saddam Hussein survived the war, there was repression throughout Iraq and, in the region as a whole, a new round of arms imports began within weeks of the war ending, with the United States, China and North Korea being among the many countries clamouring for arms orders.

Thus, even in terms of conventional arguments, we would question the wisdom of seeking a military solution to this crisis and would suggest that, at the least, it was a demonstration of an all-too-ready willingness to abandon the slower non-military means of resolving the crisis in favour of a military option which brought even greater chaos, suffering and destruction to an already dangerous crisis. Moreover, as we have seen (Chapter 8), this willingness involved direct manipulation of the UN system in pursuit of early military action.

This, in our view, is one of three factors relating to the Gulf War which most warrant attention. The second, as discussed in Chapter 7, is the crucial importance of the oil reserves of the Gulf area. It was because of these reserves that first the rapid deployment force and then US Central Command were first established. Because of these reserves, the United States established the military capability to intervene massively in the region and, once Saddam Hussein had metamorphosed from a trusted ally of the West and a buffer against Iran into a threat to those oil reserves, it determined to project military force to counter that threat.

Far from being an emergency response to a crisis, with military forces diverted from other tasks, Desert Shield and Desert Storm were the results of more than a decade of planning, investment and training. They were the products of the expansion of US force projection capabilities throughout the 1980s, a recognition of the fundamental strategic importance of Gulf oil and of the need for the US to maintain security over the region.

Carrier battle groups, battleships, amphibious warfare ships, maritime pre-positioning ships, a huge network of support facilities from the US through Europe to Diego Garcia and Guam – all were available to serve the purpose of defeating a threat to Gulf oil.

Finally, the war itself, far from being just a precision-guided war against military real estate, was a demonstration of the use of modern military firepower of a kind which is revolutionising conventional warfare and has formidable implications for the future conduct of war. Far from heralding a new world order, the Gulf War, by demonstrating the potential for resource wars fought with the most powerful conventional weapons now available, seems more likely to be an example of a new world disorder.

10

New Global Pressures

The core argument of this book is that we face the prospect of a new axis of conflict developing between the world's wealthy states and the majority of the world's population, possessors of most of the world's resources but not in control of them and facing persistent exploitation by the wealthy. By 'wealthy' we do not mean the wealthy of the developed industrialised countries alone but would include élites of then Third World.

Further, we would argue that there are a number of trends which, if analysed, give us some indication of the threat to international stability and also offer us some alternative paths to global peace and security. It is first appropriate to summarise some of the main lines of argument developed so far, and then to relate these to patterns of global development and North–South relations before applying them to possible future trends.

We will later attempt a preliminary sketch of how concepts of global security might best be developed to facilitate a more peaceful and just world, and how they might be applied over the next two decades.

The Legacy of the Cold War

In the context of the Cold War, this book has been concerned primarily with strategic military developments rather than concentrating primarily on economic and political relationships, though the former illuminate the latter and, to an extent, provide a model of the wider relationships.

A key strategic feature of the East–West axis of conflict has been the way in which it has provided a permanent and powerful motive for developments in military technology and strategic posture. More than this, the attempts to control the arms race through negotiations on arms control and disarmament have had, in comparison, remarkably little effect. The classic example of this would have to be the negotiations on the second Strategic Arms Limitation Treaty (SALT 2) from 1972 to 1979, when attempts to set ceilings on strategic nuclear arsenals had virtually no effect on the arms race beyond helping to channel it into new directions such as the development of cruise missiles. The Limited Test Ban Treaty (LTBT) resulted in most subsequent nuclear tests being carried out underground, but did not lead on to the much more significant Comprehensive Test Ban Treaty which was the ultimate aim. Nearly 30 years after the LTBT, a comprehensive test ban is still down at the bottom of the arms control agenda.

A few treaties concerned with nuclear-free zones such as the Sea-Bed Treaty and the Treaty of Tlatelolco covering Latin America were completed. They showed what was possible but did not apply to strategically significant regions. Even the much-vaunted Non-Proliferation Treaty of 1967 did little more than temper the pace of proliferation. One of its most important aspects, the demand that existing nuclear powers should engage in progressive multilateral nuclear disarmament, has simply been ignored.

With the easing of Cold War tensions in the late 1980s, there came a period of far more intensive negotiation, leading to the completion of three treaties – the Intermediate-range Nuclear Forces (INF) Treaty covering ground-launched missiles deployed by the United States and the Soviet Union principally in Europe; the first Strategic Arms Reduction Treaty (START 1) covering superpower strategic nuclear weapons; and the first Conventional Forces in Europe (CFE 1) Treaty covering NATO and Warsaw Pact conventional forces in Europe.

The INF Treaty did lead to the withdrawal of modern nuclear-armed missiles and to an intrusive verification regime – both welcome developments – but it has several major limitations. It does not cover air-launched and sea-launched missiles in any way at all, nor the ground-launched missiles deployed by countries such as France, China, Israel or several Arab states; and it does not involve the destruction of even one nuclear warhead. Delivery systems – that is the missiles – have been destroyed, but the warheads have been simply put into storage and can be recycled into new weapons.

The START 1 agreement has been reported as involving a cutback in strategic arsenals of 30–50 percent. In reality, and because of arcane counting rules, the actual cuts will be little more than 20 per cent, substantially less than the expansion in the arsenals during the nine years of negotiations! Furthermore, the weapons to be removed will be the oldest, most obsolete systems, and the Treaty will exert little control on the modernisation of the arsenals. Finally, like the INF treaty, START 1 does not involve the destruction of nuclear warheads, only the delivery vehicles. Recycling of nuclear material is not only allowed but is highly likely to happen.

The Treaty covering European conventional forces does, at first sight, represent a major step forward, as it involves substantial cuts in conventional forces across Europe and, like the other treaties, involves complex and intrusive verification procedures. Yet it also has substantial drawbacks. Like START 1, but at the conventional level, it makes no attempt whatsoever to control weapons modernisation, failing, for example, even to begin to address the development of new area-impact munitions. Secondly, it allows the major military powers to 'cascade' their slightly less modern weapons to allies or even to sell them to Third World countries. Finally, even with CFE 1, Europe remains the most heavily armed region of the world.

There is another specific criticism of Western political leadership: its blatant unwillingness to recognise Gorbachev as a reformer for nearly three years after he came to power early in 1985. Despite repeated indications such as the nuclear test moratorium and many other unilateral arms control gestures, the West, and especially the Reagan and Thatcher administrations, persistently maintained their most vigorous Cold War stance. Even when they finally declared themselves willing 'to do business' with Gorbachev, they were all too happy to preach at him instead, expecting him to make all the concessions. Not only did this delay the whole process of arms control but it also made Gorbachev's own position more difficult at home, especially after 1990 when the domestic economic problems increased.

If the conservative Western governments of the day had been genuinely committed to arms control and disarmament, the INF Treaty could have been followed within a year by a treaty covering short-range nuclear forces, START 1 could have been completed by 1988 and a much more radical START 2 within, at most, two more years. By the mid-1990s we could have achieved, at the very least, a 50 percent cut in strategic nuclear arsenals and similar cuts in short-range nuclear forces and conventional forces. This would have produced an international climate of opinion that would have been hugely more favourable to control of nuclear proliferation.

These may all sound like carping criticisms against a background of improved East–West relations, assured if sometimes modest cuts in defence budgets, verification procedures which should certainly build confidence, and the conclusion of three major treaties in five years. Yet beyond the severe limitations to the three major arms control treaties which were agreed are two highly uncomfortable problems. The first is that there is, at least for the present, little commitment to seek further progress. The INF Treaty was completed in 1987 and is now fully operational, with all the relevant missiles withdrawn and destroyed; yet there is little interest in the West in extending it to cover the many hundreds of short-range nuclear missiles in Europe and elsewhere. START 1 is complete but will take at least seven years to implement and there is no commitment to negotiate an immediate follow-up, a START 2, which would make really deep cuts, at least 50–75 percent, in arsenals and would also address the issue of modernisation. Persistent attempts to develop anti-ballistic missile defences in the US, as part of the SDI programme, are now threatening the ABM Treaty. There is no early prospect of a CFE 2 which would make for further deep cuts in Europe and would also control conventional modernisation. Haphazard unilateral cuts are easily reversed and are no substitute for mutual cuts codified in treaties.

The second problem concerns the effect of the recently concluded treaties on political and public opinion. Here we are in the same situation as in the early 1960s when the Test Ban Treaty was completed, and the mid-1970s when SALT negotiations were in progress. Put simply, we experience a false sense of security, happy with the progress so far, yet failing to concern ourselves with the much larger issues now being avoided.

Painfully slow progress in arms control, accompanied by a public belief that progress is actually much more rapid than it is, does not mean that East–West relations will remain on a knife-edge, but it does provide a context for the really dangerous legacy of the Cold War, the phenomenon of military momentum. Ten years of renewed East–West tension during the 1980s, on top of 30 years of military developments, led to a decade of heavy spending on military research and development as well as the steady build-up of nuclear and conventional arms. The latter leaves us with very substantial arsenals which are only being modestly cut back by recent arms control treaties; and other programmes; the former leaves us with a technological momentum that will yield results, in the form of new weapons systems, well after the Cold War has become a distant memory.

Furthermore, United States military policy has consistently gone well beyond the containment of Soviet power, to include a capability to protect US security interests wherever they may be 'threatened'. Even since the 'rise to globalism' of the United States during and immediately after the Second World War, a secondary pursuit of US military policy has been protecting a wide range of interests across the world. These may be grouped under the phrase 'security interests', but involve support for political allies, protection of US commercial interests, maintenance of sea lines of communication and increasingly ensuring security of US resource imports, especially oil.

As we have seen (Chapters 6 and 7), the increasing US dependence on imported strategic resources became a major concern of the military during the 1980s, leading to a considerable investment in the rapid projection of military force and, ultimately, to the major US intervention in the Gulf during 1990 and the Gulf War in early 1991.

In the post-Cold War era which we are now entering, the Soviet federation or commonwealth of states remains a major military power but is hugely preoccupied with its internal economic, social and political problems and has little capability of engaging in protracted political or economic competition outside its borders. Nor is it likely to use military force other than for purposes of internal security. Even that will be limited – one of the several happy results of the failed attempt by conservative elements to oust President Gorbachev in August 1991. One other major effect of those extraordinary events is likely to be the speeding up of reforms within the Soviet republics, including concerted action to tackle the immense economic problems. Internal preoccupations will probably dominate Soviet politics for some years to come

The United States, though, has its military power unhindered except by relatively mild budgetary restraint. Having lost its most significant enemy, the forces available for a security posture other than oriented against the Soviet Union are actually substantially larger than five or ten years ago. It also has all the legacies of the Cold War technology investment such as stealth aircraft, cruise missiles, new generations of area-impact munitions, improved command, control and reconnaissance systems, anti-ballistic missile systems, directed energy weapons and, above all, a military establishment desperate to develop new postures. Given recent trends, keeping the violent peace will be pre-eminent among these.

On present trends, this will manifest itself particularly in terms of maintaining the security of overseas economic interests in general, and strategic resource supplies in particular. Yet this is set within the wider context of a broad alliance of Northern industrial states collectively dependent on the South's resources and of a South which remains deeply constrained in its own development prospects by Northern trade and development policies but is increasingly well armed, as new weapons systems proliferate across the world.

World Development Prospects and North–South Relations

While the best prospects for self-reliant development come from within the South, the conditioning impact of the trade and development policies of the industrialised North produce immense obstacles. Looking to the future we have to combine an assessment of the current state of world development with likely trends in the coming decades. To this has to be added an analysis of the impact of current and future environmental constraints. Combining all of this gives us a tentative indication of possible patterns of North–South competition and conflict and also provides some preliminary guidelines for changing our attitudes to global security.

The three main parameters affecting development prospects are population distribution and change, wealth distribution, and North–South economic relations, including trade and development policies and, of considerable current importance, Third World debt.[1]

Population Prospects

The demographic transition from rural to urban-industrial societies includes a period of very rapid population growth, followed by a phase of near stagnation with population densities up to ten times greater than before. Most Northern countries commenced this transformation during the 19th Century and have completed the transition to near-stability; and a number of Southern countries are well through the expansion phase. Curbing population growth is rarely if ever a result of large-scale population control measures but tends to follow educational and economic improvements within a population.

World population has been growing rapidly since the mid 20th Century, especially in the past two decades, although there are preliminary signs of a slowing down. From 4.0 billion people in 1975 the population increased to 5.4 billion in 1991 and is expected to increase to 6.3 billion in 2000, and 8.3 billion in 2020. Some demographers now believe that there will be a pronounced levelling off by the middle of the 21st Century, with some degree of stabilisation at 10–12 billion during its latter half.

Almost all the population increase between 1990 and 2100 will be in what are now the less-developed regions, so that the balance of population distribution will alter drastically. In 1990, Europe, the Soviet Union and North America accounted for 20.1 percent of global population. This will decline to 17.9 percent by the year 2000 and to 14.6 percent by 2020. If we include Japan and Oceania in with the regions already mentioned, we still find that all these developed regions will comprise just 17.5 percent of global population in 2020 compared with 24 percent in 1990. Put another way, at present, about one-quarter of the population of the planet utilises about three-quarters of the energy and mineral resources and controls a similar proportion of the wealth. That wealthy population will comprise barely one-sixth of global population within 30 years.

Even this disguises the fact that much of the so-called North is relatively under-developed, especially much of the Soviet Union and parts of Eastern Europe. Similarly, some specific parts of the North are both particularly wealthy and markedly profligate in resource use, the most notable being the United States, Canada and most of Western Europe.

In essence, then, the population expansion in the North has already happened, whereas in the poorer and much more heavily populated South it is still in progress. The potential demand for food, energy and raw materials in the South is therefore immense – and likely to grow. We must also recognise that the South is making considerable progress in literacy and more general education, even against a background of considerable obstacles to development.

In 1985, some heavily-populated countries such as Bangladesh and Pakistan still had basic literacy rates of under 35 percent, heavily skewed towards the male population, but many other major countries were making rapid improvements. India had achieved a rate of 43 percent, China of 69 percent, Indonesia of 74 percent and the Philippines of 86 percent. These trends are continuing as concerted efforts are made to expand primary education to cover the great majority of populations in the South and extend the provision of secondary and higher education. The so-called 'revolution of rising expectations' was a significant political force in the industrialised world. On a global basis it has formidable potential.

Wealth Distribution

The distribution of the planet's wealth remains grotesquely uneven – though there are problems with all the major indicators used to judge wealth. The most common indicator, Gross National Product (GNP) *per capita*, tends to exclude non-monetary aspects of an economy such as subsistence food production, and can thus, to an extent, be misleading in assessing a rural economy. Even so, the differences between the major sectors of the world economy are extreme.

The World Bank uses GNP *per capita* estimates to divide countries into three broad categories – low-, middle- and high-income economies, respectively those under $580, $580–$6,000 and above $6,000 (all at 1987 figures). The high-income countries are primarily the OECD member states of the North, including most Western European states, the United States, Canada and Japan, together with a few oil-rich Middle East states such as Saudi Arabia, Kuwait and the United Arab Emirates. It also includes a few Southern states such as the Bahamas, Singapore and Hong Kong. In 1987 the total of reporting countries in this group was 29, and it included the United States on $18,530, Japan on $15,760 and West Germany (as it then was) on $14,400.

The middle income group covered a very wide range of wealth, from countries such as Greece and Portugal with GNP *per capita* of $3,000 or more, through to many states below the $1,000 level, including Bolivia, Zimbabwe, the Philippines and Egypt. Within the lower range of this category were most Latin American states and a few of the wealthier African and Asian states.

The low-income group includes many states of below $300 GNP *per capita*, and also numbers most of the world's most populous states such as Bangladesh ($160), China ($290), India ($300), Pakistan ($350) and Indonesia ($400). Most of Africa south of the Sahara and most of Southern and South-East Asia are included in this group.

The use of the terms 'South' and 'Third World' can be misleading because of the extent of poverty in industrialised countries such as the United States, and of rich élites in many poor countries. While the internal distribution of wealth is frequently appalling, it is not a phenomenon restricted to poor states with small rich élites. *Table 5* below lists a representative sample of states, showing the proportion of each state's income accruing to the wealthiest and poorest fifths of the population.

Table 5

Country	Income of richest fifth (% of total)	Income of poorest fifth (% of total)
Argentina	50	4
Brazil	67	2
Egypt	48	6
France	37	6
India	50	7
Indonesia	50	7
Japan	58	9
Mexico	67	3
United States	59	5

The quality of the data may be variable but it does suggest that industrialised countries such as the United States and Japan have sectors of their populations proportionately at least as wealthy as those of Third World countries.

Trends in wealth and poverty are difficult to assess because of the variable quality of data collected over decades, but the broad picture is one of increasing disparity between rich and poor states. Most of the poorer states of the South are getting more wealthy, although this is not true of more than a score of states, but the increase in wealth of the richest 30 or so states of the North is very much greater. As a consequence, the gap between rich and poor states is increasing rapidly. To this must be added the earlier data showing that population growth is much faster in the poorer countries so that the balance between rich and poor is moving progressively towards a smaller rich population and a larger (relatively and absolutely) poor population. There are no signs of this trend changing in the foreseeable future.

Trade, Development and Debt

A major factor determining development potential in the South is the trading relationship with the North. This, in turn, has been largely determined by the evolution of the world economy in the colonial and post-colonial periods.[2] Colonisation was initially a European phenomenon and involved the progressive control of most of Latin America, Africa and southern Asia. The main motive in the colonisation process was the acquisition of raw materials, and the process involved two distinct phases.

The first lasted until the mid-19th Century and comprised the control and use of high value resources such as precious metals and gems, spices, fine cloth and beverages and the most valuable resource of all, human slavery. The second phase was conditioned by the rising demand for low value resources following the rapid economic expansion in Europe, a consequence of the industrial revolution. This was aided by the revolution in maritime technology of the late 19th Century as sail gave way to steam and cheap raw materials from overseas could be transported to Europe to replace the depleted resource base of the continent.

By the early 20th Century a firmly-established trading pattern was in place, with colonies and ex-colonies as providers of primary commodities – raw materials such as copper, tin, bauxite, coffee, sugar and, increasingly, oil – and users of manufactured goods from the industrialised states of Europe. As we have seen, the United States was not a major colonising power, and nor was Japan, but each developed controlling interests in the economies and trade of regional neighbours in Latin America and East Asia respectively. This economic power was maintained by force on many occasions, by the United States with its Marine Corps and by Japan with its military expansion in the 1920s and 1930s.

After the Second World War there were two significant developments. The first was the establishment of the United Nations with its cluster of specialised agencies. These included just two concerned with economic relationships, the International Bank for Reconstruction and Development (World Bank) and the International Monetary Fund. Both bodies were oriented almost entirely towards the requirements of the Western market economies.

Plans for a specialised agency on trade, the International Trading Organisation, failed to materialise, but a General Agreement on Tariffs and Trade group (GATT) was established to organise a reform of trade between market economy states which had become hopelessly entangled in protectionism during the pre-war world recession. Nowhere within the UN was there established any agency concerned with North–South trade. Most Southern countries were, in any case, still colonies or, as in Latin America, closely tied to, and dominated by, Western economies.

The second post-war development was over a longer time scale and lasted 20 years. This was the process of large-scale decolonisation which commenced with India, Pakistan and Indonesia in the late 1940s and continued across Asia and Africa until the early 1960s. The acquisition of political freedom did *not* mean that newly-independent Third World countries had any means of negotiating trade reform and most found themselves in a precarious post-independence position involving several elements.

The first of these was a general reliance on trade in a few primary commodities for most of their export earnings. Jute from Pakistan, copper from Zambia and Peru, coffee and cotton from Uganda, cocoa from Ghana, tin from Bolivia, sugar and bananas from Central America are all examples of a general phenomenon. Few ex-colonies had substantial domestic industries and therefore needed to import most manufactured goods from the North. Thus was established a firm pattern to world trade – primary commodities to the North and industrial products to the South. Almost all of the trade was with the Western market economies and there was relatively little South–South trade, a pattern which persisted through the entire period of decolonisation.

After a brief boom in commodity prices at the time of the Korean War, the following two decades were characterised by stagnant commodity prices as Third World countries competed for limited markets. Industrial goods, on the other hand, showed persistent price increases so that the terms of trade (ratio of import to export prices) of Third World countries deteriorated markedly after independence. A small number of oil-producing countries were partly insulated from this trend, but non-oil-producing Third World countries experienced a 32 percent increase in import prices from the mid-1950s to 1972, compared with just an 11 percent increase in export prices. According to the UN Conference on Trade and Development (UNCTAD), by 1972:

> the terms of trade of these countries had deteriorated by about 15 percent, compared with the mid-1950s, equivalent to a loss, in 1972, of about $10,000 million, or rather more than 20 percent of these countries' aggregate exports, and considerably exceeding the total of official development assistance from developed market economy countries to developing countries in Africa, Asia and Latin America (some $8,400 million in 1972). In other words there was, in effect, a net transfer of real resources, over this period, from developing to developed countries, the flow of aid being more than offset by the adverse terms of trade of the developing countries.

Thus the structure of world trade actually involved the poor ex-colonies subsidising the rich North. Inevitably, the Third World countries attempted a number of methods of overcoming this fundamental economic handicap, including developing small-scale home industries for import substitution and large-scale industrialisation for export or processing of their own raw materials to export as higher-value secondary commodities. In all three processes they faced massive obstacles.

Import substitution frequently involved setting up industries which were too small to be economically efficient, and they also required imported expertise and machinery. If foreign companies were encouraged to set up the factories, they would repatriate profits. Similarly, attempts at large-scale industrialisation for export faced all the problems of finding investment and expertise from a position of weakness. Even then, the potential markets in the Northern industrialised countries would be subject to protection of their own industries by trade barriers such as quotas and tariffs.

Finally, the tactic with the most potential, processing Third World raw materials for export – electric cables instead of raw copper, steel instead of iron ore, or 'instant' coffee instead of roasted beans – would meet specific fiscal barriers, notably Value Added Tax.

By the early 1960s, Third World countries formed a larger part of the membership of the United Nations and were able to ensure the establishment of a new agency to provide a negotiating forum with the North. The United Nations Conference on Trade and Development (UNCTAD) held its first meeting in Geneva in 1964, with its Secretary-General, Raul Prebisch of Argentina, already establishing a blueprint for world trade reform.

The so-called Prebisch Plan, *Towards a New Trade Policy For Development*, included measures to improve commodity export potential through multilateral commodity agreements, tariff preferences to aid Third World exports of processed goods and improvements in a number of other trade issues and in foreign aid. For eight years, UNCTAD tried to negotiate trade reform to aid the Third World, but with little success. Apart from a couple of weak commodity agreements and a limited tariff programme, the Lomé Convention, introduced by the European Community and covering a tiny fraction of Third World commodity exports, the Northern states were uninterested in world trade reform. Negotiating from a position of considerable economic power, they were persistently unwilling to see any meaningful reforms.

By the third of the four-yearly sessions of UNCTAD, in Santiago, Chile, in 1972, UNCTAD was said to stand for 'Under No Circumstances Take Any Decisions'. In fact, a number of Third World states were now convinced that only united action against the industrialised North would have any impact, and were watching closely the increasing power of the oil producers' organisation, OPEC. The London *Guardian* reported on the real anger felt by some Third World delegations, commenting:

> the anger has also served to produce rather more cohesion among the Third World countries themselves. The Francophone African states have in the past been accused of slavish adherence to European interests; this time they were willing to vote solidly with the Group of 77, just as the Ivory Coast has at last been prepared to join with Brazil to stockpile coffee and force up its price, rather than wait any longer for the broken-backed International Coffee Agreement to deliver results. Producers of oil and coffee, the two biggest Third World exports, are now exploiting their market power, and these tactics may spread. This is no cure-all – too many tropical products face synthetic competition, and some key minerals are found abundantly in the rich countries – but this kind of solidarity should certainly improve the bargaining power of the Third World.

The following year, two unrelated developments combined radically to alter world trading patterns. An unco-ordinated commodities boom developed, the first since the Korean War, as rapid economic growth in the industrialised North led to demand for commodities temporarily exceeding supply. The resulting price boom sent prices of food commodities up by 37 percent during 1973, fibre prices by 60 percent and metals by a massive 133 percent.

Then, in October 1973, there was the first of a series of huge increases in oil prices following the action of a group of Arab oil-producers during the Yom Kippur/Ramadan War (*see* Chapter 9). By early 1974, the trade ministries of the industrialised countries were close to panic and the United Nations called an emergency meeting of the General Assembly in April 1974, only the sixth such Special Session in the UN's 30-year history, on the subject of world trade reform.

After four weeks of intensive negotiation, a grandiose *Declaration on a New International Economic Order* was agreed which called for comprehensive reform of commodity trade designed to stabilise commodity prices in a manner which would, in the long term, be of considerable benefit to the South. The Integrated Programme on Commodities was to be developed and implemented by UNCTAD, and agreed at the UNCTAD meeting due in Nairobi in 1978 (UNCTAD 4). By that time, though, the effect of the oil price increases of 1973–74 had been to push the Northern countries into 'stagflation', prices of most primary commodities had fallen back substantially because of falling demand, and the industrialised North was no longer prepared to entertain comprehensive world trade reform in a manner which would have benefited the South.

A number of other OPEC-type Third World commodity organisations were established but, in the absence of economic leverage or buoyant prices, they were never able to emulate OPEC to anything like the same extent. Moreover, the massive and sustained oil price rises played havoc with Third World economies, just at a time when OPEC member states were investing in the financial markets of the industrialised states. As a result, Third World countries borrowed heavily to compensate for increased energy costs, setting in process the debt crisis of the following decade.

During the 1980s, the combination of this heavy borrowing with uncommonly high interest rates led to huge economic costs for many Third World countries. By 1983, debt and interest repayments were matching the flow of capital from North to South. By

1986, the repayments had increased so much that there was a net financial flow from South to North of $20.7 billion, and by 1989 this had risen to $52.0 billion. As with terms of trade in the 1960s and 1970s, the South was subsidising the North.

To make matters worse, the prices of primary commodities, still the key exports from the South, declined in real terms throughout the 1980s. Prices in 1987–88 were, on average, almost 30 percent down on the start of the decade. Over the 30-year period since most Third World countries had acquired independence, they had experienced massive development handicaps as a result of the structure of world trade and, indeed, North-South economic relations in general.

Throughout most of the 1980s, the four key trading states of the North, the United States, Britain, Germany and Japan, were all governed by political parties generally antagonistic to any form of economic planning. There was little or no interest in trade reform designed to aid the South and, to make matters worse, even the relatively low levels of development aid deteriorated further in terms of quantity and quality.

By the early 1990s, there were no signs whatsoever of a change of outlook by the North. Negotiations in UNCTAD were either moribund or peripheral to the major issues of North–South trade, and the major area of concentration was on the GATT negotiations. These were concerned with improving trading prospects within the North and would, if successful, even be disadvantageous to the South.

Against this background of a general antagonism by most Northern states to Third World development, there have been massive and pervasive problems of misgovernment, incompetence and corruption in many parts of the South. These have led, in many states, to the development of powerful and wealthy élites at the head of commerce and government, often resulting in extreme polarities of wealth and poverty. Such élites frequently relate closely to the economic interests of Northern states and multinational corporations, and follow economic and social policies which do little to aid development across the whole population of such countries.

These problems of inefficiency and corruption exacerbate an already difficult situation of North–South inequality. They are not, however, the only causes of underdevelopment, even if frequently regarded as such in the North. Rather they severely aggravate the deep-rooted economic problems these countries face and which the far more powerful states of the North are not willing to address.

But problems of inefficiency in the Third World, while exacerbating an already difficult situation, were of limited effect compared with the deep-rooted economic problems these countries faced, and which the North was uninterested in addressing. What is surprising is the success that has been achieved in development in many parts of the South, given the persistent handicaps, and much of this has been generated by internal means and against a background of Northern indifference. In any case, the success is strictly relative; as already discussed, the gap between rich and poor has widened substantially in the past two decades and the absolute numbers of people in poverty have increased substantially.

Meanwhile, the North continues to experience economic growth, its people, a small minority of the world population, continue to control the great majority of the world's wealth and to use most of the world's physical resources, becoming more and more dependent on resources from the South as they do so. Yet the population of the South is increasing rapidly and is inevitably developing aspirations to wealth. Add to this the growing realisation that the global system as a whole imposes severe environmental limits on human activity and we have a recipe for instability and in all probability, North–South conflict.

This is in no way a new prognosis. It was widely recognised in the early 1970s among environmentalists, but the implications were uniformly ignored by politicians. One of the clearest statements of the problem came from a British ecologist writing shortly after the UN Conference on the Human Environment, held in Stockholm in May 1972. This conference had been expected to be largely about the environment problems of the 'industrial backyard' of the Northern countries, but its participants included many Third World delegations and much of the conference was influenced by a preliminary study of the possible future behaviour of the global ecosystem undertaken at the Massachusetts Institute of Technology and published as *Limits to Growth*. While somewhat superficial, its essential message was that the human impact on the global ecosystem could not increase indefinitely without damaging that very ecosystem on which human society depended.

Writing in 1973, Professor Palmer Newbould put it thus:

My own belief is that however successful population policies are, the world population is likely to treble before it reaches stability. If the expectations of this increased population were, for example, to emulate the present life-style and resource use of the USA, the demand on world resources would be increased approximately 15-fold; pollution and other forms of environmental degradation might increase similarly and global ecological carrying capacity would then be seriously exceeded. There are therefore global constraints on development set by resources and environment and these will require a reduction in the *percaput* resource use of the developed nations to accompany the increased resource use of the developing nations, a levelling down as well as up. This conflict cannot be avoided. It became the central theme of the United Nations Conference on the Human Environment.[3]

The final factor affecting future global security, then, is the limitation placed on human activity by its effect on the global environment. Before identifying the major problems concerned with environmental limits to growth, it is useful to place this in context by summarising some of the main features of the global environment.

The Global Ecosystem

The study of living organisms in their environment may aim to determine the overall behaviour of those organisms and their inter-relationships with that environment. In this context, an ecosystem comprises a defined locality in all its complexity, including all living organisms, together with the physical and chemical processes in the atmosphere, lithosphere (earth) and hydrosphere within that locality, which affect and are affected by those organisms.

At its most general, it is possible to study the complete planetary system, or global ecosystem, sometimes termed the biosphere, comprising all living organisms which occupy the planet, together with the complex of physical and chemical processes which take place on, above and below its surface. Global ecosystem studies are necessarily interdisciplinary and holistic and are concerned with hugely complex and often poorly-understood physical, chemical and biological phenomena. As a consequence, predictions of changes in global ecosystem behaviour are frequently tentative, and contradictory opinions and explanations are quite common.

Even so, there is increasing evidence that the human community is now having a considerable impact on major regional environmental systems and even on the global ecosystem. The latter tendency has fundamental implications for international relations and may be the biggest single determinant of such relations in the coming century.

The global ecosystem, although imperfectly understood so far, has five attributes relevant to us here. Firstly, it has evolved over several thousand million years to an extremely complex system which, under normal circumstances, may well have a capacity for self-regulation, with negative feed-back loops able to assist in maintaining global homeostasis. Secondly, energy flows through the global ecosystem, the principal source being solar radiation responsible for over 99.9 percent of the planet's energy source, followed by tidal, geological and fuel energy.

Thirdly, materials tend to be recycled within the biosphere, with major cycling processes existing for water, oxygen, nitrogen, carbon, calcium and many other key materials. These biogeochemical cycles vary hugely in the rate of cycling, from months or years through to many thousands of years, and it is these cycles which, in some circumstances, may be self-regulating. For example, if, for some reason, carbon dioxide accumulates in the atmosphere, oceanic phytoplankton and terrestrial vegetation may, under normal circumstances, absorb a large proportion of the excess.

Fourthly, the impact of human activity on the global ecosystem is very recent. The system has taken over 2,000 million years to develop, while tool-making humans have been around perhaps three million years, and even ten thousand years ago the global human population was probably only five million. The neolithic revolution increased that at least ten-fold in a couple of thousand years, but the pace of human activity only accelerated rapidly after the industrial revolution some 200 years ago. The combination of industrialisation and rapid population growth has meant that almost all the major human impacts on the global environment have taken place during the 20th century, little more than a blink in the eye of history for the global ecosystem.

The final factor is the rapidly-accumulating evidence that human activity is having a measurable and accelerating impact on the global environment. This includes desertification and deforestation, physical resource depletion, regional atmospheric pollution, marine pollution and planetary atmospheric and climatic change, especially in terms of damage to the ozone layer and the enhancement of global warming.

Human Environmental Impacts

There is not space to detail all the major environmental impacts now being recognised; in any case, one of the welcome developments during the late 1980s was the number of texts and journals attempting to do just that. What can be done here is to outline some of the more significant trends.

We have already discussed the question of resource conflict (Chapter 6). The industrialised countries of the North are becoming increasingly reliant on the physical resources, especially fuel and non-fuel minerals, which are produced in Third World countries. This 'resources shift' towards the Third World is progressive, increasing the dependency of the North still more. While the Soviet Federation, in whatever form it may eventually take, is well endowed with most physical resources, Western Europe, Japan and increasingly the United States are highly dependent on the South.

While the total depletion of any physical resource may be prevented by price increases and substitution, scarcities are likely to ensue, and substitution can be expensive and not wholly effective, as well as requiring the kind of foresight which is normally lacking. Progressive scarcity will therefore be viewed as a security threat, even without attempts by Third World producers to exert 'producer power' as OPEC did in 1973–74. Resource shortages will become more dominant security concerns for the industrialised North.[4]

A developing problem in many regions throughout the world is potential conflict over water resources, especially where a number of states share a major river basin. Apart from pollution problems of rivers such as the Danube, major areas of potential conflict include the basins of the Nile, Tigris, Euphrates, Ganges and Brahmaputra. All serve areas of rapidly expanding population with similarly expanding water and energy requirements.

Soil erosion and desertification are now global phenomena which are difficult to redress.[5] About 24,000 million tons of topsoil are lost each year, mainly through erosion and salinization – equivalent to the loss of the croplands of India over the past two decades. The loss of cropland and grazing land, if occurring in existing areas of low rainfall, is likely to accelerate the expansion of deserts, and desertification is currently proceeding at a rate of well over 12 million acres per year, more than the area of the Netherlands.

Although there are vast areas of the Northern Hemisphere which are managed for commercial forestry, there has been massive deforestation since the neolithic revolution and, in recent years, this has applied especially to tropical rain-forests. The earth's forests as a whole had decreased by 30 percent by the mid-20th Century, but tropical deforestation has accelerated since then.

Tropical rain-forests comprise only seven percent of the earth's land area, but the combination of high temperatures, rainfall and humidity produce a biological diversity and a concentration of biomass which is unparalleled in any other ecosystem. In addition, tropical rain-forest ecosystems maintain most of their organic material within the living organisms, primarily vegetation, unlike most land-based ecosystems in which the majority is in the soil. As a result, deforestation, if accompanied by the usual soil erosion caused by high rainfall, leads to a severe loss of nutrients and ecosystem degradation which is extremely difficult to reverse. Tropical deforestation and burning of the vegetation both increases carbon dioxide concentrations in the atmosphere and also loses the potential 'sponge' effect of forests in soaking up excess atmospheric carbon dioxide.

Although there is some successful replanting of tropical forests, commercial and financial pressures are so strong that there is a current net loss of tropical forests of over 25 million acres per year, double the rate of desertification. Furthermore, as forested areas are replaced by ranchland or, more rarely, by plantations, so natural forests are lost and, with them, considerable species diversity. This can include species which produce many potential drugs, dyes and other products. Deforestation also reduces sources of wood for fuel, leading to further pressure on isolated stands of trees and shrubs and to further loss of biomass.

The processes of deforestation, desertification and salinization, together with an increasing dependence on cash crops as Third World countries compete in stagnant commodity markets, all combine to put much greater pressure on Third World environments and decrease the potential to develop. On top of this, problems of pollution, especially in the atmosphere, affect not only industrialised countries but the entire global community.

Following major air pollution episodes in the 1950s, it became common practice to build very high smoke stacks to disperse pollutants into the upper atmosphere. The longer term effect of this was to control local pollution but to enhance regional pollution. The most common problem is now acid rain, affecting many countries in the industrialised world, especially those down-wind of the prevailing winds from major areas of industry and urbanisation. Whereas, in the 1950s, the problem was believed to relate almost entirely to sulphur dioxide, it is now recognised as being very much more complex, especially as the range of chemicals produced for diverse industrial purposes has expanded hugely, and some have physical and biological effects which were not predicted when they were first introduced.

The most notable example of this is the damage to the ozone layer being caused by a range of chemicals, principally the chloro-fluorocarbons (CFCs). These are used as refrigerants, aerosol propellants and foam agents and have been produced and used almost exclusively in the industrialised North. Ozone in the upper atmosphere absorbs certain wavelengths of solar ultra-violet radiation which would otherwise damage living organisms on the earth's surface. Loss of ozone increases the amount of such radiation penetrating to the earth's surface. Effects in humans include eye damage and skin cancer, but there are also major effects on crops leading to substantial decreases in yield. The ozone layer has already decreased by some three percent over the Northern Hemisphere but seasonal losses, especially over the polar regions, have been much greater and appear to be accelerating.

At the global level, the other major current concern is atmospheric warming, leading to substantial climate change. Since the industrial revolution, there has been an immense increase in the use of fossil fuels. The carbon dioxide produced by fossil fuel combustion has increased from 300 million tons of carbon per annum in 1890 to 1,500 million tons in 1950 and 5,500 million tons in the late 1980s. Up to two-thirds of this has been reabsorbed by the oceans and terrestrial vegetation, at least until now, but the remainder accumulates in the atmosphere where it selectively absorbs solar radiation and contributes to a warming of the atmosphere.

The effects of carbon dioxide accumulation were known at least 20 years ago but largely ignored by politicians. It is now known that many other gases, individually present in the atmosphere at much lower concentrations than carbon dioxide, have an even greater climatic effect. Because of its relatively high concentration, carbon dioxide is responsible for about half of the greenhouse effect, but CFCs produce 20 percent, methane, an increasingly common by-product of agriculture, produces 16 percent, and nitrous oxide another six percent.

Unlike the damage to the ozone layer, the greenhouse effect is a longer term phenomenon. It is expected to lead to a temperature increase of up to five degrees Celsius within a century. Even within the next two decades this may substantially change world weather patterns, producing more violent storms, especially in coastal areas, and changes in rainfall patterns resulting in droughts and floods, the total effect being severely to decrease food production potential in many of the areas of the world that are currently heavily populated.

As with ozone destruction, the great majority of the greenhouse gases originate in the industrialised North. In 1987, the United States emitted 5.0 tons of fossil fuel carbon per person, the Soviet Union 3.7 tons and the UK 2.7 tons, compared with Egypt at 0.4 tons, India at 0.2 tons and Nigeria at 0.1 tons.

Three factors emerge from these trends. The first is that regional environmental effects such as desertification and acid rain are having a direct and substantial effect on human well-being, whether by directly damaging health or by decreasing food production potential. While these effects may be regional, they affect so many large regions as to represent a phenomenon with a global impact. The second factor is that there are, separately, major global environmental problems which have accelerated in their severity in recent years. The two most significant concerns are destruction of the ozone layer and global warming; but there may be others of which we are not yet aware.

Finally, the global problems are, predominantly, the result of the behaviour and economic activities of the industrialised North. This is directly the case with global warming and ozone depletion. If Third World countries had industrialised to a similar level, the global environmental impact would already have been catastrophic.

Responses to Environmental Impacts

The major problems affecting Third World environments, such as soil erosion, desertification, deforestation and regional water conflicts, are all largely beyond the capabilities of existing Third World states to counter, given the combination of economic handicaps they face. Solutions exist for most regional environmental problems but almost all depend on a degree of international economic reform which is not remotely likely, given the economic policies of the North.

Multinational institutions such as the World Bank and the IMF pay some regard to environmental problems, but these are minimal compared with the more general economic limits facing the Third World. Moreover, there is an opposite tendency for major multi-national commercial interests to entertain activities which would not be tolerated in the industrialised North but are acceptable to economically – disadvantaged states.

Physical resource depletion is addressed by the industrialised North increasingly in terms of safeguarding resource supplies in the face of local or regional security threats. This has become a highly significant feature of US policy, especially towards the Middle East, and was a root-cause of its intensive military response to the Iraqi invasion of Kuwait. The co-opeative utilisation of Third World resources in a manner which combines resource conservation with a much higher return on exports is simply not on the international agenda.

The manner in which current global environmental problems are tackled does not give much cause for confidence in future re-sponses. Conventions on Ocean Dumping, Ship Pollution and, indeed, the Law of the Sea regime itself have all taken long periods of time to negotiate and all lack a full international control regime. The conventions on protection of the ozone layer in Vienna in 1985, Montreal in 1987 and London in 1990 have set progressively tougher limits on ozone-damaging emissions, but even the most severe agreement in London allowed 10 years for the phasing-out of CFCs, when the rate of damage to the ozone layer would indicate the need for an immediate ban, together with a comprehensive and very well funded research programme into global atmospheric pollution.

Because the problem of global warming appears to be longer term, the action of most governments has been minimal. Proposals for carbon taxes and for extensive use of alternative energy sources have been the province of minority political parties in most Northern countries.

Most major environmental problems tend to have a long ges-tation period followed by a period of accelerating effect. Action to avert that effect may need to be taken before its full entirety is even apparent, let alone assured. In practice, political and economic systems operate in the short term, normally 5–10 years at the most, and are ill-equipped for responding to longer term problems. This is particularly true of political systems. Those dependent on forms of democracy normally have an electoral period of 3–5 years. Centrally-planned economies usually operate on a 4–5-year planning cycle. Neither system is adapted to problems likely to be measured in decades.

Potential for Conflict

The major argument of this book is that global security after the Cold War will be dominated by potential conflict on a North–South axis. This is conditioned primarily by approximately one-fifth of the population of the world, principally in the industrialised market economies of the North, controlling at least three-quarters of the wealth and resources of the entire global system.

Further to this, the majority part of the world's population, in the South, is still experiencing the demographic transition, so that it will comprise six-sevenths of the world's population in the next century. If we combine the reality of global environmental constraints on development with the current disparities in wealth, it is difficult to envisage the planet being able to sustain its entire population at anything remotely like the life-style and resource use of the richest one-fifth of the population.

To this we must add several further factors. The 40 years of the Cold War have left powerful and dangerous legacies. These include formidable developments in military technology, especially nuclear weapons, area-impact munitions, ballistic missiles and, in the future, directed-energy weapons and new generations of chemical and biological weapons. They also include an abject failure seriously to address major issues of arms control. Most treaties which have been negotiated have been peripheral to the main thrust of arms races and upheavals within the Soviet system suggest that internal pre-occupations, as well as US reticence, will hinder further progress. Meanwhile, military technologies proliferate across the world.

The Northern industrialised countries, and especially the United States, have become increasingly concerned with controlling access to needed resources, and this has resulted in a concentration on long-range military strategy, especially the use of military force projection. Many systems designed for this end have been deployed with the containment of the Soviet Union partly in mind. Its decline frees them for the task of keeping the violent peace in the Third World.

Finally, global environmental problems have proved to be peculiarly resistant to any effective international response. The international political system, dependent as it is on the short-term realities of domestic political and economic behaviour, has so far been unable or unwilling to cope with global problems.

Sketching out the extent of the problem is relatively easy, as the major issues are becoming increasingly obvious. What is much more difficult is assessing the likely consequences if present political attitudes and responses persist for the next two to three decades. The following discussion must therefore be considered tentative at best.

Given current trends in population growth and distribution and economic development, the gap between rich and poor is likely to grow rapidly. Apart from the immense human suffering which will result, this will also lead to increased migratory pressures from the poorest areas. Europe will probably come under progressively greater migratory pressure from North Africa, parts of South-West Asia and poorer parts of Eastern Europe and the Soviet Union.

The phenomenon of 'militant migration' is likely to develop, and was seen in a limited form during the Summer of 1991 when many thousands of young male Albanians crossed the Adriatic to Bari in Southern Italy. Forceful police action was used to evict them. In practice, migrants comprise men and women of most ages, with the greatest burden falling on women with children, but young adult males, because of their greater mobility, are the more obvious representatives of migrant pressures. They are likely to represent the most obvious form of militant migration, and will quickly and easily be seen as a threat to industrial societies in Western Europe.

Mass migratory pressure has affected the southern border of the United States for some years but has increased greatly in the past decade. In 1990 alone, over one million illegal immigrants were arrested in the southern United States (and at least 15 were shot and killed along the border). The great majority were Mexicans, but there were thousands from El Salvador, Guatemala, Honduras and Nicaragua.

Migratory pressures will be greatest on regions of wealth lying adjacent to areas with large populations in relative poverty. Apart from Western Europe and the United States, Russia will be affected by pressures from the Central Asian states and there may ultimately even be pressures on Japan and Australia.

These migratory pressures are likely to become intense to the point of risking a siege mentality in the wealthy regions, with a greatly increased emphasis on border security. As well as leading to a fortress mentality on the part of the wealthy (a 'Fortress Europe', for example), increases in the numbers of illegal or quasi-legal immigrants are likely to exacerbate economic exploitation and racism, in turn tending to result in a radicalisation of the migrants and a developing militancy. The Bari experience must be considered no more than a preliminary indicator of future trends.

Within the South, increasing disparities of wealth and poverty, coupled with continuing population pressures and rising expectations, is likely to lead to internal instability in many countries. This may be sporadic and unpredictable but will cause disorder and, on occasions, civil war. If occurring in those many areas of the South where Northern economic interests are important, then a military commitment to support friendly governments faced with revolt is likely. This may be no more than an extension of existing practice where military training missions merge into unconventional warfare, and can then extend into direct military intervention, with all the capabilities of modern military force projection.

What is far more difficult to assess is the potential for regional or even continental responses from the developing global underclass. The idea of any kind of co-ordinated Southern Army of the Poor (as Ronald Higgins characterised it in *The Seventh Enemy*[6], 20 years ago), is still difficult to envisage, but the conditions are likely to develop which could lead to a generalised response, the loose equivalent of a pre-revolutionary situation in an individual state or district. If the global village can exist, then so too can the global ghetto. If it comprises the great majority of the human population and if their rising expectations cross international borders, then frustrated migration may give way to greater violence. Within the global ghetto, tendencies towards militant nationalism and religious fundamentalism should be expected, each in their way providing a response to exploitation.

The North, in turn, requires continuing resource supplies to maintain its wealth, and also requires to secure its major and generally lucrative economic interests in the South. We have already seen the extent to which this is a facet of security policy, especially for the United States, and how military force was used to massive effect in the Gulf, early in 1991.

There have been other examples of open conflict over resources, with much of the conflict in southern Africa in the 1970s and 1980s predicated on the struggle for control of key mineral resources. Another more specific example was the Franco-Belgian intervention in Shaba Province of Zaire in 1978. This was ostensibly to rescue European mining technicians threatened by the Shaba rebels who had invaded the province from Angola. In reality, it was to prevent the collapse of Zairean rule in the province which had long ensured that its strategically vital cobalt resources had been controlled by a pro-Western government.

For the future, the Middle East, and especially the Gulf area, remains the most crucial region of resource security, containing two-thirds of all of the world's oil reserves. It is also a region which is very heavily militarised and has three root problems of instability. The first is the continuing Israeli–Palestinian problem, which will not be solved simply by sporadic international conferences. The second is the gross inequalities in wealth distribution within the Arab world, a source of tension which has been largely unrecognised by the US and Western Europe but underlay the support given to Saddam Hussein by ordinary people, though not governments, across the Middle East in 1990. The third is the probable response to continued US and European control of oil resources, a potential catalyst for a re-born popular Arab nationalism.

While the Gulf is the most important potential zone of conflict, other resource-rich areas include central and southern Africa, the Andes and Amazonia. In all cases, progressive resource depletion over the coming decades is likely to heighten Northern control of the resource bases of a number of regions in the South, leading in turn to tension and counter-action.

The experience of the Gulf War in 1991 showed that massive military force could be readily utilised to safeguard economic interests, and it follows that Southern states will not readily make Iraq's mistake of meeting a Northern military threat on its own terms. The slow proliferation of nuclear, biological and chemical weapons and the much more rapid proliferation of conventional weapons of mass destruction all indicate that future wars may be far more damaging, especially if they involve the use of ballistic missiles equipped with chemical, biological or cluster munitions against centres of population. There is also scope for unconventional warfare, including economic terrorism, the taking of hostages, and the arming of appropriate groups with advanced weapons including chemical agents.

We also have to recognise that there is a subtle change underway in international political relations in that three major Southern states have potential to become formidable military powers. China is already in this position. It may not retain its existing political system but its combination of population, resources and military power, together with its potential alliance with the South, puts it in a strong position to provide a focus for aspirations. This may also be true for India and possibly Brazil, though China is much the most significant.

In the wider context, the global political system has to contend with a series of global environmental problems, of which atmospheric and climatic change are the most pressing. The effects of such change are too complex to predict at present but the best indications are that there will be pronounced regional impacts. Climate change and atmospheric pollution are both likely, in their own ways, to change the habitability of large parts of the world. They may improve living conditions in currently poor areas by, for example, increasing rainfall in arid regions, or make conditions more difficult in existing rich areas, perhaps by decreasing rainfall in the American Mid-West.

The movement of environmental refugees, especially in Latin America and Africa, is already a growing problem, mainly as a result of localised environmental decline such as desertification; but regional climate change will produce much more substantial effects. If the human community is distributed largely in relation to sources of food and other requisites, then relatively sudden changes in their availability will result in catastrophic migratory pressures.

Precise predictions are simply not possible at present, but the overall effect will be to put greater pressure on international systems of relationships which will already be stretched close to breaking point.

Conclusions

With the end of the Cold War and the continuing upheavals in the Soviet states, it is natural that Western security interests, hidebound by 40 years of East–West tension, will continue to orient themselves within the Northern hemisphere. Our contention is that this is fundamentally flawed and that global security interests should be dominantly oriented on a North–South axis.

The gross wealth of a small minority of the world's population, coupled with accelerating global environmental constraints, constitute the major threats to global security. This is made worse by the legacy of militarisation left by the Cold War and by the persistent refusal of the rich North seriously to address the core problems of global wealth and poverty. This attitude makes conflict more likely, and the military legacy of the Cold War makes it potentially more dangerous.

On present trends, North–South inequalities will progress through competition to tension and conflict, accelerating a trend towards Northern military action in the South. As Edwin Brooks put it, nearly two decades ago.[7]

> . . . it is vital to avoid a crowded glowering planet of massive inequalities of wealth buttressed by stark force and endlessly threatened by desperate people in the global ghettos of the underprivileged.

There is little sign that the rich countries are prepared to avoid such a future; nor have they begun to appreciate that, in terms of global security, the Cold War was little more than a sideshow. There are alternative paths to co-operative global security, but it may be many years before these are taken seriously.

11

An Arms Control Agenda for the 1990s

In order to deal effectively with the security challenges that now face the world, the traditional security agenda will have to be significantly enlarged. We will discuss such wider issues again in the next Chapter. It is clear that the dangers and waste resulting from the continuing global militarisation will have to be brought under control as an essential first element in any relevant security agenda. We therefore deal here with an agenda for arms control in the 1990s.

In May 1987 Brent Scowcroft, who was later to become President Bush's National Security Adviser, was co-chairman of an Atlantic Council Working group which produced a report on *Defending Peace and Freedom: Toward Strategic Stability in the Year 2000*.[1] Raymond Garthoff, author of many important studies of the US-Soviet relationship, was one of the experts asked to comment on the report in an appendix.

Garthoff stated first that he thought the report was a middle-of the-road assessment that could have been written at any time over the previous decade – and that the United States would have been in a much better position if such an assessment had formed the basis of official policy over that time. But he continued:

My dissent stems from the fact that the framework for the study was focused on the year 2000, not 1965 or 1975 or 1985. I believe that it fails to recognise the pitfalls of resting on familiar deterrence doctrine, and the potentialities offered by significant change underway in the thinking of the new Soviet leadership . . . unless we start soon to make a major effort to determine the extent to which the Soviet Union is prepared to work seriously toward shared security, we will never know the potential for enhancing our common security . . .

In our view the West did not respond adequately to the possibilities opened up by Gorbachev between 1985 and 1991. After the events of August 1991 – when the success of a right-wing coup in the Soviet Union could have put the political climate back into deep freeze – and particularly in the current period of uncertainty, we think that the West must recognise that it has the primary responsibility for bringing the arms race under better control. Even those who argue that the period since 1945 has been increasingly stable, as the major powers have worked out rules to guide their interaction in the nuclear age, recognise the problem of deterrence and the associated build-up of weaponry. The problem of continued reliance on nuclear deterrence will have to be confronted at some stage in the future if disarmament proceeds, but for the moment the problems, we believe, are of a different order.

It is not difficult to find complex arguments in the literature for the retention of particular weapons or the development of new ones. Some, for example, would argue for the retention of many different nuclear systems in Europe. We do not disagree with the view that complex technical issues can be important, particularly at lower armament levels. However, given the huge arsenals of weapons available, and the rate of development and spread of new systems, we believe that the major problem now is to reverse direction. We must get the process of rapid reduction, restriction and moderation firmly in train whilst the opportunity is available.

This sense of urgency is most important because the problems will not get any easier. Whilst the East–West arms race may look more benign than it was, huge technological resources are still involved in the development and production of new weapons. The situation in the South could be much more difficult to control because of the potential for major regional conflicts and new centres of arms development which are growing stronger. These two facets – East–West and North–South – of arms control should be kept in mind as we review what might be done in specific areas now.

Without wishing to return to the sterile British unilateral-versus-multilateral arguments of the 1980s, some people have questioned the value of negotiated arms control treaties when rapid disarmament is taking place in a series of unilateral decisions in different countries. Given that such decisions reflect the quickening pace of political change, there is certainly some sense in that viewpoint. Unfortunately, however, without assured rights of inspection no-one can be exactly sure what is happening in other countries, and a disjointed series of unilateral decisions do not necessarily lead to the development of larger treaty regimes. While we are in favour of unilateral measures of disarmament, particularly as a means of initiating change and speeding progress, we also favour the negotiation of major treaties to fix such developments in place and to provide broad frameworks for further change and trust-building. We will discuss more of these general issues, concerned with the building of a disarmament regime, at the end of the Chapter. First, we will structure our review of current issues in a real arms control agenda for the 1990s in the same manner as in Chapter 3, starting with nuclear weapons.

The Prevention of Proliferation

The Non-Proliferation Treaty Some regional powers have always argued that the Non-Proliferation Treaty (NPT) is a discriminatory device for the maintenance of superpower domination. Some theoreticians have also argued that the world would be a safer place if more states had nuclear weapons. Given the success they believe deterrence has had in preventing war between the US and USSR, they argue that nuclear deterrence would prevent wars in other regions. Majority opinion amongst Western analysts, however, appears strongly to favour the retention and strengthening of the NPT. The growing awareness of Iraq's nuclear programme since the 1991 Gulf War has naturally reinforced this viewpoint.

Such support for the NPT should not obscure the fundamental differences existing between the Nuclear-Weapon States (NWS) and Non-Nuclear-Weapon States (NNWS) that support the Treaty. For the NWS, the NPT is essentially an additional means of assuring security, which is based fundamentally on their nuclear deterrents. For the NNWS the idea is to use the NPT to move away from deterrence towards nuclear disarmament and a new collective security system. They view the NPT as involving the NWS in much more serious practical commitments – particularly to a comprehensive ban on nuclear testing – than has so far occurred.

These differences resulted in failure, at the Fourth (five-yearly)

Review of the NPT in 1990, to agree a final consensus document. Some NNWS, in particular Mexico, argued for a Comprehensive Test Ban Treaty but as the Director of the US Arms Control and Disarmament Agency later reported to the US Senate that the President 'is firm in his commitment to the step-by-step process and to a comprehensive test ban as a long-term objective of the United States',[2] but also that 'We are convinced that so long as the US must rely on nuclear weapons for deterrence, we must also have a sensible test programme', the basic differences over the NPT remain.

The Treaty, nevertheless, now has some 140 States Parties and is the foundation for a complex treaty regime. This involves the International Atomic Energy Agency (IAEA) for operating Safeguards Agreements to ensure that nuclear material is not mis-used, and supplier groups attempting to better regulate exports of materials (for nuclear power generation) that might similarly be misused.

It is widely agreed that the first priority is to get more countries to join the NPT. The recent decisions by France and South Africa to sign the Treaty are, therefore, very important. It is to be hoped that China can also be persuaded to join in the near future. The second priority is to extend and tighten up the control regime of the Treaty. Again the recent publicity about Iraq's nuclear programme appears to be providing a necessary impetus in the right direction. We see no reason, for example, to argue against the IAEA being able to inspect non-designated sites when it has cause for concern, or the imposition of the so-called Full-Scope Safeguards on exports to all non-parties to the NPT.

However, the most dominant concern in regard to the NPT must surely be the mandatory Extension Conference, after 25 years of operation of the Treaty, in 1995. It is vital that a decision be taken to extend the Treaty indefinitely. This Treaty is the backbone of all efforts to contain the proliferation of weapons of mass destruction, and failure to agree an indefinite extension would be very harmful not only in regard to nuclear proliferation. The US may not be willing to move rapidly to a Comprehensive Test Ban Treaty (CTBT), but it will obviously have to be able to show a continuing successful record of negotiations. Moreover, it may have to agree (with other NWS who do not agree to a CTBT) to give stronger security assurances to NNWS in order to avoid difficulties at the conference.

Five major regions have given cause for concern over proliferation of nuclear weapons: Latin America (Argentina and Brazil); Africa (South Africa); the Middle East (Israel and Iraq); South Asia (India and Pakistan); and South-East Asia (particularly now North Korea). Whilst dangers of proliferation appear to have greatly eased in the first two regions, considerable cause for concern remains in the other three – where the danger of conflict remains high. Movement towards accommodation between North Korea and South Korea is unlikely to proceed quickly, and fears must remain over North Korea's intentions while it continues to avoid concluding the required IAEA Safeguards Agreement following its acceptance of the NPT. The likelihood of any serious accommodation between the Arab States and Israel – including dealing with Israel's nuclear weapons – must surely remain low, given the inherent complexities and hatreds in the region.

A most telling comment on the control of proliferation was made by one senior analyst following Pakistan's acquisition of its nuclear capability last year. Arguing that both the US administration and its critics were misguided in believing that they could influence Pakistan, he pointed out that:

> . . . The simple truth is that when countries are determined to obtain nuclear weapons, neither a single country nor the international community can ultimately prevent them from doing so. Pakistan believed she was threatened by India's nuclear programme and sought to counter it . . . Pakistan addressed her national security concerns as she saw fit . . .[3]

Those in the rich North who support the continuation of deterrence, but oppose proliferation, need to carefully consider such arguments. We may indeed face a long-term choice between a collective security system and considerable proliferation of nuclear weapons.

The Anti-Ballistic Missile (ABM) Treaty It will be recalled from Chapter 3 that the original American arms control analysts regarded the ABM Treaty as their central achievement. It signified for them the acceptance that deterrence based on mutual vulnerability to a retaliatory second–strike was secure. The attempt to put in place nationwide defences against ballistic missiles would, they believed, inevitably trigger a compensatory build-up of strategic offensive forces. The ABM Treaty fundamentally aims to prevent the deployment of such nationwide defensive systems. One set of fixed ground-based launchers is allowed, as is limited testing of these systems. According to the traditional 'narrow' interpretation of the Treaty the development, testing and deployment of ABM systems which are sea-based, air-based, space-based or mobile land-based is not allowed.

The composition of the US Strategic Defense Initiative (SDI) has varied a good deal since President Reagan announced it in 1983. At the present time it takes the form of 'Global Protection Against Limited Strikes' (GPALS). According to the chief of the SDI organisation this consists of:

- defences against theatre/tactical ballistic missiles that can be deployed to regional hotspots;
- ground-based defences to counter strategic ballistic missiles involving about 750 interceptors at six sites;
- a space-based tier of about 1,000 so-called 'Brilliant Pebbles' interceptors.[4]

The exact date of deployment of SDI remains unclear, and a great deal of testing of new systems – for example various sensors and lasers – is underway.

What is quite clear, and openly accepted by US officials, is that SDI must inevitably come up against the restrictions in the ABM Treaty. Since the resumption of negotiations in 1985, the US has therefore attempted to persuade the Soviet Union to join it in a cooperative transition to deterrence based on a mixture of offensive and defensive strategic systems. According to the chief US negotiator at what the Americans call the 'Defense, and Space Talks' in Geneva there are three reasons for their move in this direction:

- to make a first strike even more unthinkable;
- to provide extra insurance as strategic offensive forces are reduced; and
- to provide substantial protection against threats from countries developing ballistic missiles.[5]

After the Gulf War the third rationale has a resonance with the public and is being used determinedly as a means of increasing Congressional funding for SDI programmes.

Detailed investigation of the Soviet attitude to the ABM Treaty shows that it has been given consistent support. This support is likely to continue even if the Soviet Union shrinks to the Russian Federation. They still accept the original view that nation-wide ABM systems will lead to a compensatory increase in strategic offensive systems, and they certainly do not wish to expend huge resources in developing space-based defences at this time.

Four outcomes from the negotiations, which were scheduled to follow on immediately from the signing of the START Treaty, are possible. The two sides could agree to stay within the confines of the ABM Treaty or they could jointly decide to move away from the Treaty. Alternatively either side could unilaterally break the Treaty. At the present time a Russian breakout seems most unlikely. It is possible, however, that they might agree to some limited additional deployments in order to counter threats from the Third World. There were also suggestions that the Soviet Union would have gone beyond this to negotiate further space defence and strategic offensive reductions: perhaps to develop a joint accord for long-term minimal deterrence with the USA. The real choice remains with the US. Does it wish to use its technical advantages to develop SDI unilaterally – even at the risk of forcing a Soviet/Russian response? Or will it decide on a more moderate course of action?

Reduction of Nuclear Arsenals

The required destruction of INF missiles was completed on time by mid-1991. Then the START Treaty was signed and required large cuts in superpower offensive forces over the next seven years. The first question that might arise, therefore, is whether any more cuts in nuclear forces are necessary or sensible.

The question can be answered by recalling the two basic theories of how to deter an opponent from starting a nuclear war. It is possible to rely on:
- assured destruction in which each side knows that it cannot attack without receiving a devastating nuclear response; and
- counterforce or warfighting in which, much more ambitiously, it is intended to prevail over an opponent, particularly by attacking its nuclear forces first.

While both the US and USSR have carefully maintained an assured destruction capability, they have also pursued counterforce strategies. The problem with counterforce strategies, of course, is that they can be very destabilising in crises.

An important question, therefore, is whether the cuts in strategic forces in START have been sufficient to eliminate counterforce strategies. Here there is a quite clear-cut answer: no, they have not.

On the US side, for example, the current SIOP-7 has removed some 1,000–2,000 targets from the list. These are mainly in Eastern Europe, but many thousands remain. Indeed, it has been suggested that the START cuts were carefully crafted to preserve bomber forces in order that sufficient remained to search out and destroy mobile (*ie* new ICBM) targets. The eminent American scientist, Wolfgang Panofsky, put the issue clearly when he said:

> . . . The enactment of START will in no way require a revision of the strategic doctrine now established by either government, although the target lists will have to be moderately shortened . . . under reductions by a factor of two these relationships will hardly change at all . . .[6]

In order to move away from counterforce doctrines we would, therefore, have to see reductions in START 2 at the level that Richard Burt, the US START chief negotiator, is now proposing. As he put it: '. . . Taking advantage of Moscow's existing readiness to cut, we should follow up soon and reach an accord that reduces both sides to about 2,500 warheads'.[7] A number of plans for cuts at this kind of level have been put forward.

Reiveson and von Hippel[8] have suggested, for example, what they call 'finite deterrence' with each superpower having just 2,000 strategic nuclear warheads. They suggest that this would have the benefit of minimising fears of large-scale counterforce attack. They argue that such deep cuts could only be made if the ABM Treaty was retained in something like its present form and the medium nuclear powers (Britain, France and China) could be persuaded to cut their strategic forces to 200–500 each.

They suggest that each superpower should maintain its triad of strategic forces at these lower levels, and that the value of the nuclear targets should be reduced by de-MIRVing and cutting the number of launchers on ballistic missile submarines. Dangerous trends such as depressed trajectory SLBM attacks could be eliminated by bans on testing, and as only assured deterrence would be required there would be less fear of disruptive 'decapitation' attacks on command and control systems. Complex verification systems such as 'tagging' individual warheads would also be required. Finally, they suggest that eventually a verifiable cut-off in production of fissile material and stockpile control could be developed. Given that such cuts could be made at the strategic level, and there is clearly a strong trend to reduce levels of theatre and tactical nuclear systems across the board, the question arises whether much lower limits on strategic weapons might be possible?

While ideas of making nuclear weapons obsolete by the construction of perfect defences is widely seen as impossible, there is a long history of suggestions for minimal levels of deterrent forces. Numbers in the hundreds for each superpower are frequently suggested. Given the destructive potential of just one such weapon being detonated on a major city there is clearly force in these arguments. Counter-arguments concern the greater difficulties of effective verification and detection of cheating at such levels. It could, perhaps, be argued that once we have found the means to live with each other at 'finite' levels of deterrence we could, in fact, move towards President Gorbachev's denuclearised world, rather than stop along the way. Whilst a straightforward reduction down to finite deterrence (assured destruction) levels in START 2 is less likely than an agreement on an intermediate position, protracted negotiations do seem unnecessary. START can probably be used as a framework for further reductions within its already agreed categories.

Bans on Testing

There are over 100 states now party to the Limited Test Ban Treaty (LTBT). These include the so-called 'threshold' states – Israel, India, Pakistan, South Africa, Brazil and Argentina – which resisted joining the more discriminatory Non-Proliferation Treaty. Both the Limited Test Ban Treaty and the Non-Proliferation Treaty have strong Preambular commitments to achievement of a complete cessation of nuclear tests, and the Non-Proliferation Treaty also has a strong commitment to the cessation of the nuclear arms race in Article VI. As noted previously, it was the lack of progress towards a Comprehensive Test Ban Treaty which led to non-agreement at the Fourth Review Conference of the NPT in late 1990 and the stalemate at the LTBT Amendment Conference in early 1991.

On the other hand, the US and USSR did manage to ratify the two testing treaties – the Threshold Test Ban Treaty and the Peaceful Nuclear Explosions Treaty – that they had negotiated in the mid-1970s. Work on these two treaties since the mid-1980s had considerably developed the verification procedures. While the USSR was prepared to proceed towards a Comprehensive Test Ban

Treaty immediately, it was also prepared to go along with the United States in a step-by-step approach. France and China have indicated that, under certain conditions, they would consider a comprehensive ban. The real question is whether the US and UK are truly interested.

A variety of reasons have been advanced by these two states during the 1980s to justify their reluctance to accept a comprehensive ban. These have included doubts about verification, and reliability and safety of the weapons stockpile in the absence of testing. Such doubts have been vigorously questioned by independent scientists and many analysts have come to suspect that the reluctance is rooted in a desire to develop 'third-generation' nuclear weapons to support warfighting strategies.

First-generation weapons were fission weapons, second-generation were fusion weapons and third-generation nuclear weapons are '. . . nuclear-explosion-powered devices that transform, select or direct their energy in a unique way'.[9] Examples are X-ray lasers, nuclear kinetic energy weapons, microwave weapons and particle beams. Associated developments – although not third-generation weapons – are earth/ice penetration and manoeuvrable warheads.

Some testing and development of these advanced weapon systems can be carried out in very low-yield explosions in the laboratory. It seems generally agreed, however, that full development would require series of underground tests. A Comprehensive Test Ban Treaty involving a worldwide network of seismic detection centres, on-site inspections etc. would make effective cheating and development of such new weapons extremely unlikely. Some people argue that given the institutional resistance in the US, a more politically feasible move is first to a low-threshold ban or a low number of tests per year.

The real issue was stated by Tom Zomora of Friends of the Earth:

> . . . If President Bush is truly committed to creating a new world order based on mutual respect and the rule of law, he should begin by honouring the United States' international obligation to end nuclear testing for all time . . .[10]

It is probable that if President Bush does not at least make progress in that direction, the Extension Conference of the NPT in 1995 will be difficult. After blocking any discussions on this subject for years at the Conference on Disarmament, the US has at least now allowed an *Ad Hoc* Committee to begin consideration of the issue. The outcome, however, remains quite uncertain.

Restrictions on Distribution

Geographical restrictions on the distribution of nuclear weapons occur as part of the Antarctic Treaty, the Outer Space Treaty and the Sea-bed Treaty. Perhaps more importantly, the Treaty of Tlatelolco aimed to create a nuclear weapon-free zone in Latin America. Though this treaty was signed in the late 1960s, both Argentina and Brazil have been strongly suspected of having nuclear programmes directed at bomb-making capability. Recently, however, the installation of civilian governments in both countries has led to a significant improvement in relations, an opening up of information on their nuclear programmes, and disavowal of the intent to go nuclear. While some people harbour doubts that the military really have changed their aims, both Presidents have recently announced that they will negotiate safeguards agreements with the IAEA.

The Non-Proliferation Treaty's Article VII specifically favours the setting up of such nuclear weapon-free zones. Another was negotiated by the countries of the South Pacific and came into force as the Treaty of Rarotonga in 1986. That treaty clearly takes a very tough line against the extremely unpopular French nuclear testing in the Pacific, but considerable efforts were made to accommodate potential US objections over the transit of nuclear weapons. Unfortunately, the US (and the UK) have not supported the treaty, the US even suggesting that it was 'destabilising'.

Further possible nuclear weapon-free zones and broader zones of peace have been discussed for other areas of the world. Even in regions of conflict, progress seems possible. The recent decisions of South Africa, Zambia and Tanzania to join the NPT *de facto* creates a large nuclear-free zone in Southern Africa. In Korea the United States exerted great pressure to persuade the South to halt its nuclear weapons programme. There are now some indications that an implicit deal might be possible in which the North signs and implements IAEA safeguards to signify the halting of its programme and the US removes its nuclear weapons from South Korea.

It is to be hoped that, as the international political climate

improves, a flexible and pragmatic build-up of such zones continues in areas where the absence of indigenous nuclear forces
make it possible. Of course, where indigenous nuclear weapons are
already in place – for example, on the Indian sub-continent or in
the Middle East – a much longer and more difficult preceding
period of confidence-building will be required before removal of
these weapons is possible.

Moderation of the Dangers of Operation

The original 'Hot Line' agreement was set up between Moscow and
Washington following the Cuban missile crisis. It was subsequently
improved, and various other notification and risk-reduction
measures have been put in place. Analytical opinion strongly
favours further development of such measures to help guard
against inadvertent nuclear war, particularly during periods of
crisis when safeguards against accidental use have to be relaxed in
order to ensure that firing takes place if ordered.

The critical problem results from the fact that both superpowers
have counterforce doctrines and therefore launch-on-warning strategies so as to be able to ensure use of their strategic forces. This
leaves little time for decision, one recent review noting that:

> The commander of the North American Air Defense Command
> (NORAD), for example, would have only three minutes from the time of
> an initial attack indication to pass judgement on whether the continent is
> under fire or not. Clearly, this decision . . . entails major risks of prema-
> ture release of weapons based on false alarms, miscalculations or
> confusion.[11]

Numerous, almost unbelievable, examples of disordered decision-
making in such circumstances have been documented in recent
years.

Clearly, some unilateral actions that can be taken to reduce the
risks – such as instituting better controls from the centre and
reducing alert rates – would be advisable. Other ideas suggested
include fitting systems that allow destruction of missiles after they
are launched. It has also been pointed out that even the upgraded
'Hot Line' would not function well if a nuclear exchange ever
began. A new agreement might therefore involve special radiation-
resistant satellite linkages. Reduction of forces to 'finite' deterrent
levels would allow other agreements – verifiable separation of

warheads from launchers for example – which would further extend decision-time, and therefore safety, in crises. While the risks of accidental war may be small, the agreements already reached indicate that they are real and that further progress should be made in this area.

As we have seen in Chapter 5, advances in science and technology are producing further problems of control in relation to other weapons of mass destruction. We now turn to these non-nuclear systems.

Chemical Weapons

At the Conference on Disarmament in Geneva, negotiations on a multilateral Chemical Weapons Convention (CWC) have been in progress for over a decade. The Convention sets out to prevent the development and production of chemical weapons and encourage the destruction of all present stocks of such weapons. The very long 'rolling text' consists of some 20 Articles, a Verification Protocol and several Annexes.

The Convention, in a similar manner to previous recent treaties, requires detailed declarations of stocks and facilities and will set up an international organisation to deal with verification. This will be very complex because of the possible manufacture of chemical weapons in civilian chemical production facilities, and because challenge verification at some sites could risk national security in matters in no way connected with chemical weapons.

Despite some signs of opposition in the US government, President Bush appears to be personally committed to the Convention. His administration has certainly taken a number of initiatives aimed at achieving agreement. Very significantly in May 1991 it was announced by the White House that, 'the United States will call for the resolution of all major outstanding issues in the CD talks in Geneva on the CWC by the end of 1991 and the completion of the CWC within 12 months'.[12]

To back this up, the US suggested that negotiations on the final draft text should be held in continuous session. More importantly, some telling concessions were made:

> The US will drop its position that states retain a right of retaliation with CW as long as they have CW stocks if CW are used against them first. The US will formally forswear the use of CW for any reason; and:

The US will drop its position that we must be allowed to keep two percent of our CW stockpile (500 tons) until all CW-capable states have joined the Convention . . .

The US also signalled its willingness to help resolve the difficulties over challenge verifications. Many analysts are therefore beginning to think that a CWC will be agreed in 1992.

If it is agreed, a CWC will have one very important difference from the NPT. While both will have 'carrots' to tempt states to join (in Articles on assistance with relevant industrial development) and sanctions against hold-out states, the CWC will be non-discriminatory. It will enforce a total ban on chemical weapons. A situation corresponding to the nuclear 'haves' and 'have-nots' of the NPT regime will not arise. While it may well be difficult to persuade some states to join the CWC initially, it is nevertheless possible to envisage the development of a universal norm – a collective security system – against these weapons.

Biological Weapons

It is widely understood that the Biological Weapons Convention (BWC) was only agreed because the military saw little use for such weapons at the time. Consequently the verification provisions of the Convention were not at all stringent. Subsequently, the development of genetic engineering techniques and the spread of such biological research capabilities around the world have increased fears of what might be occurring in various countries. Given the relative simplicity of the techniques involved and the small scale of operations required, controlling the proliferation of biological weapons will undoubtedly be very difficult.

To date, five-yearly Review Conferences have made some improvements, notably the agreement on data exchanges in 1986. This required annual reporting on research centres and unusual outbreaks of disease. Unfortunately, reporting has been incomplete, and lack of adequate central resources has limited the use to which the information could be put.

Nevertheless, implementing such confidence-building measures has proved to be a useful interim development, as most experts have anticipated that more far-reaching advances in the control of biological weapons will have to await the agreement of a verifiable Chemical Weapons Convention. The Review Conference of

Autumn 1991 agreed further data exchanges. There is also a variety of ways in which the organisational resources available to help implement the Convention could be improved; for example, a small, continuously operating Secretariat should be set up to care for the Convention between reviews but this has, so far, not been possible to arrange.

Thus, though major developments on the Biological Weapons Convention may have to await the final agreement of the Chemical Weapons Convention and some experience gained with its implementation, it is clearly necessary in the meantime, to continue striving for more states to become parties to the Convention. We believe that it will eventually be necessary, and also possible, to develop a tough Verification Protocol for the BWC.

Other Weapons of Mass Destruction

In 1979–80, the United Nations held a major conference on 'Prohibition or Restrictions of Use of Certain Conventional Weapons which may be Deemed to be Excessively Injurious or to Have Indiscriminate Effects'. A recent UN publication noted:

> . . . various proposals were discussed. They concerned the prohibition of napalm and other incendiary weapons; blast weapons relying on shock waves caused by the detonation of substances spread in the air and fuel-air explosives; anti-personnel cluster warheads or other devices with many bomblets which eject a great number of small fragments or which release projectiles in the form of flechettes or needles; mines and booby-traps; and new types of small-calibre projectiles or bullets whose effects were said to be comparable to those of the dum-dum bullet.[13]

This catalogue would appear to cover many of the horrors we have seen used increasingly during the 1980s. It certainly includes the modern conventional weapons which cause death and destruction over wide areas.

The Convention on Inhumane Weapons, agreed in 1981, had Protocols covering non-detectable fragments, mines and booby-traps and incendiary weapons. There is clearly a need for a concerted effort to get more states to become parties to the Convention.

Additionally, the Convention allows for the holding of a new Conference to tighten up the present Protocols and to add new ones. This is a matter of urgency and we think that particular attention should be paid to new conventional weapons – such as cluster-bombs – which are now, in effect, weapons of mass destruction. The military effectiveness of such weapons in the war against Iraq suggests that this will not be easily achieved.

The Coalition attacks on Iraqi nuclear facilities again raises the question of how to deal with so-called radiological weapons. While the production of weapons which kill just by radiation is not thought militarily useful, Sweden has led a group of countries thwarting the agreement of a Convention on such weapons at the Conference on Disarmament. These critics argue that the important practical issue is to prevent attacks on nuclear facilities which could be catastrophic. This is, in effect, being blocked by the US and its allies, who argue that the matter should be dealt with separately from radiological weapons as traditionally defined.

In our view, both radiological weapons as traditionally defined, and attacks on nuclear facilities should be banned. Attacks on nuclear facilities as a 'final' means of preventing a state developing nuclear weapons could be an increasingly ominous problem if the NPT regime disintegrates.

Conventional Weapons

Naval Arms Control The highly successful bilateral agreement between the US and USSR on the Prevention of Naval Incidents was agreed in the early 1970s. It did a great deal to contain the dangerous interactions between the superpowers' naval forces. It was subsequently developed both in similar agreements between other navies and the USSR, and in the expansion to other superpower forces in the 1989 Agreement on the Prevention of Dangerous Military Activities. These improvements in what is called 'operational arms control', however, highlight the overall question of naval arms control.

Naval arms control can be sub-divided into four different categories:

- *structural*, which deals with the numbers of ships, planes, and weapons;
- *qualitative*, which deals with the kinds of weapons;
- *operational*, which covers restrictions on what the forces can do; and
- *confidence-building measures*, which reduce uncertainty by making more information available to potential antagonists.

Historically, the Soviet Union has favoured naval arms control and since 1985 it has pushed many ideas very strongly.

The US, and the West in general, have not been at all receptive to these ideas because as one US navy commentator put it:

> . . . Maritime power is obviously the prerequisite for defence of the West, literally the physical tie that binds. Even if the Soviet threat has been greatly reduced, the need for capable naval forces . . . and power projection (aircraft, SLCMs, and amphibious forces) obviously remains . . . there would seem little to gain in agreeing to limitations . . .[14]

Certainly, there appears to be a widespread consensus amongst analysts that very little arms control will be agreed in relation to naval forces in the near future.

Yet the Soviet threat *is* much reduced, a fact which is having an effect on Western military – including naval – budgets. Moreover, both the US and USSR have been removing large numbers of tactical nuclear weapons from their surface ships. As these processes continue and other arms control measures are agreed, it does seem probable that further naval operational and confidence-building measures should be possible. A multilateral incidents-at-sea regime and much enhanced notification and observation of exercises are frequently suggested as initial stages.

More radical ideas include the banning of non-strategic naval nuclear weapons, and large-scale negotiated cuts in attack submarines. Such agreements could contribute to the stabilisation of East–West relations. They could also help to focus attention on longer-term issues. While the strong Western navies can project power around the world now, technological development continues also in the Third World. New and diverse threats – for example, from small, quiet submarines – could make such worldwide operations much more dangerous in the future. Consideration of a very different agenda – such as Zones of Peace like the one much discussed for the Indian Ocean – rather than confrontation might then become possible.

Conventional Forces in Europe There are numerous heavily militarised land borders between states around the world. One of the most heavily militarised, the border between East and West in Europe, has recently seen a very rapid de-escalation following the political changes in the Soviet Union. Two main approaches have been adopted: force reductions and confidence-building measures.

Implementation of the first Conventional Forces in Europe Treaty (CFE 1) will essentially remove the risk of surprise attack in

Europe. It will, however, leave the problem of a sustained, prepared, offensive attack which constituted the second part of the CFE mandate. Negotiation of the CFE 1 A follow-on was expected to begin to deal with this problem by agreeing cuts in personnel levels. Some people argue that further reductions will be unnecessary, or very difficult to organise. We agree with those who suggest, on the other hand, that there is a great deal more that could be done. A huge concentration of military forces will remain in Europe after the completion of the CFE cuts. The experienced negotiator and analyst, Jonathan Dean, has suggested that:

> . . . security in Europe could be further enhanced . . . by cuts of 40–50 percent from post-CFE NATO holdings of the same armaments which CFE negotiators have already identified as those indispensable for offensive attack: tanks, armoured personnel carriers, artillery, combat aircraft and combat helicopters . . .[15]

In short CFE could be used as a framework for further cuts in a second round.

Various new means could also be agreed to make mobilisation of forces more difficult, for example by putting more restrictions on the forward deployment of equipment needed to move forces, and by restricting numbers of trained reservists. The continued development of new modernised offensive conventional forces might also be restricted by agreed limits on procurement.

The new political situation in Europe, however, raises a different agenda as well as the completion of the original one. All kinds of new possibilities for conflict appear likely to arise in Eastern Europe and the old Soviet Union now that central control has been removed. Much new thinking will be required to find means of keeping such potential conflict under control. One means that should be considered is the restructuring of all forces in a more defensive orientation.

While the CFE talks have taken place within the framework of the Conference on Security and Co-operation in Europe (CSCE) process, they have involved so far only the 23 nations of NATO and the old Warsaw Pact. The 35 nations of the CSCE as a whole have been involved in the parallel talks on Confidence- and Security-Building Measures (CSBMs). The current negotiations build on the limited agreements in the original 1975 Helsinki accord and the 1986 Stockholm and 1990 Vienna documents. These negotiations are intended to produce a more comprehensive document for the 1992 Helsinki CSCE Review. The 1990 Vienna agreement put into place complex arrangements for data exchanges, notification of exercises and inspections. High-level seminars to clarify military doctrine are continuing, and the foundations of an organisational system – a Council of Ministers, a Secretariat, a Conflict Prevention Centre and an Office of Free Elections – are being laid. As James Goodby, former leader of the US delegation to the CSCE, noted recently in regard to future developments:

> . . . There will undoubtedly be continued negotiations on arms reductions and confidence-building. But such measures alone cannot ensure that nascent disputes will not lead to war. Building institutions that will help states resolve their disputes without violence is perhaps the greatest task now facing the CSCE.[16]

Goodby looks forward to a steady evolution of organisational capabilities and norms of state behaviour but with accords continuing to be politically rather than legally binding.

Some analysts are concerned that such measures will not be adequate and that a much stronger development of the CSCE will be required. They also fear that efforts to retain NATO as the centre point of a European security system – and with 'out of area' potential – will distort the process of building a widely respected and effective European-wide system. We share those concerns and agree with those who think that a pan-European organisation will be needed. This will not come about quickly, but the objective is, in our opinion, much more likely to lead to a secure future for Europe.

Open Skies In early 1989 President Bush revived President Eisenhower's 'Open Skies' idea. While it might be argued that satellite observations have made this a much less useful proposal, there would be some technical advantages in being able, for example, to fly observation planes under cloud cover. Moreover, for countries that do not have satellites there would be considerable gains.

The Soviet Union's response was initially quite enthusiastic, Foreign Minister Shevardnadze noting additionally that 'open seas' ideas – unacceptable to Washington – should be included. The subsequent discussions have become bogged down in differences over the level of technology available to different countries and

Soviet concerns to restrict access. Specifically, NATO proposed that the annual number of overflights should be proportional to the geographical size of the various parties. The Soviet Union wanted a much lower number than that formula would produce. It also wanted to be able to overfly US bases outside Europe (for example, in Japan), and to close off certain 'sensitive' areas within the USSR. In order to equalise technological differences, it further wanted to be able to designate which aircraft overflew, to greatly restrict possible sensors used, and to have access to all data gathered. While both sides have made small concessions, at the present time these negotiations are deadlocked. It is to be hoped that differences can be resolved because that would obviously assist in the process of building trust in what might be difficult times in the near future.

If the Soviet Union has been most resistant to 'Open Skies' proposals, it is the United States that appears to be the block on a treaty on anti-satellite weapons. The importance of satellites was re-emphasised during the Gulf War and, although the Soviet Union had a primitive anti-satellite (ASAT) system, it has not been operative since the early 1980s. The US, though, has continued trying to develop new weaponry despite a widespread view that an ASAT ban could be verified. The development of ASAT weapons could clearly become quite destabilising. Yet the US Deputy Assistant Secretary of Strategic Defense, Space and Verification was quoted as arguing recently that:

> . . . Space control requires an integrated combination of anti-satellite (ASAT) capabilities, space surveillance, and enduring space assets. In view of our continued need to project power, deter war and control escalation during conflict, it is essential for the USA to develop and deploy an operational ASAT system to counter Soviet exploitation of their present space control and space-based targeting capabilities . . .[17]

Little sign of new thinking here!

The Control of Military Exports

The Missile Technology Control Regime (MTCR) has continued to be an effective means of preventing the spread of ballistic missiles. The membership has grown and the controls have been developed and better implemented. These welcome trends can be expected to continue. Similarly, in regard to chemical and biological weapons, the work of the Australia Group of exporters has become more effective.

Yet despite some calls for better monitoring and control of conventional weapons exports after the Gulf War the prospects for control are not good in the short term. At present the three dozen supplier countries compete for an annual arms market worth $30 billion. The reasons this trade is so difficult to control range from supplier governments long used to viewing sales as a means of foreign policy and manufacturers needing sales to survive and finance R&D, through to recipients being involved in regional conflicts or viewing export restrictions as discriminatory. An alarming example of the problem was the US announcement of huge arms exports to the Middle East immediately after the Gulf War.

Progress in effective control is going to need greater determination – for example helping arms companies to diversify into civilian production – and discrimination from suppliers. Key exports will have to be identified and sufficient resources – governmental and industrial – put together to track these items. It also will be necessary to work with Third World states to develop a cooperative regime in which they feel that they have a stake. In this perspective export controls are seen as a means of buying time in which more peaceful conditions in regions of conflict can be developed – for example through defensive restructuring – and thus the demand for new armaments reduced.

A Developing Arms Control Regime?

The main bearing of this Chapter has been that there is a need for new political thinking in the West. Now is the time to seize the opportunity to reverse the arms race. That will require political decisions, such as abolishing strategic-level counterforce targeting.

When arms control negotiations are possible it is also necessary to recognise that arms control law is in need of development. While arms control apparently involves special problems in dealing with complex scientific issues and multiple countries, patent law already deals with complex science, and international commercial law is very effective. If the will is there, the expertise can be found. There is an urgent need to reflect on the process of arms control in order to find better methods of operation.

12

Wider Concepts of Security – Preventing New World Disorder

One pleasant side-effect of the failure of the Right-wing coup in the Soviet Union in August 1991 was the reuniting of the KGB double agent, Oleg Gordievsky, with his family. In the context of this book, Gordievsky's story also has a much darker side which was reported in various journals in the mid- to late-1980s after his defection to Britain. It was written up in some detail on 16 October 1988, when the London newspaper, *The Sunday Telegraph*, carried an article entitled 'When the World Almost Went to War'. Written by Gordon Brook-Shepherd, a writer specialising in the study of Soviet defectors, it was said to be based on two days of interviews with Gordievsky, centring on his account of how, in the Autumn of 1983, in the depths of the renewed Cold War, there was almost an inadvertent nuclear war between the Soviet Union and NATO.

According to Gordievsky's account, at the beginning of the 1980s, the ageing Soviet leadership had expected the new President Reagan to repeat what had happened with the incoming President Nixon. They expected that the Americans would quickly turn off the tough talk and 'go in for détente'. The fact that this did not happen, in combination with the developing US nuclear modernisation programme – M-X, Trident 2, Pershing 2, cruise missiles etc. – and talk of new countervailing (war-winning) strategies, was reported to have thoroughly alarmed the Politburo and its advisers.

The alarm was such that the KGB and the GRU (military intelligence) were instructed specifically to watch for the signs of the approximately 10-day build-up which was thought to be required to prepare for a NATO nuclear first strike against the Soviet Union. The first KGB instructions of this nature were sent out at the end of November 1981 under the code name RYAN – *Raketno Yadernoye Napadeniye*, or Nuclear Missile Attack.

Gordievsky, who was in charge of the British desk at the KGB Moscow Centre, sent the RYAN order to London. By *The Sunday Telegraph*'s account:

> It required the KGB in Britain . . . to keep the closest scrutiny over the comings and goings of ministers, noting whether Mrs Thatcher was driving more often than usual to the Palace; to look out for any unusual movements of troops or increased activity at airbases and ports; to watch for any signs of official stockpiling of food, the build-up of emergency blood banks . . .[1]

Regular status reports were required from all important locations around the world and 'Flash' telegrams were required in the event of indications of an emergency.

This system was said to be still in operation two years later when Andropov was dying and when 'in that closed and highly suspicious atmosphere, the leadership was more than usually nervous'.

Then NATO began one of its occasional and highly secret exercises to practise its methods of releasing nuclear warheads in the event of all-out nuclear war. Code-named 'Able Archer', the exercise was due to run from 2–11 November 1983. As was expected, and normal practice, Warsaw Pact surveillance facilities began to monitor this exercise, and again, as was normal practice, Western intelligence was monitoring the Pact's monitoring. In this case, however, 'it soon became clear to both the British and the American listening centres that something was going badly wrong . . .' In fact:

> Instead of the normal monitoring to be expected from across the Iron Curtain, a sharp increase was registered in both volume and urgency of the Eastern Bloc traffic. The incredible seemed to be happening, namely that the Warsaw Pact suspected it might really be facing nuclear attack at any moment.

According to Gordievsky's account, while the West would have understood standard Soviet nervousness about an attack developing from an exercise:

> . . . What they [the West] were totally unaware of at the time was how far they had really passed through a war danger zone in those days . . . on

8–9 November . . . the Kremlin had pressed what came close to a panic button.

In his account of these events, Brook-Shepherd suggests that significant subsequent changes in the 'Able Archer' type exercises were made to avoid triggering such panic. He further suggests that no further such episodes occurred in the early 1980s.

When Gordievsky defected to the West in 1985, he was debriefed by the British with whom he was apparently in contact from the early 1970s. In September and October 1985, Gordievsky's information on the dangerous state of Soviet strategy and psychology in relation to the West's current activities was passed to the US authorities in a paper titled 'Soviet Perceptions of Nuclear Warfare'. This was reported to have been read fully by President Reagan and the 'evil empire' onslaught against the Soviet Union quickly run down.

While we do not have precise corroboration of Gordievsky's claims, what is clear is that the high hopes of the early 1970s did degenerate into the renewed Cold War of the 1980s. Moreover, the almost half-century of the nuclear age has been marked by a series of thaws and freezes between East and West and this has included periods of intense political confrontation such as the Berlin crisis, the Cuban missile crisis and the Korean jet incident. Even 40 years after the East–West confrontation had started, it was possible for a potentially dangerous crisis of misunderstanding to occur.

Thus while we, at the moment, appear to be living through a much more hopeful period in East–West relations, it would be foolish to imagine that no new crises will arise. They are inherent in the nuclear deterrence system as practised in the past, and will be an inevitable part of a polarised world equipped with nuclear, chemical and other weapons of mass destruction.

The risks inherent in nuclear deterrence were among the factors that motivated the change of policy engineered by Gorbachev and also caused many people in the West to ponder the consequences of the failure of détente. A debate developed on alternative approaches to defence, and this involved the development of ideas of common security and greater attention to the rule of international law. Many of the ideas were utilised in the changes initiated from Moscow under Gorbachev, but they have a saliency which moves us on from the Cold War to a considerable relevance to the new global polarisation.

Common Security and The Rule of Law

One of the earliest attempts to map out a form of common security as a response to the Cold War was the work of the Palme Commission which issued its report, *Common Security: A Programme for Disarmament*, in 1982. The Commission argued

> All nations would be united in destruction if nuclear war were to occur. Recognition of this interdependence means that nations must begin to organise their security policies in co-operation with one another. Obviously, this will not happen overnight. But a political process can be started which – if carefully managed and consistently pursued – can develop sufficient momentum to outrun the effects of past failures.[2]

It argued for a policy of common security based on the principles that, for example, all nations have a legitimate right to security; military force is not a legitimate instrument for solving disputes between nations; and security cannot be attained through military superiority. These are fine sentiments and represent worthy aims, and they are as appropriate in pursuit of a new world order after the Cold War as they were within the tensions of the early 1980s. What has to be at issue is whether the Northern states, dominated by the United States and its allies with their emphasis on 'realist' power politics, can be brought to an understanding of the imperative of implementing them.

The influence of 'realism' in the international politics practised especially by the United States should not be underestimated. The realist view first came to prominence in the United States and was best illustrated initially by Hans Morgenthau's *Politics Among Nations*, published in 1948. The Truman administration was ultimately converted to its outlook, as it replaced the more idealistic attitudes dating from Woodrow Wilson and including, to an extent, Roosevelt. While international relations theory has moved well beyond realism, it has remained the dominant outlook of successive US administrations, with the partial exception of the Carter years.

As a theory it is deeply flawed as a means of explaining the world, let alone providing for stable and peaceful relations, and even more so as we move out of the period dominated by the Cold War into a more complex period without the presence of a single clear-cut enemy available to make simplistic analysis so much easier. Realism succeeded for some decades, probably because it was a reaction to what was perceived to be the failure of Wilsonian idealism and the attempts to build a rule of law between the two world wars.

Yet the American arms controllers of the 1950s and 1960s saw, while accepting the political *Status Quo* dominated by realist power politics, that there must be limits to military competition in the nuclear age. In his important book *World Politics and International Law*, Francis Boyle noted this and explained that such theorists argue for the maintenance of a 'balance of power'. But he argues that this sits very uneasily with their Machiavellian power politics because:

> The principal (and fatal) defect of modern 'realist' theory is its supposition that Machiavellianism can actually be subordinated to the objective of preserving a balance of power system . . . By its very nature, Machiavellian power politics requires the employment of violence against putative adversaries in order to achieve ultimate objectives. This dictate traps governments into an interminable cycle of force and counterforce . . . [3]

He goes on to argue that US policy for a quarter of a century (previous to his writing in 1985) had been an unmitigated disaster and a subversion of the very international legal order that the US was involved in trying to establish in the United Nations system at the end of the Second World War. Moreover, and perhaps crucially for the future, he also points out that:

> . . . Machiavellian power politics violently contradicts several of the most fundamental normative principles upon which the United States is supposed to be founded: the inalienable rights of the individual, the self-determination of peoples, the sovereign equality and independence of states, non-interventionism, respect for international law and organisations, and the peaceful settlement of international disputes . . .

It is perhaps ironic that Boyle is able to show that at the end of his life, in 1980, Hans Morgenthau, the founding father of modern American realism, agreed strongly with Boyle's concerns and feared that the practice of realism was leading towards nuclear war.

The contrast can clearly be seen between John Steinbrunner's recent description of practice under the rule of law and the view of a senior official in the Bush administration of US defence strategy. Steinbrunner suggests that it would be advisable for the US to follow certain guidelines, for example, that:

- Military forces are to be configured only for the defence of existing national territory.

- Any change in political jurisdiction is to be accompanied by legitimate methods of political consent.
- Military power is to be projected only with the consent of the whole international community, and only in defence of the above principles.[4]

Lewis Libby, Principle Deputy Under-Secretary of Defense (Strategy and Resources) speaking in 1990 argued for 'several key building blocks to the force structure of a new strategy'. At the conventional level he suggested:

- . . . First, forward presence through forward-deployed forces is of critical importance to help shape the future strategic environment in ways favourable to the US . . .
- Second, is the need for the US to maintain an ability to respond to regional threats that concern it . . .
- Third, the US must keep an eye on the future and plan to reconstitute larger forces if necessary . . .

On top of that, in Libby's view,

> . . . On the strategic side, the US must maintain a robust ability, through both strategic offensive and defensive forces, to respond to the threat of nuclear weapons . . . In addition, it must maintain the quality of its military leadership and personnel, and stress innovations to keep or gain the competitive edge in key areas of warfare.[5]

The contrast could hardly be more clear-cut.

The foundation for progress is therefore, in our opinion, the need for the United States and its allies to recapture and further develop the idealism that has sometimes been apparent in the past, matching the liberals who started the remarkable changes in the Soviet Union in the mid-1980s, in moving forward to construct a really new world order. The accelerating global pressures, coupled with the diffusion of military technology around the world will eventually force the US and its allies to give up power politics, but not necessarily soon enough.

Once the fundamental change in approach is made, it is not too difficult to see the outlines of what needs to be done. The final statement of the Palme Commission in 1989 was called *A World At Peace: Common Security in the Twenty-First Century*. In a section titled 'Common Security Through the Rule of Law', it argued for transforming the international system through three developments: the development of norms of behaviour requiring the peaceful settlement of disputes; strengthening of international institutions to support such norms; and mobilisation of public opinion.

The Palme Commission was just one of a number of independent commissions during the 1970s and 1980s, others being chaired by Brandt, Brundtland and Nyerere; all of them tried to come to terms with the world's problems. Building on this work, a group of those involved produced a new report in April 1991 entitled *Common Responsibilities In The 1990s: The Stockholm Initiative On Global Security And Governance*. The proposals on 'Peace and Security' are dominated by a series of proposals for strengthening the United Nations. They suggest that:

> On the global level, the time is ripe to implement the international security regime based on the Charter of the United Nations . . . The system of international peace and security which we seek must be comprehensive and universal, and protect the interests of the weak as well as the strong . . . For a new world order, it is vitally important that the United Nations is made stronger and more effective.[6]

They then put forward a series of proposals to improve the UN's ability to monitor conflicts, enforce the law, and carry out peace-keeping operations. They also include means of monitoring, regulating and limiting the arms trade, arguing that part of the peace dividend achieved by the reduction in military expenditure in the rich North should be allocated to the South, just as the South should take measures to cut military spending.

Bertrand has presented a clear view of the overall problem. He sees a forthcoming clash of two basic views of security. The first will continue to preserve the main structures and trends in the present military apparatus. It will attempt to continue the present qualitative arms race and resist the development of arms control. The second:

> . . . will attempt to considerably reduce the present levels of armaments, to do away completely with certain types of weapons, to develop control measures and institutionalise them so as not to reduce but to eliminate threats of aggression between countries which accept these regimes of permanent inspection. It will attempt to reinforce and reform world institutions to enable them to guarantee an effective system of collective security.[7]

Such a view is expressed in the context of a concern principally with militarisation and its risks, but it applies even more in the wider context which we have been considering, and it would seem to be on this basis that those wider issues of security can begin to be approached effectively.[8]

Wider Security Issues

Our analysis of future global security issues has taken as its starting point the patterns of militarisation over the past 40 years and indicates four determining factors. One is the extent of that global militarisation – largely a result of the massive military legacy resulting from 40 years of the Cold War. The second is the deep polarisation of the world into a wealthy minority located mainly in the North and an impoverished majority, primarily in the South. The third is the increased dependency of that Northern minority on the resource wealth of the South; and overlying all these are the environmental constraints increasingly affecting human activity across the world.

Our contention is that this combination of factors is likely to lead, on present trends, to a period of instability, tension and conflict. Yet in trying to set an agenda for controlling these global trends, we are constrained by this intellectual legacy of Western thinking on international security. This is partly a result of the intense East–West confrontation of the past 40 years which has dominated strategic thinking, almost to the total exclusion of wider global issues. This is made worse by the continuing ethnocentricity of Western strategic analysis, with its well-nigh total preoccupation with a small minority of the world's population. It is as though there has been an unwritten assumption that concentration on East–West issues must be the dominant concern throughout the whole world, not just in the North.

In so far as nuclear war threatens the entire world, there is some truth in this, and it must also be accepted that East–West rivalries have had their effect on many parts of the South, from the Caribbean to Angola and from Vietnam to Korea. Yet for most of the peoples of the world, the Cold War was scarcely relevant to the daily pursuit of a better life; the increasing problems of poverty and environmental degradation have for long made it little more than a sideshow.

The core problems of poverty, environmental constraint and militarisation require five responses. Processes of militarisation have to be reversed. Northern industrialised countries have radically to change their policies towards the Third World. Development policies encouraged by such change must be in a form that will ensure accelerated yet environmentally sustainable development. Future development in the industrialised countries must itself be sustainable, recognising that the major global environmental problems are caused primarily by the activities of these countries. Finally, there must be a change in international behaviour to ensure a rapid and effective response to any future changes in the global ecosystem.

We have already discussed, in Chapter 11, an agenda for arms control and disarmament which would amount to a rapid reversal of the patterns of militarisation which have affected the world in the past 40 years, leading to the point where, at the end of the 1980s, worldwide military spending was around $1,000 billion per year.

While the ending of the Cold War will certainly see significant cuts in that spending, especially as over 80 percent of it has originated in the countries involved directly in the Cold War, our concern has been with the wider issue of global militarisation. The agenda has therefore extended to addressing those threats which, while usually originating within the context of the Cold War, also carry global risks.

We would contend that this kind of agenda is essential if we are to curb the destructiveness of military technology but would also point to the potential for redistributing resources on a massive scale to more fruitful areas of human endeavour. While the processes of demilitarisation and arms industry conversion are complex and have, in themselves, certain costs, the prospect of cutting up to half of global military spending over the next decade would release resources hugely in excess of anything previously committed to development assistance and environmental repair in the past.

As to the four other areas of actions listed above, the first and foremost is the reordering of North–South relations. This requires comprehensive trade, debt and aid reform. Trade reform entails the general implementation of commodity agreements, along the lines of the *Integrated Programme on Commodities* as originally envisaged, providing for progressively higher and stable primary commodity earnings for the South. Tariff preferences and commodity-processing incentives are essential to encourage substantially higher export earnings, giving greater potential for considerable investment in internal development. Debt cancellation rather than debt rescheduling is required to counter the debt crisis, and development assistance is required in grant rather than loan form and aimed principally at basic needs.

These necessary changes in North–South development relationships are both radical and fundamental. They represent a near-total reordering of attitudes and would, over a period of years, involve a redistribution of wealth from North to South – a reversal of the pattern of the last several decades. While they involve a basic shift in the approach to international development, they do not, alone, address two aspects of the wider context, political and social reform within the Third World and the response to environmental constraints.

The deep polarities of wealth and poverty which exist globally are mirrored by similar polarities within most Southern states, exacerbated by extensive corruption, itself frequently connected directly to North–South economic relationships. Internal reform has to proceed in parallel with international reform, but could itself be aided by much stronger patterns of South–South cooperation, especially in such areas as regional industrialisation and market development. Such cooperation is already developing and could have the additional advantage of improving the bargaining strength of Southern states in their relations with the North.

Addressing the wider context of environmental constraints applies in different ways to the approaches to development followed in the South and North. The requirement is to seek patterns of development which are, to the best of our knowledge of environmental processes, sustainable in the long term.

Conditions for sustainable development are several and varied, with the overall aim of preventing local, regional and especially global environmental deterioration.[9] Renewable resources, whether they be crops, forests, rangeland or fisheries, must be maintained in a manner which ensures their sustained productivity. Over-exploitation, whether it leads to desertification, salinization, deforestation or other patterns of damage and decline, has to be avoided.

Furthermore, exploitation of renewable resources must be done in a manner which fills three further requirements. The first is that exploited ecosystems which have already deteriorated must be returned to the state in which sustainable exploitation is possible. More generally, any exploited ecosystem must contribute to the planetary system a broadly similar level of energy-flows and

materials-recycling to the natural ecosystem it replaces, and substantial areas of natural ecosystem must be preserved to maintain
species diversity.

Any depletion of non-renewable resources must involve depletion only to a level of a defined minimal stock, below which
exploitation will not be permitted. Any further exploitation must
be consequent on the availability of newly-discovered reserves.
Part of the earnings from the exploitation of non-renewable resources should be invested in more efficient use of these resources
or their replacement with renewable resources. Thus, more
efficient use might be by a combination of improved repair, recon-
ditioning, re-use and recycling, together with the avoidance of
wastage due to such processes as corrosion or leakage.

While the zero emission of pollutants into the biosphere may
rarely be possible, the capacity of the biosphere to handle emissions
must be recognised as limited, and emissions must not exceed those
limits, whether they are of a local, regional or global nature.

It follows that a greatly improved lifestyle for the majority of the
world's population must be achieved, using patterns of development greatly different to those pursued by the industrialised
North, and the massive and ecologically inefficient over-use of
resources by the North must be curbed. If, for example, the global
ecosystem cannot cope with a given form of pollution originating
primarily in the industrialised North, then the pollution output
must decline not just to an environmentally sustainable level, but
to well below that level, in order to allow for at least a modest
increase in pollution output from the South as development takes
place.

If, for example, it was determined that carbon emissions needed
to be halved worldwide to control global warming, then emissions
from the North might have to be cut by three-quarters, as even the
sustainable forms of development that might be introduced in the
South would involve some increase in carbon output.

In many ways, the transformation of North–South economic
relations might be accomplished in a manner which simultaneously
redresses North–South inequalities and also allows for environmentally sustainable resource use. A commodity agreement covering a
major non-renewable resource such as tin could involve a progressive increase in tin prices which would encourage conservation in
consumption while allowing an increased potential for sustainable
economic and social development in the areas of production.

There is no guarantee that this would happen but policies have to be constructed which encourage it to happen.

This brings us on to three core forms of opposition likely to face such changed policies. The first is that of political and economic timescales. Political systems tend to support planning which shows a social or economic return on political investment commencing within 5–10 years at the most. One to two years is often preferable, and even weeks or months can be desirable prior to an election! Similarly, economic returns are normally sought within much less than 10 years. Political and economic planning to counter environmental degradation may show little positive return in one or even two decades yet, if it is not undertaken, the effects could be disastrous and even irreversible. It follows that the process of implementing sustainable development which also addresses North-South polarisation will involve a degree of planning and co-ordination that is antagonistic to the broadly free market approach which has dominated much of Western politics in the 1980s.

Secondly, the longer term effects of major environmental trends are difficult to predict with any kind of certainty. It is therefore easy to adopt best-case scenarios in order to avoid facing up to uncomfortable choices.

Finally, and most intractably, evolving a sustainable and peaceful global economic system inevitably means considerable costs for the wealthy industrialised states of the North, especially the Group of Seven – the United States, Canada, Britain, France, Germany, Italy and Japan.

Common global security implies radical cuts in resource use by the North, together with the transition to stable economies and a costly commitment to sustainable development in the South. This will be in direct opposition to those schools of thought which believe that existing levels of wealth and consumption can be maintained in the North, whose countries have a legitimate international right to maintain their standards and styles of living, if need be by military force.

The easing of Cold War tensions leaves a massive military complex searching for a new role. Protecting the interests of the wealthier North against any kind of threat from the South, whether from migratory pressures or threats to economic interests or resource supplies, is an eminently saleable policy and one for which some military strategists have been preparing for many years. The search for a new enemy to replace the Soviet threat is both urgent and intense. The threat from the global ghettos might be just too good to ignore.

Security Issues for Britain

Transforming attitudes and policies in the North which will prevent this 'close the castle gates' mentality and will help ensure the changes in international behaviour is an extraordinarily ambitious task, and one suspects that it will be difficult to make much progress until the current policies are demonstrated to be inadequate. Yet it is necessary to relate the requirements previously indicated to the particular circumstances of the present, and examining a particular country can provide some indications of the processes to be encouraged.

In the wake of the Cold War, Britain is in an unusually good position to influence ideas of global security. As we move into an era of potential environmental and resource conflict, the experience of a state whose recent history has spanned North–South and East–West relationships to the full means that it has considerable potential for promoting the policies most likely to lead to a more peaceful and stable world. Unfortunately, its past history, in both defence and foreign policy, indicates that its experience and outlook has hardly been positive, being far too much concerned with the legacy of empire. Even the progressive integration into Europe in the past two decades has been accompanied by the maintenance of a crippling defence posture, part of a hankering after world status that reached its peak in the rarefied anomaly of Thatcher's Britain after the Falklands War.

Yet scope exists for a more rational approach to global security, and Britain's particular experience has much to offer. So far, the post-Cold War changes in defence posture have been small-scale, led primarily by a need to save money rather than any concern for a fundamental reconsideration of policies. This could change though, and Britain could, as just one middle-ranking power, develop defence, foreign and trade policies which could hasten the more general acceptance of those attitudes to security which we have been discussing.

Britain's persistently high defence budget, despite weak attempts to curb it in the 1950s and 1960s, has resulted from a willingness to take on too many roles within NATO and a desire to maintain great power status, not least through maintenance of nuclear forces. Its response to the collapse of the Warsaw Pact has been hesitant, and the fact has signally failed to be used as an opportunity to conduct a full security review.

More generally, Britain's foreign and trade policy has been all too typical of a Northern industrial power, intent on ensuring that the world economy works in a manner best suited to its immediate domestic requirements, even if continually damaging to the South. Apart from occasional rhetoric, the commitment to environmentally sound politics has been minimal, and a recognition of the need fundamentally to redress global inequalities has been absent. On current trends, the defence posture will be maintained at close to present levels, Britain will slowly integrate itself into Europe, and its foreign and trade policies will be devoted to maintaining the global *Status Quo*.

Applying the arguments of this book to Britain, we would stress that the greatest threat to the security of Britain comes from the prime threat to global security. This is a planet of deep divisions of wealth and poverty in which the entire potential for global development will be increasingly constrained by fundamental environmental limitations. One-fifth of the population controlling three-quarters of the wealth and requiring an increasing proportion of its physical resources from the poor South is a recipe for instability and conflict.

Exacerbating this are two further factors. First, the process of global militarisation and the legacy of 40 years of an East–West arms race has greatly increased the potential for devastation and human suffering which can be produced by war. Secondly, the capacity of the monetarily-rich but resource-poor North to intervene in the South in pursuit of its requirements for wealth has increased massively in the 1980s, just as its trade and aid policies have become steadily more regressive.

We would argue that a security policy for Britain must recognise that it is in the fundamental security interests of the country to avoid such a crowded, glowering planet, and that a policy of self-interest as well as plain justice dictates an orientation to global needs. We should add, though, that Britain's capacity to act shows weaknesses as well as strength. The greatest weakness is that the country itself is in severe long-term economic decline. This has been a phenomenon of at least the past 40 years, but the tragedy of the 1980s was that a unique opportunity to reverse the trend and redevelop the country's industrial infrastructure using oil revenues was thrown away in over a decade of destructive free market dogmatism.

If the few remaining years of oil revenues are not also to be wasted, drastic action to reverse Britain's industrial decline will have to be taken, in parallel with developing a security policy designed to prevent the new North–South divisions developing. Defence policy will have to be redirected towards very much smaller and less offensive forces, with budgets cut by at least half during the present decade and forces made available for a much-strengthened UN security system.

The reform of Britain's trade and international development policies should entail a commitment to those reforms which enhance sustainable Third World development. This would cover all the major trade and development issues such as commodity agreements, selective Third World preferences and debt cancellation. Domestic and international environmental policies will require radical redefinition, especially in relation to energy and resource conservation and pollution control, and this must be integrated into the redevelopment of Britain's industrial capabilities.

None of these issues should be addressed unilaterally; all should be pursued through the many multilateral organisations to which Britain relates. Thus, the role within Europe, through NATO, WEU, CSCE and especially the European Community, should be to promote these policies persistently. Membership of the World Bank, IMF and many other UN agencies as well as the Security Council and the UN itself all provide impressive opportunities for promoting wider concepts of security, and will increasingly involve the opportunity to work with other like-minded governments. The much-neglected mechanisms available within the Commonwealth should be given far greater prominence, as that unusual collection of states has the capacity to act as a model for the wider world community.

In all, Britain's experience as a former imperial power, its relative economic decline and its roles within NATO and the EC all provide it with an opportunity to adopt patterns of development and a foreign policy which could be quite influential in the coming decades. It remains necessary to effect the change in political and public opinion that will enable these policies to be implemented.

A Sense of Reality

It can be argued that the 'realist' political outlook favoured by Western states over the past 40 years has resulted in their maintaining considerable global power and prestige, and has been responsible, finally, for the demise of the major threat to their security.

It can further be argued that such power politics provide the best approach to the uncertainties of a polarised world, that it is legitimate for the advanced industrialised states of the North to maintain their position of power, using military force if no other way exists. Finally, it can be argued that the alternative proposals which have been outlined, for the North as a whole and for Britain in particular, are so absurdly idealistic as to be naive in the extreme.

Contrary to this, we would argue that the alternate view – recognition of deep global divisions and environmental constraints as causes of dangerous instability and conflict as well as continuing human suffering – is fully realistic as well as containing elements of idealism.

For the moment, the new world order appears to be all too readily an order implemented, and on occasions imposed, by the United States and its allies. In time it will be seen to be self-defeating, but by then much more damage will have been done and much human suffering experienced. The task is therefore to encourage, in every way possible, the vital re-assessment of our understanding of security and to move towards an era of common security in which we begin to construct a new world order based not on coercion and the use of military power but on peace and justice.

Notes and Further Reading

Chapter 1

1. Smith, R. Jeffrey (1986) Arms Talks: 20 Years of Duds? Study for ACDA Finds Few Benefits. *Washington Post*, 5 November.
2. Leffler, M.P., (1983) From Truman Doctrine to the Carter Doctrine: Lessons and Dilemmas of the Cold War. *Diplomatic History*, 7, 245–266.
3. Messer, R.L. (1977) Paths Not Taken: The United States Department of State and Alternatives to Containment, 1945–46. *Diplomatic History*, 1, 297–320.
4. See, First Committee Convenes in New Political Landscape: Third Disarmament Decade Launched. *UN Chronicle*, March, 1991
5. Baker, J. (1991) The Euro-Atlantic Architecture: From West to East. Address in Berlin, 18 June. United States Information Service, London.
6. Saunders, J.W. (1991) Retreat from World Order: The Perils of Triumphalism. World Policy Journal, **VIII**, 227–255.

Chapter 2

1. For a primer on arms and arms control which includes a general description of the growth of superpower nuclear arsenals, see the US Arms Control Association's publication, (1989) *Arms Control and National Security*. ACA, Washington, D.C.
2. Details of nuclear weapons developments up to the mid-1980s are available in Rogers, Paul (1988) *Guide to Nuclear Weapons*. Berg Publications.
3. A comprehensive text on nuclear strategy and targeting is Ball, Desmond and Richelson, Jeffrey, (editors), (1986) *Strategic Nuclear Targeting*. Cornell University Press.

Chapter 3

1. Bertrand, M. (1991) The Difficult Transformation from 'Arms Control' into a 'World Security System'. *International Social Science Journal*, **127**, 87–102.
2. Schelling, T.C. (1986) What Went Wrong With Arms Control? *Foreign Affairs* (Winter) 219–233.

3. Rogers, Paul and Dando, Malcolm (1990) *The Directory of Nuclear, Biological and Chemical Arms and Disarmament.* Tri-Service Press.
4. For detailed reviews of the original ideas and their impact see: Krepon, M. (1989) Has Arms Control Worked? *Bulletin of the Atomic Scientists*, May, 27–45; and Adler, E. (1991) Arms Control: Thirty Years On. *Daedalus*, **120**, (1), 1–272.
5. Ball, D. (1989) A Sad Record. In Krepon (4).
6. Hines, J.G., Petersen, P.A. and Trulock III, N. (1986) Soviet Military Theory from 1945–2000: Implications for NATO. *The Washington Quarterly* (Fall) 117–137.
7. Lee, W.T. (1986) Soviet Nuclear Targeting Strategy. In Ball, Desmond and Richelson, Jeffrey (editors), *Strategic Nuclear Targeting*, Cornell University Press.
8. Parrott, B. (1988) Soviet National Security Under Gorbachev. *Problems of Communism*, **XXXVII**, 1–37.

Chapter 4

1. For details of major strategic weapons developments see Rogers, Paul and Dando, Malcolm (1990) *Directory of Nuclear, Biological and Chemical Arms and Disarmament 1990.* Tri-Service Press.
2. For a wide-ranging analysis of the dynamics of military technology see Gunter-Brauch, Hans (editor), (1989). *Military Technology, Armaments Dynamics and Disarmament.* Macmillan.

Chapter 5

1. An examination of trends in nuclear, chemical and ballistic missile proliferation is included in Rogers, Paul and Dando, Malcolm (1990) *Directory of Nuclear, Biological and Chemical Arms and Disarmament, 1990.* Tri-Service Press.
2. For a valuable analysis of the history of nuclear crisis management, which includes assessments of the Quemoy-Matsu Crisis and the Cuban Missile Crisis, see Lynn-Jones, Sean M., Miller, Steven E. and Van Evera, Stephen (1990) *Nuclear Diplomacy and Crisis Management.* MIT Press.

Chapter 6

1. The quotation from General Smedley Butler is included in Pearce, Jenny (1981) *Under the Eagle*, Latin America Bureau, a study of US policy towards Latin America.
2. A general account of the maritime strategy is given in Freidman, Norman (1988) *The US Maritime Strategy.* Jane's Publishers.
3. US force projection policy in the 1980s is chronicled most clearly in issues of *The Proceedings of the US Naval Institute*. The quotations from Admiral Watkin are in a supplement to the January, 1986 issue of the *Proceedings* which was devoted entirely to the maritime strategy.

Chapter 7

1. A comprehensive volume on the recent history of the Middle East is Yapp, M.E. (1991) *The Near East Since the First World War*, Longmans.
2. An indication of the US Department of Defense's thinking on oil and US security in the early 1980s is to be found in the *Military Posture Statement* of the US Joint Chiefs of Staff for Fiscal Year 1982.

Chapter 8

1. The origins and development of the 1990–91 Gulf crisis and war are covered in some detail under the heading *The Second Persian Gulf War* in the 1992 edition of *Collier's Cyclopaedia*. In addition, for a comprehensive month-by-month description, see appropriate issues of *Keesing's Contemporary Archives*.
2. Much of the detailed military data on the crisis and war was supplied by *Dfax Associates*, security data specialists (Vassalli House, Leeds, LS1 6DE, UK) whose help is gratefully acknowledged.

Chapter 9

1. Detailed referencing of the data on munitions and casualties will be found in Rogers, Paul (1991) The Myth of the Clean War, *Covert Action Information Bulletin*, Summer, 1991.
2. Quoted in Richard Sadler (1991), Carpet of Death is Allies Legacy, *Yorkshire Post*, Leeds, UK, 29 April.
3. The first major radical assessment of the Gulf crisis and war is Phyllis Bennis (editor) (1991) *Beyond the Storm: A Gulf Crisis Reader*, Interlink Books, US, and Canongate Press, UK.
4. One of the early military assessments of the war is Watson, Bruce M., George, Bruce, Tsouras, Peter and Cyr, B.L. (editors) (1991) *Military Lessons of the Gulf War*, Greenhill Books.

Chapter 10

1. Data on population, wealth and development trends comes primarily from *Third World Guide 91/92* (ITM, 1991), which in turn draws primarily on UN agencies.
2. Data on Third World trade uses the *Third World Guide* (see above) and also material provided directly by the Commodities Division of UNCTAD for an earlier volume.
3. The papers by Palmer Newbould and Edwin Brooks (below), from which quotations are drawn, were published originally in Vann, Anthony and Rogers, Paul (editors) (1974) *Human Ecology and World Development*, Plenum Press.
4. There are useful contributions on resources and security in Westing, Arthur (editor) *Global Resources and International Conflict*, OUP.
5. Sivard, Ruth Leger (1991) *World Military and Social Expenditures 1991*, World Priorities Inc. As well as providing the usual excellent summary of budgetary trends, the 1991 edition gives an assessment of global environmental problems.

6. Higgins, Ronald (1982) *The Seventh Enemy*. (third edition), Hodder and Stoughton.
7. See n. 3 above.

Chapter 11

1. Scowcroft, B. and Woolsey, R.J. (1987) *Defending Peace and Freedom: Toward Strategic Stability in the Year 2000*. Atlantic Council, Washington, D.C.
2. Official Text (1990) *Lehman Calls the NPT Review Conference Successful*. United States Information Service, 18 September.
3. Reiss, M. (1991) The Illusion of Influence: The United States and Pakistan's Nuclear Programme. *RUSI Journal*, (Summer), 47–50.
4. *Arms Control Reporter* (1991) SDIO Chief Henry Cooper Outlined Again the Three Parts of GPALS. 24 April, 575. E. 24.
5. Smith, D.J. (1990) The Defense and Space Talks Moving Tonards Non-Nuclear Strategic Defenses. United States Information Service, 8 November. Reprint of article in *NATO Review*.
6. Panofsky, W. (1989) Introductory Remarks: From INF to New Agreements. In *Challenges for the 1990s for Arms Control and International Security*. National Academy of Scientists, Washington, D.C.
7. Burt, R. (1991) Opinion. *Sunday Times*, London, 4 August.
8. Reiveson, H.A. and von Hippel, F.N. (1990) Beyond START: How to Make Much Deeper Cuts. *International Security*, **15**, (1), 154–180.
9. Fenstermacher, D. (1991) Arms Race: The Next Generation. *Bulletin of the Atomic Scientists*, March, 29–33.
10. Zomora, T.A. (1991) LTBT Amendment Conference to Continue, But No Test Ban in Sight. *Arms Control Today*, March, 14–17.
11. Blair, B.G. and Kendall, A.W. (1990) Accidental Nuclear War. *Scientific American*, **263**, (6), 19–24.
12. White House (1991) *Fact Sheet on Chemical Weapons Initiative*. 13th May, Washington.
13. Disarmament Facts 71 (1990) *Convention on Inhumane Weapons*. Department of Disarmament Affairs, UN, New York.
14. Tangredi, S. (1991) Naval Strategy and Arms Control. *The Washington Quarterly*, Summer, 201–209.
15. Dean, J. (1990) Building a Post-Cold War European Security System. *Arms Control Today*, June, 8–12.
16. Goodby, J.E. (1991) A New European Concert: Settling Disputes in CSCE. *Arms Control Today*, January/February, 3–6.
17. *SIPRI Yearbook* (1991) Military Use of Outer Space. OUP.

Chapter 12

1. Brook-Shepherd, G. (1988) When the World Almost Went to War. *Sunday Telegraph*, 16 October.
2. Palme, O. (1982) *Common Security: A Programme for Disarmament*. Pan Books, London.

3. Boyle, F. (1985) *World Politics and International Law*. Duke University Press.
4. Steinbrunner, J. (1991) The Rule of Law. *Bulletin of the Atomic Scientists*, page 20, June.
5. Libby, L. (1991) *Remarks on Shaping US Defence Strategy: Persistent Challenges and Enduring Strengths*. Adelphi Papers, **257**, IISS, London.
6. Palme Commission (1989) *A World at Peace: Common Security in the Twenty-First Century*. Palme Commission, Sweden.
7. Bertrand, M. (1991) The Difficult Transformation From 'Arms Control' into a 'World Security System'. *International Social Science Journal*, **127**, 87–102.
8. A wide-ranging contribution to the developing literature on post-Cold War strategic thinking is Booth, Ken (editor) (1991) *New Thinking About Strategy and International Security*. HarperCollins.
9. A text which includes an introductory analysis of options for sustainable development is Ekins, Paul (1992) *A New World Order: Grass Roots Movements for Social Change*. Routledge, London. A more advanced treatment of the issues is Ekins, Paul and Max-Neff, Manfred, (editors) (1992) *Real Life Economics: Understanding Wealth Creation*. Routledge, London.

Index